D1462447

THE GREATEST AMERICAN WOMAN

Lucretia Mott

LUCRETIA MOTT

From a bust by Adelaide Johnson, sculptor of Washington, D. C., whose monument of Lucretia Mott, Elizabeth Cady Stanton and Susan B. Anthony is in the Capitol at Washington. Mrs. Johnson's bust of Susan B. Anthony is a part of the permanent collection of the Metropolitan Museum of Art, New York City.

THE GREATEST AMERICAN WOMAN
Lucretia Mott

By LLOYD C. M. HARE

T1

NEGRO UNIVERSITIES PRESS
NEW YORK

To

BRIZAIDE G. HARE

"IN the same sense in which the greatest man ever produced in this country was Benjamin Franklin, the greatest woman ever produced in this country is Lucretia Mott."
—Theodore Tilton

"From her mother Lucretia Mott was descended from Peter Folger. . . . He was a remarkable man, the father of the mother of Benjamin Franklin."
—May Clemmer in "Our Famous Women"

In Preface

LUCRETIA MOTT was the real founder and the soul of the woman's rights movement in America and England. She was the outstanding feminine worker in the struggle to rid our country of slavery. She advocated labor unions in a day when they were almost unknown and generally considered illegal. She proscribed war and worked diligently for liberal religion.

A woman of rare refinement, yet she was not afraid to challenge the evils of her day, or to speak upon the public platform, an act then considered unwomanly and indecent.

These achievements, combined with her undeniably beautiful character and innate spirituality, do much to fulfill the author's title, "The Greatest American Woman." Of her contemporaries Harriet Beecher Stowe and Margaret Fuller were superior writers; Elizabeth Cady Stanton, Lucy Stone, and Susan B. Anthony devoted greater energy and longer service to the cause of suffrage, but no woman in American history ever combined so many outstanding talents or participated influentially in so many varied movements, and with such grace of charm, as Lucretia Mott. She was great in deeds, great in womanhood, and great in those attributes of femininity that women strive for, and men demand.

In her many controversies she never lost the poise of womanly dignity. She was always essentially true to her sex. We are told she grew old beautifully, so that every wrinkle in her face was the accolade of Time in the ripeness of experience.

In reading this book one should keep in mind the fact that, despite all the interests that absorbed her attention, Lucretia Mott was the mother of six children and found time to be "a paragon of housewifely excellence," as she was once described.

The reader need not agree with all the policies that Lucretia Mott propounded to concede the woman's great abilities and the influence of her life upon her own generation, and ours.

In her day America, as now, was rocked with a great economic problem—slavery—defended as entrenched greed always is defended. America had its nation-shaking disputes over the Constitution, its vigilantes, and a Supreme Court controversy that came to a climax with the Dred Scott decision. America had its conservatives, reactionaries, radicals, liberals and that inert mass of people who talk up progress until suddenly they discover it cannot be accomplished without ridicule and the sacrifice of social and business prestige, whereupon they become suddenly very "sound" in their views and adhere to old abuses.

No woman loved approbation more than Lucretia Mott, but public persecution never swerved her from duty as she conceived it.

In this modern world torn with dissensions we may look back upon Lucretia Mott as a steady light to make sure the path of progress. We profit from the fact that she adhered to the highest ideals of morality as a cure for the ills of society. She never succumbed to the tempting sophistry that the ends justify the means. Violence as a social solvent she abhorred.

Our Nation needs today the enlightened liberalism, the sanity, and the sincerity of purpose of this great woman who did much to give us, the women of America, the right to go upon the public forum to discuss living issues of our century. Let us not fail as carriers of the responsibility she entrusted to our hands.

As we hold aloft the burning torch let us bear in mind the sentiment Lucretia Mott loved so well, and repeated so often:

Truth for Authority, Not Authority for Truth.

ROBERTA CAMPBELL LAWSON,
President General Federation of Women's Clubs.

Illustrations

Table of Contents

CHAPTER I

THE BURNING OF PENNSYLVANIA HALL

FIRE bells clanged. Pennsylvania Hall was afire. People rushed bareheaded from their homes. A red glow brightened the sky. Billowing banners of fire streamed flamboyantly into space; snapping breadths of flame, the fearful heraldry of destruction, darted across blackened walls like tongues of dragon flies unleashed for food.

The crowd in the street surged to and fro. Men pushed and ran and shouted, but no one made effort to extinguish the blaze. The people of Philadelphia detested the owners of the burning building, who were Abolitionists.

Within a few hours Pennsylvania Hall was gutted. Where on the morning had stood a temple, at night lay a heap of twisted iron, smoldering fire, and embers fast resolving into winrows and ashes. There laid charred ruins and walls blackened by waves of flames. The Goddess of Liberty had been insulted and defiled.

The next day pandemonium broke loose. Maddened rioters cavorted about the ruins of the conflagration and paraded the streets of the city shouting imprecations at the mention of the names of Abolition leaders. By evenfall the heaving crowd, embraced by darkness, was ready to wreak vengeance on the city's most active Abolitionist—Lucretia Mott.

With wild yells, turning, writhing, headless, like some fabulous monster of a thousand legs, the mob poured along the thoroughfares of the city, its rat-like tail of hangers-on straggling around each corner. Through the night, without eyes, without soul, and without reason, paralyzing all who came within sound of the murmur of its polyglot tongue and panting breath, it glided from the ruins of Pennsylvania Hall.

In 1835 Lucretia Mott and her husband, James, were not popular in the city of Philadelphia. They had given the negro food when he was hungry and clothed him when he was naked, and spoken for him when he was dumb; and they must be punished.

Out of the mob darted a friend. He sped into a side street where alone and phantom-like, through gloomy and deserted byways, he raced on ahead to the Motts. He would warn them. His body took shape as he hastened across a patch of light on the sidewalk which was cast by a lamp that shone through an uncurtained window. Turning into Ninth Street, he drew panting before his destination. The hollow reverberations that resounded to his knock echoed with startling loudness. He could hear the growing murmur of the mob as it approached the intersection of Race Street.

He wondered if the door was barricaded . . . . if there were armed people in the house . . . . if ever a Quaker had need of arms . . . . if ever a Quaker had the right to fight in defense of home and property . . . . would the door never open? . . . . now was the time . . . . his thoughts were as jerky as his breath . . . . eternity passed . . . . could he not warn them? . . . . footsteps . . . . slow, composed . . . . the door opened . . . . a man loomed before him with a lighted lamp in hand which cast shadows on the walls about him, distorted, weird, ever changing . . . . the crowd was at the head of the street . . . . the visitor slipped into the house. . . . .

Into another world.

The scene was one he never forgot. It was that of Lucretia Mott, youngish Quaker matron, poised and serene, entertaining friends in the parlor while she and James awaited the wrath of the multitude. They feared no mob. If it could not be cowed by non-resistance, they would accept courageously any fate that might be theirs. Conscience was clear. They had done no wrong.

More than any of the reformers in the Nation engaged in the Abolition movement, the Motts and their associates of Philadelphia were locked in a death grapple with slavery itself.

Less than forty miles separated the city from the soil of Maryland. Slaveholders visited Philadelphia and sent their sons to its medical schools. Fugitive slave hunters armed with whips and guns crossed the border and trampled freedom's soil in quest of prey. In the darkness of night, negroes flitted across Mason and Dixon's line, and cowered by day in the Mott house.

Many influential Philadelphians were related by marriage to the county families of Maryland and Tidewater Virginia. Much of the city's trade flowed southward. There was consequently little sympathy for Abolitionists, and everywhere they were ridiculed and persecuted. The clergy of all denominations preached at, or against them. The politicians abused them, the penny sheets hawked about the streets caricatured their leaders. It was impossible to obtain a hall for public meetings. Everywhere the doors of society were closed against them.

For these reasons the humanitarians of Philadelphia had erected Pennsylvania Hall as a forum open to the discussion of anti-slavery and other reforms.

When ready for dedication, the poet Whittier had come to Philadelphia and fitted an office in the edifice, to edit the anti-slavery paper called "The Pennsylvania Freeman."

Young, diffident, almost unknown, he had been warned by kindly attentions received from the Motts, who had taken him into their home, introduced him to friends of anti-slavery, and encouraged him in moments of homesickness for far-away Haverhill.

The editor discovered the Abolitionists of the city were of the right stuff. He described them admiringly as staunch men and unflinching women in the face of danger. Many of them, he later said, did not believe in the devil, and those who did were not afraid of him.

The opening ceremonies of Pennsylvania Hall had brought Abolitionists of all degrees of zeal, courage, and sincerity into the city. John Quincy Adams, Thaddeus Stevens, and a host of eminent men had been requested to give the "keynote" speech, but a strange epidemic of ill health had descended upon the Nation. Invalids were in charge of the government of the United States. One by one the politicians had sent their regrets and described their several ailments or explained the pressure of business which necessitated their immediate attention at Washington, but all rejoiced with the friends of liberty and free speech, and so worded their regretful epistles as to lose as few votes as possible.

Not until the National and State civil lists had been near exhausted was a local prodigy found in one David Paul Brown, Esq., of the Philadelphia bar, who had accepted the invitation, and let it be known that he was "ready to fight the battle of Liberty" so long as he had "a shot in the locker." And incidentally that he was a busy man and that the Abolitionists were fortunate to obtain his services in opening Pennsylvania Hall.

Came Mr. Brown, and the hall had been dedicated to "Free Discussion, Virtue, Liberty, and Independence." People gazed at the building and called it stately and beautiful. Enthusiasts hailed it as "the most commodious in the republic," and a magnificent temple. Curious visitors stalked its halls and noted that the first floor was fitted with a small auditorium, committee rooms, offices and stores, and that overhead in the second story was a large hall with galleries, and that the building was brilliantly lighted with modern gas. They observed chairs on the forum lined with blue silk plush, and sofas upholstered in blue damask moreen, and tables hung with blue silk. It had been all very elegant for plain Quaker advocates of freedom and reform.

A mild literary program under the auspices of the Philadelphia Lyceum consumed the afternoon of the first day's dedicatory exercises. An address on the physical education of children was delivered by a physician, and numerous compositions were read on stilted queries such as: "What is the cause of Earthquakes?" and "What is the origin of those Meteoric Stones which have fallen to the earth, at various periods of time since the creation?"

The second day's proceedings had been not so innocent. A speaker had orated on the "Right of Free Discussion" which everywhere in America, he alleged, had been denied the advocates of anti-slavery. He suggested that the cold corpse of Freedom should have a shroud purchased for her funeral, little knowing that the magnificent hall wherein he stood was soon to be its crematory.

This speech awakened the people of Philadelphia to the realization that a menace had risen in their midst in the sacred name of Liberty.

If any there were who doubted, every constraint was obliterated when on the third day Mr. William Lloyd Garrison, of Boston (and late of Baltimore jail), and three "females" had addressed an immense audience convened to hear not only the notorious Garrison, but to witness the spectacle of women who so far had forgotten their feminine delicacy as to publicly orate before a mixed audience of men and women.

The pro-slavery element of the city was by now in an uproar of virtuous excitement. Large numbers of visitors were in from the South, and these, combined with the riff-raff that mysteriously gathers in any large city at the hint of trouble, filled the air with the breath of lawlessness. Soon after Garrison's speech, plead as he fondly believed "in good old Saxon language," a mob had rushed in and swirled around the hall and stormed out like a torrent in the aimless manner of mobs, everybody waiting for somebody else to start something. Outside, men whetted the primitive instinct for destruction by insane cavortings and wild screeches.

A speaker, at the sound of tinkling glass from brickbats hurled against windows, expressed satisfaction that for once the "stupid repose" of Philadelphia had been aroused.

The mob in the street shuffled about, and someone started the cry of "fire" in the hope that it would precipitate the audience into a panic.

At the rostrum a valiant little figure in starched Quaker garb vainly protested the attitude of persons who thought it improper for women to make public addresses. Lucretia Mott expressed the "hope that such false notions of delicacy and propriety would not longer obtain in this enlightened country."

These were perhaps the last words of the day, for the meeting was adjourned soon after when it became evident that the speakers could no longer be heard.

The next morning a small band of undaunted women reconvened at a session of the Woman's Anti-Slavery Convention. Lucretia exhorted the delegates to be steadfast and solemn in the prosecution of the business for which they were assembled. Coming to the hall she had seen the ominous forecast of placards that had been posted in public places during the night, announcing that a convention to effect the immediate emancipation of slaves throughout the country was in session in the city and that it behooved all citizens who entertained "a proper regard for the right of property and the preservation of the Constitution of this Union to interfere *forcibly* if they must."

All that day Lucretia heard the cries and threats of infuriated men seep in from the street. Virtuous males jeered and shouted down her voice. Conditions became so intolerable that the managers of the auditorium feared bodily violence and made haste to call upon the mayor and sheriff for protection.

Response had come not until sundown when the mayor arrived and gave the situation an appraising eye. He gathered the Abolition leaders about him and informed them that public opinion was against them; something they had suspected. Pontifically, his honor pointed out that it was public opinion that made mobs. He could promise protection of the building only if it were vacated and the keys delivered into his possession. This done, he mounted a place of vantage and addressed the persons present as "fellow citizens."

In general terms he deprecated disorder. He pointed out that the Abolitionists had the legal right to hold a meeting, but being good citizens they had, at his request, surrendered the keys of the hall and called off their evening meeting rather than add to the discord of the occasion. Shamelessly—charged the Abolitionists—he called the mob's attention to the fact that in Philadelphia the authorities never called out the military to preserve order. He looked upon the members of the mob as his police. He "trusted" they would obey the law and keep order. He then bade them farewell for the night.

Three rousing cheers followed the departing official, who no more had disappeared than mobsters quickly came forward from among those who remained. Under their directions pieces of heavy timber were struck against the locked doors of the hall in battering-ram fashion. Poundings were continued until locks and hinges yielded, and entrance was effected.

Through the breach thus made the ruffians of Philadelphia had swarmed like terrorists of France. Everything that would burn was piled on the speaker's stand. Offices were pillaged. Blinds were ripped from windows, wood shavings were brought up from the cellar, and highly "inflammable" anti-slavery books and papers from Whittier's office were added to the pyre. A flame had been kindled and the gas turned on. The mob had thundered out in glee and disorder.

This is the story of four days of rapine and fire that Lucretia's friends talked of in the parlor in Ninth Street as they awaited the coming of the mob from the site of Pennsylvania Hall.

Aware of the cowardice of rabbles, the Motts had made preparations for the threatened onslaught only so far as Quaker principles would permit. The younger children of the household and some clothing had been sent to the house next door. A few light pieces of furniture likewise had been removed out of temptation's way.

Throughout the evening their son Thomas dashed out and back upon trips of reconnaissance and made breathless reports of what was going on outside. Friends of the family dropped in with words of cheer and offers of assistance. Several uninvited young men appeared, who seemed to the Motts suspiciously ready for any emergency that might require their services. They suspected the younger generation of Quakers were not averse upon occasion to the use of violence.

Several callers, tremulous with agitation, clustered about Lucretia's chair where she sat as "calm as a summer evening" and exhorted her to keep cool. Good Dr. Parrish bustled in, much frightened, and recommended that the anti-slavery societies be gradually dissolved. Immediate emancipation of slaves had its drawbacks, he perceived. Better the women abandon their activities than arouse so great a storm, jeopardizing life and property. Let things go on in the old way.

In the course of the exciting evening, if anything came near to discomposing Lucretia, it was probably Dr. Parrish. He was a kindly soul and meant well, but he was not of the stuff of which reformers are made. Lucretia, on the other hand, was a person not to deviate from the path of duty, once identified.

She was to face other mobs before the years of her long and eventful life were to close in the sunset of old age, yet always, as tonight while she awaited this early contact with impassioned humanity, she was calm in the face of danger.

Fear had no part in her make-up. Self-possessed and unshrinking in the stormiest turmoil, with mobs howling about convention halls, assailing windows with stones, hooting and yelling at the doors, clamoring down aisles, scattering vitriol among the audience, leaping onto the platform, drowning the speakers with shrieks and cries, Lucretia Mott was to hold fast to her integrity, never to compromise in the slightest degree that which she discerned to be a matter of principle.

About eight of the clock Thomas came running in with the cry, "They're coming!"

The shouts of the excited throng pouring down Race Street now could be distinctly heard. The supreme moment had come. Everybody in the room stiffened. Ears were strained for the slightest change of sound. The mob at the intersection seemed not to turn, nor halt. Like a great wave of humanity gone mad, it pounded across Ninth Street, and passed out of sound.

The occupants of the room relaxed in wonderment. They were later to learn that at the critical moment a family friend had jumped into the lead and shouting, "On to the Motts!" had misled the mob up Race Street away from their prey, the ruffians following their new leader with unsuspecting confidence.

The passage of the mob across the head of the street did not entirely dissipate the tension of the parlor in the Mott house. Family and friends remained seated, receiving reports every few minutes from anti-slavery associates throughout the city as to what movements were going on. Intermittently fire bells tolled and the sunless air of night was made mysterious with the scarlet mantle of fire.

The rioters were not entirely denied. Unable to find their original prey they spent a not unprofitable evening setting fire to an orphanage and otherwise disported themselves in the manner of freeborn citizens expressing their disapproval of Abolitionists who would do away with law and order and the status of property in slaves.

At length learning that the mob had become broken and scattered and spent its strength, the group at the Motts' broke up. Friends bade farewell, lights were dimmed and the family retired. Quiet descended on the torn city of Philadelphia, and only the dull glow of embers, fading out in various pyres, gave visible evidence of the mad carnival of disorder that had all day gripped the City of Brotherly Love.

CHAPTER II

THE NANTUCKET BREED

Lucretia Mott has been variously called "the black man's Goddess of Liberty," "the soul of the woman's movement," and "the flower of Quakerism."

Few persons whose names have survived the ordeal of death have possessed an heredity so completely in harmony with environment, an ancestry so uniformly similar in traits, a foundation more securely based on mental vigor, bodily health, and spiritual excellence, than Lucretia Mott.

Philosophers do not accord whether man is a photographic plate producing a picture of character in coördination with the lights and shadows of mortal existence, or whether man is a mosaic formed of generations of ancestors.

Across the pages of history there flashes a Napoleon in whose soul surges the fates of empires; a Luther whose mind ferments the drama of religious reform; a John Brown who dies ignominiously on the banks of the Potomac; but no one knows from what mysterious source, from what spring of genius upon some mountain top of idealism, man gathers the fateful drop which exalts the one above the many.

The humble peasant plows his furrow in the field of life, and dies unhonored and unsung. The thoughts that may have seared his soul, no Boswell has recorded. But there has been a union of chemicals. A son springs full armed into the tapestry of life. His hot breath withers the leaves of history. Empires fall, and nations rise, and men think new thoughts—and the world wonders whence he came.

Perhaps it may be said that dead, forgotten forebears are either the clay of which peasants are imaged or the marble from which genius is hewed.

Lucretia (Coffin) Mott was born of Quaker ancestry in the island town of Nantucket, Massachusetts, January 3, 1793.

The family of Coffin has sent out into the world more than its share of distinguished sons and daughters. Seventeen of the family are recorded in Appleton's "Cyclopædia of American Biography" and the names of fifteen appear in the "National Cyclopædia." "Who's Who in America" has been perennially supplied.

The Coffins for centuries were masters of ships in the whaling fleets, captains in the merchant service, and admirals in the royal navy of England. The sea was their heritage, its formless, changing waters the family estate that had come down to them through generations of mariners and traders. The cultivation of their proud acres bred a race of brave men, enduring men, who loved freedom and space.

The men of Nantucket were encompassed by the sea. As boys they played in the water just as children of other climes frolicked in nursery and park. They could go but a few miles from its sight and never from its sound.

Everything they saw was a memorial to the sea; the lighthouse on the point, the green-slimed piers and oil-soaked wharves, the sail-maker's lofts and the shops of the blacksmiths and coopers that clustered the waterfront; every employment was connected with the trade of the mariner, every thought was directed to fathers and uncles in the unknown world beyond the distant horizon.

The archives of the Coffins are soaked with salt water. The sea epoch is gone, but the leaves of its history are brittle with brine. Salt water in their veins and seaweed dripping from the family tree, theirs is the salt water aristocracy of New England. Individualistic, capable of meeting emergencies with skill and daring in a world where the fearful mind must wither upon the bosom of Neptune's kingdom, these autocrats of the quarter-deck and merchants of the counting room bred a race that feared as little the artificial compresses of human thought as they feared to sail into a strange sea merely because its waters seemed to have no end.

In the year of Lucretia's birth, Nantucket town stood on wharves like a boy on stilts. Its cobble-stone streets were immersed in lapping waters along the harbor front and rose in eminence through a town of shops and homes to the old North Church on Beacon Hill. Unidentified as yet, these narrow idling lanes that seemed to be going nowhere and yet took in everything on the way, were soon to be named.

Names fragrant and quaint, like old Nantucket! Here was to be Whale Street and Try Works Lane, remindful of Nantucket's great industry, the whale fishery pursued by sons in far off workshops called the Java and Pacific Oceans; Federal, Independence, and Liberty streets, shades of the elder John Adams and screaming eagles; Milk, Orange, Quincy, and Gay, a euphonious grab-bag of names; these were the crazy-quilt lanes that connected the town's great square houses each with the other, like threads of a drawn-work pattern.

The island of Nantucket lies like something spewed into the sea, far-flung off the coast of Cape Cod, on the water route to Virginia. It is a land pungent with the odor of cedar and bayberry and the breath of pine from windswept moors. Over all is the spell of unceasing waters.

Outside the town's harbor the foam churns the bar, scrub oaks on the downs lean crazily from centuries of buffeting winds. Sea gulls wing bold and free in air cleansed by sun and sea. Behind every hill, around every turn, at the end of every path, lies the water—the sobbing, grieving, restless sea—mysterious as the Sphynx in Egypt's sands, luring and treacherous and inscrutable as the smile of a fallen woman, sombre, greedy, and grasping.

Now, beneath turquoise skies it surges peacefully onto sandy beaches, wavelets run gleefully to the shore, break and fall away like children at play. Now, under heavy oppressive mists, it rolls moody and sullen, silent and fearful. In seasons of storm it hurls infuriated waters day and night upon island shores with crashes that sound like cymbals of judgment; its breakers are no longer a lullaby, its waters no longer a shimmering sheen. All nature is an instrument of death and terror. In paroxysms of fury it gathers to its breasts the frail ships of men, gathers into its lair the bones of Nantucket's sons, and only when its greed is satiated does it become again a crooning song, a thing of beauty, a woman with a serpent around her head.

Even so early as the close of the eighteenth century, Nantucket was a land of tradition, the tradition of the American whale fishery, of ships and tar and oil, and florid-faced, sandy-haired sea captains, in whose veins ran the Norse blood of Old England, of merchants and shipowners, Puritans, and Quakers with the "thee" and "thou" of a simplicity that was as carefully effected as the wordy effusions of the cavalier.

Social history has recorded comparatively little of the wives of the grizzled captains and the solid merchants, and still less of taproom wenches, loving females who filled the dreams of Jack in the fo'castle at night and made topics of conversation by day.

We know little of the women of the eighteenth century, for in that era women were social appendages, "Mistress" Roe or "Goody" Doe, or merely "the wife of" John Smith. Individually they had small existence, yet in their veins flowed as much good blood of England as in the stalwart male; the saga blood, the pioneer spirit, the honest God-fearing attributes with which the male of America has been apotheosized in history, were as much the qualities of the early mother as the early father.

Fortunately more is known of the wives and mothers and daughters of Nantucket than elsewhere, for the women of Nantucket were an extraordinary race with a flair for solving their own problems while men folk roved the sea. It is meet that the desirable attributes of the island should best be exemplified in a woman—Lucretia Mott—who combined in her makeup the boldness of hardy and adventurous seamen, the simplicity of Quaker antecedents, and the pride of generations of magistrates who had ruled for centuries in England and America.

Of forty-three male ancestors in America that are traceable, twenty-six held prominent public office in town or county; twenty-two were judges and eleven governors.

Lucretia's ancestry affords an interesting study of the interbreeding of a virile stock. Four ancestral lines are traced from Tristram Coffin, three from Richard Gardner, and two from Thomas Macy, all of whom were governors of Nantucket in colonial days when the island was a part of the Province of New York. One set of grandparents were full second cousins, but no other marriage is recorded among the related families of so close a degree of consanguinity.

The first of the name of Coffin in America was Tristram, than whom no other man may so accurately be called the patriarch of Nantucket. He was a gentleman of dominant personality, born in Devonshire, England, where the family of Coffin is said to have been seated since the days of the Norman Conquest at Alwington Manor by the Severn Sea. Tristram was twice chief magistrate of Nantucket. He and his family were the largest owners of land on the island, and owned the lesser island of Tuckernuck, adjoining.

Tristram was father of five sons and three daughters who reached maturity. The eldest son Peter became Chief Justice of New Hampshire and was for a time acting Governor of that Province. Perhaps

TRISTRAM COFFIN,
THE FIRST OF THE RACE THAT SETTLED IN AMERICA
FIRST CHIEF MAGISTRATE OF
NANTUCKET, 1671.

BE UNITED. DO HONOR TO HIS NAME.

the most noted of the children was a daughter named Mary, known as "the Great Woman." She married an influential citizen by the name of Starbuck and became the mother of the first white child born at Nantucket. It is thought that she was the most gifted of all the early settlers.

Scarcely a political, social, or domestic movement prevailed but she maintained a leading part, being esteemed as a judge among them by the people. Her home, wherein many of the public assemblies of Nantucket were held, was known as the Parliament House.

Past the prime of life she became a convert to Quakerism, and the recognized religious leader of the community. To her must be accredited the guiding influence that made Nantucket the Quaker center of America second to Philadelphia. No one person played so large a share in molding the striking qualities of the Nantucket character as Mary (Coffin) Starbuck, the twice great-grandaunt of Lucretia (Coffin) Mott.

In the paternal line, Lucretia traced to Mary's brother James, a wealthy merchant and shipowner, who was judge of probate and the first Chief Justice of Nantucket's Court of Common Pleas.

Nathaniel, son of James, was a shipmaster in the merchant marine and made voyages to Europe. He was united in marriage to the daughter of Judge William Gayer, of Nantucket, brother of Sir John Gayer, of Bombay, captain-general and admiral of the East India Company.

The chief interest in the life of Nathaniel Coffin is the fact that, like his father and other members of his family in subsequent generations, he was once captured by pirates. The inventory of the estate of this great-grandfather of a distinguished Abolitionist discloses three negro slaves.

The father, James, also owned a slave, and the will of William Gayer makes mention of a negro once his "servant."

Notwithstanding these early evidences of slaveholding on the island, the people of Nantucket were, in general, opposed to the holding of humans in bondage. Elihu Coleman, one of the preaching brethren of the Society of Friends and a grandson of Mary (Coffin) Starbuck, published, as early as 1733, a remonstrance against slavery, which was one of the first books in America on the subject.

The family furnished in its numerous ramifications many members of prominence in the anti-slavery cause in which Lucretia towered in importance above all other members of her sex. The founder of the Underground Railroad was Vestal Coffin, who organized the institution near the present Guilford College in North Carolina in 1819. His son, Addison Coffin, entered its service as a conductor in early youth, and his cousin, Levi Coffin, was many years reputed president of the railroad.

It was Levi Coffin who helped Eliza Harris to freedom in the famous flight across the ice described in Uncle Tom's Cabin which has thrilled the readers of several generations. Levi was Simeon and his wife the Rachel Halliday of that book.

A distant kinsman, Joshua Coffin, the Massachusetts antiquarian, was likewise an Abolitionist, closely associated with William Lloyd Garrison and the poet Whittier at the beginning of their crusade against slavery.

Whittier, too, was a scion of the first Tristram Coffin in two lines of descent.

Crossing the strains of Coffin and Gayer was biologically sound, for the descendants of the union of Nathaniel Coffin and Damaris Gayer have been famous in numerous vocations.

The couple were great-grandparents of the Hon. Nathaniel Gorham, president of the Congress of the United States under the Articles of Confederation. Nathaniel's daughter Anna married Charles Francis Adams the ambassador (and was mother of the great Henry Adams), another married Edward Everett the orator, and a third became the wife of Rev. N. L. Frothingham, whose son Octavius was a leader in the movement that had for its object the promotion of rationalistic ideas in theology. Octavius Frothingham was first president of the Free Religious Association, in which Lucretia took prominent part.

William Coffin, eldest son of Nathaniel and Damaris Coffin, removed to Boston, where he and his family became prominent in the mercantile life of that city, and were Tories during the Revolution. A spirited stock, they for generations maintained high positions in the military and naval establishments of Great Britain and distinguished themselves by bravery in numerous wars the world over. Their history is a story of deeds of loyalty and honorable service to king and nation.

William's brother, Benjamin, was Lucretia's grandfather. He did not remove to Boston, but remained at Nantucket, where he followed the non-militant career of school-teaching. He was maritally, if not martially, inclined, being twice married and having seventeen children.

The sixteenth child was named Thomas, for his mother's father, Thomas Macy, county treasurer of Nantucket.

Thomas Coffin was Lucretia's father; a courteous and refined gentleman, intelligent in appearance rather than handsome, and somewhat formal but kindly in manner. He possessed the strong religious feeling that was a trait prominent in his daughter. An unwavering integrity is said to have been his most marked characteristic. Although a follower of the sea, and later a merchant, he was a man of studious habits.

Thomas Coffin was scarcely more than a youth when he secured command of his first ship. Ready to haul anchor on a long voyage he did what many a Nantucket captain has done before and since—he took a wife, established a home, and left them both for the unknown perils of a distant voyage.

He did not long follow the occupation of shipmaster. When Lucretia was seven years old he made his last voyage, sailing from Wood's Hole as master and owner of the ship "Tryal," on a trading cruise to China. His purpose was to acquire seal skins en route to exchange for silks, nankeens, and tea. This was the latest and most profitable trade established by the enterprising mariners of New England who, in the employment, went half the world around and sometimes circumnavigated the earth.

Captain Coffin had been out about a year when his ship was seized by the Spaniards off the Pacific Coast and taken into Valparaiso. Here the master undertook his own defense in the Spanish courts but, after much delay, having reason to believe that redress was not forthcoming, he left the Spanish city, crossed the Andes, and found passage at a Brazilian port.

After an absence of three years from loved ones, who had heard nothing of him for a year and who had given him up for dead, Captain Coffin arrived safely home "from foreign shores."

The event that broke the monotony of Nantucket life was the arrival home of a vessel from China or from the still longer peril of a whaling voyage.

Whenever a vessel was sighted a crier went his rounds shouting the news at the street corners and in village byways. Then all would become bustle; the whole population would betake itself to the "walks" that extended along the peak of Nantucket houses. These were railed-in platforms, accessible by trapdoor, where retired captains and anxious shipowners, pipes in mouth, and wives "widowed" and children "orphaned" during a voyage of four years, could anxiously watch over the horizon with glasses to identify the ship that was coming in. What excitement and what joy, and what sorrow, the final decision brought.

By the time the incoming vessel had crossed the bar and was rounding the point, the town's wharf was filled with an expectant crowd, and touching were the scenes of welcome its old planks have known. Grizzly captains who had not lived with their wives so long as a youthful married couple inland, met the mother of their several children, of whom they had dreamt so many times upon the silent restless bosom of the sea in long nights of solitude off Zanzibar or the wild islands of the South Sea. A sire was introduced to his youngest child whom he had never seen and who shyly met father, that strange, half mythical god of whom it had heard so much in evenings by the fireside.

Death, too, the uninvited guest who stalks about the fringe of every human gathering, often thrust its silhouette into the midst of the merrymakers. A waiting wife learned that her loved one was never again to greet her at the wharf, but had met a death common to those who go down to the sea in ships and do their business on great waters. Many a Nantucket son lies buried in the alien soil of a distant isle and many another has found his last resting place where ceaseless tides froth the uncharted waters of the Indian Ocean or the South Pacific, far from the quiet island of his birth and the home of his fathers.

The unexpected return of Captain Coffin was cause of great rejoicing, not alone in the Coffin home, but over all the island where relatives and friends resided. The story of Lazarus returned from the dead was not an uncommon one at Nantucket, yet it brought joy to the hearts of her people who knew the terror of loved ones at sea and long years of anxious waiting.

Lucretia and her sisters and brother loved to recall their delight at their father's return; how they clustered about him over and again to hear him recount the wonderful story of his adventures. And being a mariner he was never loath to comply with their demands.

During his stay on the West Coast (as Nantucketers commonly called the coast of South America bordering the Pacific) Captain Coffin had acquired a stock of Spanish phrases, the use of which always aroused the admiration of his children, reared in the provincialisms of the eighteenth century. He took amusement in teaching them some of these phrases and often required them to bid him "good morning" and "good night" in Spanish. More than seventy years afterwards Lucretia was able to repeat these words and phrases as if she had learned them the day before.

Brilliant as was the Coffin tradition, the greatness of Lucretia's character came not entirely from that source. Maternal forebears supplied her, preëminently, the characteristic of individuality.

Lucretia's mother, Anna Folger, was descendant of a family of little less worth than the Coffins.

Anna was just seventeen at the time of her marriage to Thomas Coffin, whose boyhood neighbor and playmate she had been. A portrait painted some ten years after her marriage represents a stately woman with large penetrating eyes, dark hair, a low broad forehead, and firm mouth.

Anna Folger's father was William, a merchant known to his Nantucket contemporaries as "Tory Bill" Folger, for reasons adequately expressed by the nickname. Whether he aroused the antagonism of his neighbors because he was a large capitalist, or whether he was contemptuous of anyone who deviated from the King's cause during the Revolution, or carried his head high because of the blood of his mother's family—the Mayhews—is not known, but tradition recounts a story that the only thing "Tory Bill" ever found was a jackknife, and that was "stuck in a post over his head."

The Folgers were shipowners and merchants prominent in the development of the whale fishery both in its earlier and later years.

The first generations of Folgers possessed, to an extraordinary degree, that happy combination necessary for pioneers of a nation— the union of native intelligence with skilled hands. There were combinations of blacksmiths and innkeepers, and one had "some skill" as a shoemaker, combined with public service in offices requiring clerical ability and education, as then known. The wife of one was a sister to New England's famed Indian fighter, Colonel Benjamin Church. Through this line Lucretia traced her ancestry to Richard Warren of the "Mayflower" company and his wife. The latter displayed marked talents in the management of her estates after the death of her merchant husband.

The founder of the Folger tribe was Peter. A veritable composition of versatility, he acted on Nantucket and elsewhere as school teacher, missionary and Indian interpreter, magistrate, clerk of the courts, surveyor of land, and miller.

In addition to this miscellany of talents, he is known as the author of a poem criticizing the conduct of Puritan magistrates, and was the maternal grandfather of Benjamin Franklin.

Franklin writes, in his humorous way, of hunting up some Folger relatives in France just arrived by ship, and being told in response to an invitation to dine with America's most fêted envoy that they would accept, provided they found nothing else to do.

Although Anna Folger sprang from one of the proud families of the island, the traditions of thrift and labor were as much hers as that of any poor Nantucket girl. From earliest days the people of Nantucket had been compelled to struggle for a livelihood. A barren soil, a bar beyond the harbor that prevented deeply laden vessels of large draft to pass over, and the exigencies of war which ruined, time and again, the whale fishery, had sustained the thrift and energy of the inhabitants.

Idleness was the most heinous sin that could be perpetrated. An idle man at Nantucket was soon pointed out as an object of compassion, for on this barren sod, idleness was a synonym for want and hunger. It took persistent labor to wrest a sustentation or to amass a competency sufficient to provide for the shadowing years of life.

The mothers of Nantucket were proverbially busy. They raised large families of children, nurtured them with affectionate care, and clad them "in decent plainness," we are told. In odd moments butter was churned, floors scrubbed and baking done, wool carded and spun and cloth woven. That family was forever disgraced whose members were not clad in good, neat and sufficient homespun cloth. So tenacious were the people of their ancient habits of industry and frugality that an inhabitant seen with a long coat made of English cloth on any day other than Sunday was sure to be ridiculed and censured and looked on as a careless spendthrift whom it would not be safe to trust in financial matters.

It is characteristic of the thrift of the people that at one time the Presbyterians on the island, being outnumbered by the Quakers, joined with that church in the worship of God in order to avoid the expense of maintaining a separate establishment!

Men going down to the market place, either to transact business or to gossip, carried always a piece of cedar in their hands so that while they were talking they might automatically employ themselves whittling bungs for oil casks, or other useful articles.

They had a great ingenuity with the knife. Though they held everything that was called "fashion" in the utmost contempt, they were as difficult to please and as extravagant in the choice and price of these implements as any young buck in Boston would be about his hat, buckles or coat. As soon as a knife was damaged or superseded by a more convenient one, it was carefully laid up in some corner of a desk. One of the worthiest men on the island had a collection of upwards of fifty knives, among the whole of which there was not one that perfectly resembled another.

Bride or widow, Anna Folger was forever knitting, the feminine counterpart of the masculine whittling. Her heart was always young, and although she lived to the age of seventy-three, her children, some of them with children and grandchildren of their own, looked to her as a guide, relying on her judgment and valuing her approbation, as in childhood days.

She was very observant with a quick perception of the ludicrous, and was apt in the witty application of old Nantucket sayings to passing events. A great-granddaughter remembers her as always sitting up very straight, and generally humming in an undertone to herself as she knitted. She seldom indulged in the ease of a rocking chair, unless for a short time at twilight. Even in her last years she seldom laid down in the day time for a nap, or reclined on a sofa. Sometimes she would be overcome by drowsiness, and her head would drop forward, her busy hands would cease their task, and for a few minutes she would "lose herself," as she said, but this was not for long.

A number of the scions of old Peter Folger, closely related to Anna Folger, are worthy of brief biographies because they exemplify the energy of the stock as a whole. Many of the female members of the family have been poets, notable Quaker ministers, educators, and reformers. Maria Mitchell, the astronomer, was a descendant.

A picturesque woman was Keziah Folger, born 1723, who married a Coffin and became the heroine of Colonel Hart's whaling novel "Miriam Coffin." Like many a Nantucket matron she started trading in pins and needles while her husband was away at sea. She eventually became an extensive shipowner, with vessels on every ocean. Around this nebulous character much tradition has accreted, and she is romantically described as a smuggler in whose country home vaults and caches secreted illicit goods.

Another ancient figure in the family picture gallery, looming mightily out of the dim vista of the past, is the Hon. Walter Folger, who greatly resembled his gifted kinsman Franklin for mechanical skill and inquisitive thirst for knowledge. This versatile man studied medicine and law and has been classed as a very talented scientist by an eminent authority, although he had nothing but home study to guide his investigations.

Attorney-at-law, Chief Justice of the Court of Sessions, member of Congress and of both branches of the State Legislature, he acted as surveyor of land, repaired watches, clocks, and chronometers, made compasses, engraved on copper and other metals, made several chemical and other scientific discoveries, calculated eclipses, spoke the French language, and was one of the best astronomers, mathematicians, and mechanics of his day. His fame rests on an astronomical clock which he conceived and built while a young man between the ages of twenty-three and twenty-five, the equal of which is not known, and which has been running since 1790.

Naturally so gifted a man was not without peculiarities. He had a propensity, when sent to market on an errand to replenish the household larder, to wander into the local hardware store to buy something needed for the invention then under way, much to the distress of his good wife. A neighbor, sympathizing with Mrs. Folger that her husband must indeed be trying, was met with the typical Nantucket retort, "Yes, he is, and I sometimes wish that he didn't know any more than thy husband." Which closed the conversation, perhaps for a good long time.

LUCRETIA MOTT, SOCIAL PIONEER

Captain Timothy Folger, magistrate and shipowner, was the first to chart the course of the Gulf Stream, at the request of his cousin Benjamin Franklin. He was Anna Folger's uncle.

Captain Mayhew Folger, Anna's brother, was a shipmaster whose discovery of the whereabouts of the mutineers of H. M. S. "Bounty" on Pitcairn Island in the South Pacific Ocean aroused international excitement.

———

Lucretia once referred to her island background and childhood, writing: "In those early years I was actively useful to my mother, who, in the absence of my father on his long voyages, was engaged in the mercantile business, often going to Boston to purchase goods in exchange for oil and candles, the staples of the island.

"The exercise of women's talents in this line, as well as the general care which devolved on them in the absence of their husbands, tended to develop and strengthen them mentally and physically."

Before her father retired from sea and for a short time after marriage, Lucretia experienced the vexations of a genteel poverty. She never forgot the lessons of those early years of skimping, although the greater part of her life was spent in comfortable, even prosperous circumstances.

Throughout life she aroused comment by economies in stationery and her practice of sorting ravelings for use as sewing thread, and similar needless habits. She wrote letters upon scraps of paper which she had carefully preserved. A friend tells of a letter received from her two and a half inches wide by two inches long, written on both sides, containing one hundred and forty-one words treating on seven distinct subjects. She apologized for her paper and enclosed five dollars for a benevolent object.

Her economy was not parsimonious. She conserved her wealth for the betterment of others. In days of affluence she pinched herself that she might give more abundantly. She contributed freely to philanthropic and social causes. Nearly the whole of her life was dedicated to the welfare of persons less fortunate than herself. Not content to have the poor come to her, she went forth to give them succor, in extreme age walking from house to house, dealing out with her own hands food and clothing.

A member of her family tells of the great cloak and heavy saddle-bags stuffed with food which encircled her frail body as she sallied forth on these daily errands of mercy. In ancient years she placed apples on the fence railings of her home for children to find on their way to school. And when bedridden, shelves were built about her bed that her own hands might deal out Christmas offerings to the poor of the countryside.

It was Ralph Waldo Emerson, no idle flatterer, who called Lucretia "a noblewoman" and "the flower of Quakerism." All that was beautiful and flexible, meek but spirited and bold in thought, he found in the character of this woman who was an instrument in breaking down the prejudices of accumulated centuries, and in building more beautiful mansions in their stead.

Small wonder Lucretia Mott, born of the Nantucket breed, was an incipient preacher, an inspired seer, while yet a girl. No opposition, contumely nor persecution, was ever to lessen one iota the distinctive quality of her convictions, the breadth of her comprehension, nor the beneficence of her work as a human being. Ridiculed, scorned, and shunned, she was never to forget that she was a woman. It is fitting that she should be called the "soul" of the woman's cause to which Elizabeth Cady Stanton supplied the brilliant esprit and Susan B. Anthony long years of determined toil and energy.

One sees in the courage of Lucretia Mott mariners sailing beyond the sunset, voyaging into unknown spaces, plumbing uncharted seas and mapping lanes like rivers through ocean tides, discovering and naming new lands, and returning to their home ports with full cargoes of lives well spent.

CHAPTER III

EARLY LIFE

Lucretia was in her twelfth year when for the first time she left the sea-girt land of her birth. Not again was Nantucket to be her residence, yet she was to regard the island always with an affection different from that felt toward any subsequent dwelling place. The cradle of her childhood she never ceased to love with all the passionate patriotism one is likely to feel for an island home.

In later years Lucretia taught her children and her children's children to cherish its tradition. "Nantucket way" became household law. The Abolitionist, the advocate of sex equality, and world peace, took root in the soil that nurtured her forebears, although the flower blossomed in a transplanted clime. Always about the roots clung something of the soil of Nantucket.

The family's first mainland residence was established at Boston in the west side of the city. The garden at the back of the Coffin house sloped down to the fields beyond which the Causeway crossed to Charlestown. In this vicinity the blended waters of the rivers Mystic and Charles became lost in Boston Bay. From her window Lucretia had an unobstructed view of both streams and the low hills on the farther side. Listening, she could hear the sound of travel on the drawbridges. The activity and bustle of a great city was strongly exhilarating, and she found life very much worth while.

Lucretia and other children of the family at first attended private school, but afterwards were sent to the public school of the district "to mingle with all classes without distinction."

Of this change, Lucretia later commented: "It was the custom then to send the children of such families to select schools; but my parents feared that would minister to a feeling of class pride, which they felt was sinful to cultivate in their children. And this I am glad to remember, because it gave me a feeling of sympathy for the patient and struggling poor, which, but for this experience, I might never have known."

Another change in education came when the girl was thirteen years of age. This time she was sent to a Friend's boarding school at Nine

35

Partners, New York, a considerable distance from home in days of inferior transportation.

The school at Nine Partners had been founded for the purpose of providing a superior education to sons and daughters of Quaker families. Co-educational in theory, boys and girls were admitted to the school, but were taught in separate classrooms under different teachers and divided into what was known as the "boys' side" and the "girls' side."

At Nine Partners boys and girls were not permitted to speak with each other, unless they were near relatives, in which case they might converse together for a limited time on certain days over a particular corner of the fence that divided the play yards.

Occasionally little boys attempted to look through knot holes in the fence at the girls' side and were promptly punished for this evidence of moral turpitude.

Lucretia was accompanied to school by a younger sister, "desirable little Elizabeth," as her father called her, a girl of loving disposition and excellent abilities, but retiring to such an extreme that she invariably placed herself in every background. In seventy years of almost daily intercourse, the elder sister seldom failed to take counsel with this shy companion whose judgment she valued highly.

The years at school were passed in quiet happiness, although the spirit of Lucretia sometimes rebelled at what she considered the unreasonable severity of the system of "discipline." The doctrine of infallible judgment prevailed, and punishment was sure and swift, although not always just.

Lucretia's inclination to substitute her code of justice for authoritative standards was tempered by a conscientious readiness to acknowledge her faults as she was quick to see them.

Lucretia took punishment easier than she could see it inflicted on others. When a boy favorite was confined in a closet on bread and water, she and her sister contrived to get into the forbidden side of the house, and supply the culprit with bread and butter. As the food passed under the door, the same feelings filled her breast as when, in defiance of law, in later years she harbored and fed in her home escaping slaves on their way to Canada.

One of the favorite amusements of the girls at Nine Partners was to play "Quaker Meeting." The fantasy was one rich in material, and afforded peculiar opportunity for mimicry. On one occasion the girls with proper gloom and solemnity held a pretended "meeting for business" to consider an alleged case of violation of the Society's Discipline. Lucretia was on the committee appointed to visit the offender and report to the meeting the results of its inquisition, which she did in the following words, given with the drawling tone affected by Quakers as an evidence of piety: "Friends, we have visited Tabitha Field—and—we labored with her—and we—think—we—*mellowed* her—some."

Among playmates at school, Lucretia liked best a girl named Sarah Mott whom she accompanied one vacation to the Mott home in Westchester County. There she met for the first time the family whose name she was to make illustrious.

The neighborhood where the Motts lived was called Cowneck by the practical minded yeomen of the district, but under the rooftree of the old Mott farmhouse romance blossomed, for here Lucretia, yet a girl, met her future husband. Her life and his were destined to flow as parallel as the two banks of a meadow stream, and to lead into the great ocean of human kindness that touches and makes kin all lands regardless of creed or color.

The principal teacher at Nine Partners was a woman of no mean attributes, if we may believe the tradition that she harbored not only a fondness for the study of grammar, but was able to impart to her pupils a similar taste. She was very critical of their pronunciation and their choice of language, and made nice distinctions between words which Lucretia often repeated in after life to the vast amusement of her grandchildren, and with capital imitation of the old teacher's precise and antiquated style.

The woman taught her "scholars" (as grammar school pupils were optimistically identified) to appreciate English poetry. Selected passages were learnt by heart, as a regular school activity. It was, doubtless, this influence to which Lucretia owed her familiarity with Cowper and Young.

In these school girl years, American education knew nothing of expensive plants and highly certificated teachers. Education was preeminently a matter of memory work. Children were trained to absorb a vast amount of ofttimes inconsequential data, called fundamentals. Graduated, they resembled nothing so much as animated encyclopædias and gazetteers, able to tell on a moment's demand the height of the Himalaya Mountains or the imports and exports of Patagonia.

Elias Hicks, a radical Quaker preacher, on a visit to Nine Partners, once interrupted a recitation in geography when the height of Chimborazo was in question, by sharply criticizing the time wasted in teaching girls such useless things as the height of a mountain. Testily, the old Quaker had demanded: "Teach them something that will be useful to them in after life."

This utterance, coming as it did from so respected a source, made a profound impression on sensitive Lucretia, sitting at attention. She had not ceased to relate the scene three-quarters of a century after, and she maintained always definite ideas on the education of girls.

The courses of study at Nine Partners were neither wide nor deep, but they were all that "select schools" taught girls in days when it was seriously maintained by approved authorities that women were possessed of "delicate and tender minds" unable to endure for any length of time the strain of concerted reasoning.

The care of the school at Nine Partners was largely under the observation of a Quaker by the name of James Mott, a gentleman of culture and character. Through his influence was called to the faculty of the school his grandson and namesake, James Mott, Jr., son of his daughter Anne, of Mamaroneck, who had married Adam Mott, of Cowneck, hard by.

The boy James Mott was a sober youth who had shortly before passed his nineteenth year. He assumed his new duties with such earnestness that he forever after looked upon school teaching with repugnance. Contemplating his class for the first time, he felt himself "loaded as it were with heavy shackles, grievous to be borne." Four years later memories of his pedagogical experiences lingered so vividly in mind that he wrote, relative to a sister in a like position, saying: "I can sympathize with her, having tasted of the same cup, mixed with ingredients more bitter than she ever knew, or can have an idea of. . . . . "

The drabness of life at Nine Partners was brightened by reacquaintance with Lucretia Coffin. James makes mention of her in an early letter to his parents. Writes he: "Lucretia Coffin says she is very lonely since sister Sarah is gone, for there is nobody in school that fills her place." Then he proceeded to do so himself with equal seriousness, but with more satisfaction than attended his teaching.

LUCRETIA MOTT, SOCIAL PIONEER

The tall, silent, grave-looking youth, with sandy hair and kindly blue eyes, grew in the estimation of his sister's former chum. Greater opportunity for intimacy prevailed when at the age of eighteen Lucretia was made assistant teacher on the girls' side. The friendship rapidly ripened into affection.

Small as was the pecuniary reward of teaching—being only about one hundred dollars per annum the first year in addition to her board —Lucretia was gratified when at the end of the year she was promoted to the position of regular teacher. Captain Coffin was successful in business at Boston, but becasue of his views on the importance of training women to usefulness, he consented that his daughter should remain another year at Nine Partners.

The twelvemonth was not altogether unpleasant. This may be gathered from the fact that a French class was formed among some of the teachers and that James and Lucretia found themselves often in each other's company.

It was while at Nine Partners that the unequal condition of woman impressed Lucretia's mind. She learnt that the charge for tuition of girls was the same as that for boys, but that when they became teachers women received only half as much as men for similar services. The injustice of this distinction was so apparent that she early resolved to claim for her sex all that an impartial Creator had bestowed.

At the end of the next school year she rejoined her parents at Philadelphia, where her father had charge of a factory in the new and thriving business of manufacturing cut nails.

So bright were the prospects of the manufactory that in 1810 James Mott forsook his meagre salary as a teacher at Nine Partners, and bursting the pedagogical shackles of slavery, removed to the same city to take a position in the enterprise.

The youth found Philadelphia a beautiful town. It had a feature about it startling to the stranger. Its streets did not run hither and yon in a dissipated manner, as did the streets of Boston or the alleys of London. Instead, everything was order and method in this admirable town, befitting a city of smug Quaker merchants. Philadelphia streets were stiffly laid out; they ran across the city in parallel lines from the Delaware to the Schuylkill. Cross streets intersected chastely at right angles. No slipshod alleys or bewildering lanes darted at variance from the straight and narrow paths that led to the waters' edges, where land left off and commerce began.

All was premeditated simplicity. Highways one way were named largely for trees; the old couplet runs,

> Chestnut, walnut, spruce and pine,
> Mulberry, cherry, race and vine.

In the other direction James discovered a novelty which has since worn off; streets were known numerically, First Street, Second Street, Third Street; no one could make them rhyme, nor could any one get lost.

The houses of the city were handsome, generally of brick, but closely set together. Pavements of the same material, neatly cleaned, were sheltered in the business district by awnings which, in all the principal streets, were spread from shop windows to the edge of the pavement. The soft red tones of houses and sidewalks blended prettily with the verdant trees which lined the avenues of the city. Philadelphia was known as the green city, sometimes the red city, depending whether the visitor was impressed by trees or dwellings.

Such was the city where James and Lucretia were to spend long years of usefulness—the city of Lucretia's kinsman, Benjamin Franklin.

James was not many months in Philadelphia when it was agreed that he and Lucretia should "pass meeting" and be married. The engagement was regarded with much favor by the families of the two young people, and an early alliance was encouraged.

As is often the case, the engaged pair appeared to be opposites. James was tall and slow. He spoke little, and that little gravely.

In marked contrast, Lucretia was short of stature, a sprightly girl of quick bodily movements and vivacious manner. Her figure was slender and petite. There was about her an air of dignified simplicity and grace of conduct that has been described as being almost peculiar unto herself.

Many observers thought her handsome, others not certain called her more than "quite good looking." Her features, scrutinized carefully, did not possess the symmetry of proportion which constitutes formal beauty, but the animated and agreeable expressions of her face made her acceptable to all who saw her as a woman of more than ordinary comeliness—in fact, a woman of considerable fascination, if we may believe enthusiastic male pens.

Two features ruled Lucretia's face. A benignant mouth softened an otherwise dominant chin and lofty brow, and beautiful eyes riveted attention; limpid-gray eyes widely set and full that seemed to grow appealingly darker whenever the girl was moved by the excitement of sympathy or the animation of conversation.

The keen appreciation of humor that characterized the Nantucket stock was hers, and what is rare in woman, she was able to appreciate a joke at her own expense.

Typical of her humor was an incident of later life. Coming into a darkened room she discovered James and his brother sitting in contented silence, one on either side of a large wood fire. She exclaimed, "Oh, I thought you must both be here, it was so quiet."

Although Lucretia and James were distant in external attributes, their souls were blended in harmonious understanding. Beneath the woman's lively exterior lay a nature as deep and sober as that of the man. Where James would perceive everything in a serious way, Lucretia did no less, but with an inclination likewise to discern the humorous side. Traits common to both were tenderness and a high degree of practical spirituality.

James, announcing to his "honored parents" the nearness of the intended marriage, informed them stiffly that "You will please write me on the subject, and should you concur, will recollect that your consent signified in writing will be necessary."

The formal consent of the Quaker sect was a prerequisite not idly obtained. The ordeal of "passing meeting," as it was called, was looked upon by the Society as a prophylactic to prevent young couples "from the dangerous bias of forward, brittle, and uncertain affections."

On a day set the candidates for the office of matrimony were duly examined by a committee appointed by the Society. James, who had nothing more reprehensible in his character than school teaching, admitted afterwards that anticipation of the ordeal had proved worse than reality. With the inelegant relief of youth he bragged that he had felt as calm and composed during the ordeal as if he had "been speaking before so many cabbage stumps."

This excellent choice of metaphor was uttered with no intent of disrespect. Probably James himself did not appreciate the mellow flavor. It may be attributed to a burst of inspiration over which he had no control, a flaring up of the Inner Light which never failed the Quaker.

We have no comment by Lucretia.

On the tenth of April, 1811, in the Pine Street Meeting House in Philadelphia, sober James took his place by the side of the woman he loved, sprite-like in simple dress with a white muslin kerchief crossed upon her breast and a quaint little Quaker cap framing the beautiful face. Standing in the presence of a congregation of friends and relatives, the twenty-two-year-old boy and the eighteen-year-old girl, joined hands in Quaker fashion and announced to the meeting that henceforth in the eyes of God they were husband and wife. No "hireling priest" chanted words of "honor" and "obey." No civil magistrate sealed the union of love.

By so simple a rite they became lifelong lovers in a union of fifty-seven years, terminated only by the angel who steals the breath of men. The years of their wedded life fulfilled not short of beautifully the promise that was theirs that April day in the spring of youth and love and comradeship.

In speaking of this union, Robert Collyer, many years later said: "If James and Lucretia had gone around the world in search of a mate, I think they would have made the choice that heaven made for them. They had lived together more than forty years when I first knew them. I thought then, as I think now, that it was the most perfect wedded life to be found on earth. They were both of a most beautiful presence. . . . . Both of the sunniest spirit; both free to take their own way, as such fine souls always are, yet their lives were so perfectly one that neither of them led or followed the other, so far as one could observe, by the breadth of a line. He could speak well in a slow, wise way, when the spirit moved him, and the words were all the choicer because they were so few. But his greatness—for he was a great man—lay still in that fine, silent manhood, which would break into fluent speech while you sat with him by the bright wood fire in winter, while the good wife went on with her knitting, putting it swiftly down a score of times in an hour to pound a vagrant spark which had snapped on the carpet, or as we sat under the trees in the summer twilight. Then James Mott would open his heart to those he loved, and touch you with wonder at the beauty of his thoughts; or tell you stories of the city where, when a young man, he lived; or of the choice humor of ancient Quakers, who went through the world esteeming laughter vain, and yet set the whole world laughing at their own quaint ways and curious fancies."

LUCRETIA MOTT, SOCIAL PIONEER

The glory of the married life of James and Lucretia Mott was the result of a oneness of moral purpose, a oneness in devotion to what they believed to be right, a oneness of sympathy with the oppressed and wronged everywhere. Said Lucretia when she and her husband had become famous in reform work: "James and I have loved each other more than ever since we worked together for a great cause."

However auspicious the couple's spiritual outlook at time of marriage, they could not ignore the fact that omens of business depression on every side intruded with unwholesome persistency. The times were gloomy. Entanglements with foreign countries, impending war with Great Britain, and the distresses occasioned in financial circles by the circumstance of the charter of the Bank of the United States not being renewed, made serious the outlook of traders and shippers.

The wedded pair for a few months resided with Lucretia's folks, feeling not justified in undertaking for themselves the heavy expenses of housekeeping. But shortly the hope (expressed before marriage by James, that the next time his parents should visit Philadelphia they would be entertained in a house of his own) was materialized, and James and Lucretia were able to rent a new structure in Union Street —a situation reported ideal, located near Father Coffin's, the meeting-house, and business; rent $300 per year.

The joy of establishing their first home was adulterated by the knowledge that failures in the business world continued apace.

The news came to Philadelphia that in the dusk of May, Commodore Rodgers of the American frigate "President" had met the British sloop of war "Little Belt" off the mouth of the Delaware and, receiving a cannonball in reply to his hail, had retaliated with gunfire. War frowned across the sea.

In the Northwest, Indian aggressions were of common occurrence attributed to the instigations of the British in Canada. Tecumseh and the Prophet gathered forces on the Tippecanoe and clashed with Harrison's militia.

The straggling little country of the United States, sprawled along the seaboard of a continent, faced extinction.

Its inhabitants were not Americans. They were New Englanders, Pennsylvanians, Virginians. They talked of State rights and were jealous of the Federal Government which sat supinely in the swamp holes of the District of Columbia.

So acute became affairs that members of the Coffin and Folger families seriously began to think of winding up their interests in Philadelphia, and pioneering to the frontier State of Ohio. Rovers of the sea turned faces inland where ships and embargoes and the slogan "freedom of the seas" would be things of a distant world. The Motts referred to it as a fever which was making inroads into the family, commonly called the "Ohio fever."

Captain Thomas and Anna Coffin actually made the journey on horseback to the site of Massillon, Ohio, with a view to permanent settlement. But a month later James wrote that the fever had "considerably abated." The Coffins had returned.

On the sixth of August, 1812, Lucretia gave birth to the first of six children, a daughter named Anna.

In the excitement of caring for a succession of babies, thoughts of Ohio gradually became less frequent until lost in the turmoil of years of perplexing struggle.

The spiritual flame of the people, which might otherwise have flickered in the strife for existence, was kept bright by letters from the elder James Mott, letters full of wise admonitions and loving encouragement. The grandfather considered the trials of the young man and woman the crucial test of their lives. He wrote to stress how important it was that they should set out with correct views upon the highway of life.

Five years of dark uncertainty were before them, but as yet no great blow had befallen the couple, happy in the fortunes of family life.

In July, 1814, a son was born and named after his grandfather, Thomas Coffin. Six months later James mentions that Anna, two years and a half old, "learns quickly, and begins to spell," and that "little Thomas says many words, and will soon talk."

Then fell the crushing blow that took away the first of those whom Lucretia loved. In 1815 typhus fever laid her father low after a short but distressing illness. The demise was untimely. In an unfortunate hour the captain had endorsed for a friend, and lost heavily. His family survived him in straitened circumstances, after having known years of affluence.

The death was a shock to James, who recently had been taken into his father-in-law's business as a partner. In an excess of grief, he wrote: "My business is suddenly changed; I have now to settle the

44

affairs of one whom I have tenderly loved, for whom I have felt a
filial attachment, and upon whom I depended for advice and instruction. I feel a responsibility unknown before."

The widow Anna, with dependent children, resorted again to shop-
keeping. An establishment opened by her gained such local popularity
that James and Lucretia were encouraged to try a like venture. They
opened a shop on Fourth Street, near Arch, but were obliged to sell
out at a considerable loss. This was a second affliction from which
James found it difficult to rally. The only profit the struggling pair
derived from the experience was the lesson that there is no such thing
as friendship in trade, for friends whom they had supposed would be
willing to give them their custom had avoided the shop.

The course of a few years saw several changes of occupation.
Once James removed to New York City to work in a bank while
Lucretia remained at home. This did not prove satisfactory, and
there was a scurrying around to bring James back to Philadelphia as
bookkeeper in a friend's store.

Lucretia, meantime, was not idle. She was not one to sit by and
complain about her husband's income. The restless urge of New England blood to "pitch in" stirred her. She was good cheer to James,
but this was not enough. In conjunction with a cousin she opened a
school for children under the patronage of the Pine Street Monthly
Meeting of the Quaker Society.

Unlike the shop experience, the school proved a success. The
only drawback, according to Lucretia, was that "our walk is long:
and, as there are two sessions, we take our dinner with us; but if we
can get a large school, we shall not mind the walk."

Just as things were brightening, the typhus fever struck again.
"Unsearchable are the ways of Providence," wrenched James in
anguish, " . . . . We are the children of mourning, for it hath
pleased the Almighty in his inscrutable wisdom to visit our habitation
with the messenger of death, and take from us our darling little
Thomas. . . . . His disposition was the most affectionate," continued
the stricken father, "he loved everybody, and all loved him. The last
he said was, 'I love thee, mother.' . . . . It is a close trial; it is hard
to give him up, and say, 'Thy will be done.'"

Lucretia, too, developed symptoms of the dread scourge, and
became very feeble.

45

It was a mournful experience to the mother. Only a few weeks ago and her baby had been active, fat, and rosy-cheeked; her boy child. Now the ground had closed upon the tiny form she would see no more, nor feel its trusting confidence close to heart. She had given life to this child and nature had reached forth a hand and cheated her of flesh and blood born in pain and travail—an empty sacrifice.

Under the solemn influence of death Lucretia devoted herself to deep religious reflection. The loss of her father, business difficulties, financial worries, all were nothing. For the first time life was stark.

The bereaved mother was moved one day to express herself in Friends' Meeting; a simple prayer. She met with such sympathy and encouragement that she afterwards spoke often and became a minister.

Quaker ministers drew no salary. They were called to office by the approval of their society, not because of education, but because of special gifts of spiritual thought or example. They did not devote their full time to religious duties, and preached only when the spirit moved.

Lucretia loved the Quaker church and its meetings with long and restful silences.

It was Charles Lamb who wrote: "Would'st thou know what true peace and quiet mean; would'st thou possess the depth of thine own spirit in stillness, without being shut out from the consolatory faces of thy species, come with me into a Quakers' Meeting."

One suspects the silent introspection of Quakers at church was occasionally a vacuous contemplation of nothing. Without doubt the young maiden wondered if her bonnet was properly adjusted, and the wandering eye of youth sought a vision not so much of God as a goddess in mouse colored silk and white kerchief.

In the midst of silence, a voice would speak—known in Quaker parlance as "breaking the silence." Sometimes it would be the quavering voice of a woman, timid at first, but gathering strength as the speaker became accustomed to the sound of her voice in the stillness of the room. Not infrequently it was a rambling and unlearned discourse, the result of a ministry untrained for speech-making, occasionally it was an appeal to the noble and beautiful in man, more often a discourse on practical morality.

Public discourses delivered in "Friendly Meetings," being always extemporaneous, few of Lucretia's sermons are extant, but for more than half a century in America and abroad her voice was heard in behalf of the oppressed and the poor.

The exemplary daily life of the woman of twenty-five, her dignified presence and correct style of expression, together with the earnest simplicity which marked her public testimonies, gained her the reputation of being an attractive speaker. She was free from the faults and peculiarities which too often attended the manner of preachers. She had a fine scorn for the whining voice thought necessary in preaching the word of God. Humorously she referred to it as what "we Friends call the preaching tone."

An old Friend in Lancaster County, Pennsylvania, told Robert Collyer of his first hearing Lucretia in early days when she was almost unknown.

Writes Collyer: "He had had a dreary time with the Friends that day, but at last a woman stood up he had not seen before, whose appearance touched him with strange, new expectations. She looked, he said, as if she had no great hold on life, and began to speak in low tones, with just a touch of hesitation as one who is feeling after her thought, and there was a tremor as if she felt the burden of the Spirit. But she found her way out of all this, and then he began to hold his breath. He had not heard such speaking in all his life. It was so born of all conviction, so surely out of the inner heart of the truth, and so radiant with the inward light for which he had been waiting, that he went home feeling as he supposed they must have felt in the old time who thought they had heard an angel."

To this Collyer adds his own experience: "I once heard such an out-pouring. It was at a wood-meeting up among the hills. She was well on in years then, but the old fire burned clear, and God's breath touched her out of heaven, and she prophesied. . . . . For two hours she held the multitude spellbound, waiting on her words. . . . . I have said she prophesied. No other term would answer to her speech. Her eyes had seen the glory of the coming of the Lord and she testified of that she had seen; and this was all the more wonderful to me, because it was the habit of her mind in her later years to reason from premise to conclusion. . . . . But she had seen a vision sitting there in the August splendor, and the vision had sent the heart high above the brain.

"I think I should not quite have known my friend but for that wood-meeting, as we should not quite have known Christ but for the Sermon on the Mount."

47

CHAPTER IV

HERESIES

The key to Lucretia's power in the ministry lay in her primal declaration, "My conviction led me to adhere to the sufficiency of the light within us, resting on truth for authority, not on authority for truth."

Truth for authority, not authority for truth! In seven words is written the character of Lucretia Mott.

Whenever she questioned an institution, sacred or profane, she was answered, "It has the sanction of time, antiquity, the Fathers, custom, the Bible, or the law of the land as authority," but she would reply, "That is not sufficient, I do not seek authority to prove true a point, but Truth to be my authority."

This set her at once beyond the pale of man's theology. It carried her beyond the canons of the Christian Church. It left her unreached by the dicta of St. Paul and other administrative leaders, both ancient and modern. She read their eloquent declarations by the illumination of her own seeking spirit, as they themselves had read the words of Christ.

Had she lived in St. Paul's stead, Christianity might have been more tolerant—especially to women.

Lucretia sought mental freedom and spiritual light that she might consecrate herself to the service of humanity. "How," she asked, "can I follow the light of God without a free, fearless, single-minded use of the power He gives me?" "Proving all things, trying all things, and holding fast only to that which is good, is the great religious duty of this age," she wrote. "I desire to escape the narrow walls of a particular church, and to live under the open sky, in the broad light, looking far and wide, seeing with my own eyes, hearing with my own ears, and following truth *meekly* but *resolutely*, however arduous or solitary may be the path in which she leads. . . . . I thank God that I live at a time and under circumstances which make it my duty to lay open my whole mind with freedom and sincerity."

Lucretia's first physical surroundings had been those of a Quaker community, her earliest admonitions had been those of a Quaker mother. She had learnt as a child the attributes of simplicity and free thought, tolerance, gentleness, and love of humanity.

This early training she never forgot, and when she came to the Quaker ministry her first sermons were pleas that the members of the Society should return to the simplicity and tolerance of the church that had known Fox and William Penn. She looked backwards to these elements, but forward in every other respect.

Even in old age when one is apt to deplore the degeneracy of the times, she expressed her theory of life, saying: "I never look back to the past as the Golden Age, but always forward to it, as coming. . . . . "

In the ultimate analysis Lucretia, like all religionists, did good not for love of posterity so much as to win the commendation of St. Peter, although, perhaps, she never completely realized this fact. In the nineteenth century the basis of the Christian religion was Salvation, and the Quaker, despite every effort on his part, was a human being. He was prominent in deeds of philanthropy because he wished to save his soul.

Man seldom removed his eyes from the hand that held the Keys of Heaven.

In Lucretia's day Christian salvation fell into three primary classifications—Catholic, Evangelical Protestant, and Quaker.

Catholics thought that salvation could be attained only by the consent of the Catholic Church, and that good deeds alone were not sufficient. The church was the medium by which God revealed Himself to man and intervened in his affairs, and its priests were the experts who interpreted God's wishes.

The Evangelical Protestants likewise believed in the necessity of good standing in the true church, but disagreed with the Catholics, and among themselves, as to the identity of that church. They were prone to place less faith in the powers of the clergy and more in the lessons of the Bible. The Bible alone was the medium through which God directed the affairs of man.

In contrast to these theories, Quakers believed that God revealed himself to man, not through the conduit of the Bible or a hired priesthood, but as a voice in man's soul communing with man individually through the Inner Light.

As democracy had made every man a patrician in defiance of the established political order, so in defiance of church, Quakerism mitred

49

every individual and made him personally responsible to God in spiritual matters.

The Quaker searched the Bible in vain for what Christ said about valid ordination or sound creed or efficacious sacraments, hence he was opposed to theological "systems" and sermons prepared by uninspired clergymen on points argumentative or speculative, and which neither could be proved nor disproved.

Lucretia expressed it thus: "The highest evidence of a sound faith being the practical life of a Christian, I have felt a far greater interest in the moral movements of the age than in any theological discussion."

To Elizabeth Cady Stanton she once expressed the opinion that religion was a natural, human experience common to all well-organized minds, but that theology was a system of speculation about the unseen and unknowable which the human mind had no power to grasp or explain, and that these speculations varied with every sect, age, and type of civilization.

At the time Lucretia entered the Quaker ministry, theology ruled religion, and religion dominated America. The average American was a voracious reader of sermons. To brag that one had read the Bible from cover to cover the greatest number of times was to achieve intellectual reputation.

Literature, education, and national thinking flowed in arteries of theology. A foreign visitor made the assertion that in the United States there were but two amusements—politics for men and religion for women.

Men left church duties largely to women along with housework and other non-profit enterprises, but if men did not dominate the activity of church work, they at least reaped the glories. Wives, sisters, and mothers decorated the meetinghouses, sewed knickknacks, planned fairs and bazaars, cooked delicacies for the elders and washed the dishes afterwards, but when honors were bestowed, men alone were eligible to the cloth and the deacon's chair, and women were silent in voting assemblies.

The men active in church life were few in number, nevertheless the whole fabric of masculine expression was woven with the motif of theology. Men spoke continuously of God and his divine grace, in politics, in business, and in war, and on every public occasion.

THE GREATEST AMERICAN WOMAN

The great books dealt with religion, the popular interest centered in theological controversy, the chitchat of parlor conversation was sermons. Nothing passed the time so brightly in stagecoach or tavern as a heated argument over the meaning of some battle-scarred passage in the Bible.

The clergy dominated the country's learning. They were the persons who could afford the avocation of letters in a day when popular opinion considered literature a dilettant hobby for gentlemen of leisure. Unless a man had an assured income from another source, or was physically incapacitated for the ruder vocations of life, he was considered indolent who worshipped the muses while so many forests remained uncut and there were fishes in the sea to be caught.

The American muses were three old spinsters who hobbled like hags behind a penguin priesthood.

Lucretia found the world asleep in the trundle bed of medievalism, with the windows shut tightly that the devil might not poke in its head and pollute with the breath of heresy the religious stagnation of the chamber. Shades were drawn tightly by day against the sun that theological whatnots, which had come down from the workshops of early monks, might not fade.

Science was a babe in swaddling clothes suckling its milk from religion; an heir who threatened to inherit the earth from its bachelor uncle, the church. Accordingly the church sought papers of guardianship and early sent the child to Sabbath school to be instructed in the lesson that science must not infringe where religion had gone before.

Darwin had not spoken, and every finding of the naturalist was weighed with the Bible before its truth was accepted or rejected.

Against the black curtain of ignorance, clergymen performed miraculous feats of hand, and retailed salvation.

Camp meetings broke out like a rash along the frontier, where life was drab and stern and full of the dread of Indian wars. Ranting clergymen traveled the country like carnival showmen, confident they could solve every moral and social problem of the age by reference to the Bible; each different from the other.

In rustling forests, lighted by the glare of great camp fires, souls were harvested to God amidst sights and sounds that would defy belief were they not completely authenticated. Exhorters from the platform screeched hell and damnation while men and women writhed

51

before them on the ground, and grew black in the face. Orgies of spiritual debauchery took place within the pulpit's shadow that have been equaled only by the antics of frenzied savages in the wilds of Africa. The ear heard the thump of falling bodies, the "holy laugh" of maddened men; the eye perceived converts on all fours barking like dogs who had "treed the devil."

The forest gloaming became an unreal bedlam. Hysterical maidens screamed in the night, women staggered to the *anxious seat* more sadly in need of a psychiatrist than the threats of unwholesome clergymen who gleefully proclaimed that each such convert now "had Jesus in her!"

In contrast to these barbarisms Lucretia taught a religion in which future punishment bore no part, and sanity had, at least, a polite reception.

She saw nothing beautiful or possible in the picture drawn by the evangelist in his sermon on "The Justice of God in the Eternal Damnation of the Wicked" when he described the sinful sufferer after millions of years of anguish lifting up his face to God and beseeching, "How long, O Lord, how long?" and the answer coming from the throne of an inexorable ruler, "Eternally, eternally!"

All this, perhaps not because of any heinous crime, but because of the fall of Adam, or because the sinner had failed to join the right church.

Ministers profaned Sabbath mornings describing with ghastly detail the last fleeting moments of human life on earth; raising their voices they would screech the terrible scenes of hell, the gleaming fire and rivers of molten lead, and the limbs of human beings quivering in eternal damnation.

An entire Sabbath morning at a child's school was consumed in prayer to God and in "solemn conversation" with the little tots in respect to their hopes of salvation. We are piously informed that many of the children wept, and that a generally bad time was had by all.

In nursery, schoolroom, and pulpit, little children and adults alike were taught that mankind by the fall of Adam had lost communion with God and was under his wrath and curse and so liable to all the miseries of the present life, and many of them to the pains of hell.

Gardens might flower, shrubbery grow green and orchards bear fruit, the sun might shine, bees hum and birds sing, yet when the corpse of some frail child too young to consciously sin was lowered beneath the sod, men knew in that awful heartwrenching moment that a stern, awful, jealous, implacable God was visiting upon it the punishments of hell as a just reward for an hereditary guilt committed by the first parents of mankind.

The God who ruled the religious world had as many sides as a prism. He was a crabbed, arbitrary, eccentric being who was forever demanding propitiation and threatening hell-fire to those who displeased him. In another capacity he was a magnificent king. Kings demand obedience and humility and pageantry, so primitive man in the nineteenth century thought of God as a transcendent king, and knelt in prayer and bowed his head, instead of raising his eyes to the glory of the heavens and the stars above.

God made man in his own image, declares the Bible, and Lucretia was wont to add that equally it might be said that man has made God in man's image with all of man's imperfections. She did not think it strange that there should be atheism in the world while such false ideas of God were inculcated in the minds of the people.

In the Quaker church Lucretia bore testimony against melancholy views of the Creator.

On the whole she found that the respectable people of her generation believed the old concepts without suspicion that they might be fallacious. They had been infused into prayers and sermons and religious literature. They had been handed down by the wise and good of many generations of Christians. The wise and good of people who were not Christians did not count. Pagans were ciphers in the drama of eternity.

Theology had early interpreted the meaning of the boundless regions that lie beyond the horizon of accurate knowledge, and whenever science pushed the horizon a step and proved the theologian wrong, the theologian would cling to his presupposition and cry "heretic!"

Clergymen had known nothing of gravitation, so Galileo had been persecuted. Clergymen in 1859 knew nothing of evolution, so persisted that man was God's especial creation, and when an occasional human was born with a tail they were deeply offended. It was evident that God indulged occasionally in a bit of humor—perhaps to appease the monkeys.

53

Because of the limitations of knowledge, the bold investigators of Lucretia's day were not much more scientific than those whom they denied. Today the scientific mind justly raises the inquiry whether the "TRUTH" which played so prominent a part in Lucretia's philosophy is not as lacking of proof as any dogma of the churches.

The virtue of Lucretia's religion was that she was willing to assume new perspectives on theology, to see with eyes that had been freshened. She disputed dogmatism. She opposed intolerance and the suppression of reason. She aided in the task of clearing the ground of the primitive shacks of superstition.

The astounding growth of liberal religion during the years of her life may be attributed to the ideals of a new social gospel that followed the rise of eighteenth century democracy.

Three sermons mark the progress of liberal religion in America, and each had its influence upon the life of one who at the preaching of the first was a girlish matron holding the amateurish position of minister in the Quaker society.

At Baltimore on the fifth day of May, 1819, frail, ascetic William Ellery Channing spilled the first great heresy of the century, in a sermon at the ordination of Jared Sparks, that was to be a milestone on the path of liberal religion.

Channing upheld the exercise of reason in religious matters and declared the Bible to be "a book written for men in the language of men and its meaning to be sought in the same manner as that of other books." Christ, he asserted, was a great moral teacher and not a mediator between erring man and offended deity.

The repercussions of Channing's Unitarianism stirred anew the running battle of the ages. It was as though Channing had thrust a stick into a nest of hornets. The fact that theology was not on solid ground did not prevent the battle being kept up with immense learning and little knowledge on either side.

Channing's idea of the transfer of authority from external scriptures to the reason within man could not fail to attract the attention of so liberal a Quaker as Lucretia. She was always to love Channing's works.

By 1836 the shocking excrescences of the old theology were removed among Unitarians by a criticism not very searching or profound, perhaps, but at least sufficient for the day. Things painful and incredible in the Bible were either explained away in good faith or unsuspectingly ignored.

This tranquil and grateful sense of intellectual rest was rudely broken by a retired clergyman—Ralph Waldo Emerson, whose pulpit was the lyceum platform.

Emerson's address to the graduating class at the Harvard Divinity School pushed back the horizon drawn by Channing, and started a controversy within the Unitarian ranks that was not to end until traditional views were practically eliminated.

Emerson's message was the birth of Transcendentalism. It taught that, whereas religious truth was properly intuitive in man, current religious philosophy regarded it as external to him, founded on persons and events in historical Christianity, and that the religion of the day could be revitalized only as men came to look within, rather than without, for the revelation of God.

Transcendentalism was the poetic side of the liberal religious movement. It was the warm stream of spirituality blended in the chilly current of rationalism. Emerson reaffirmed the soul's inherent power to grasp "The Truth." He spoke a great deal of the Inner Light. The sage had said upon leaving his Boston pulpit: "I believe I am more of a Quaker than anything else. I believe in the still small voice; and that voice is Christ within us."

Scholars dispute any similarity between the Transcendental "oversoul" and the Quaker "Eternal Goodness," yet there were numerous likenesses.

Lucretia held with Emerson the hypothesis that the religious sense is inherent in man and grows with increased knowledge, and is not solely dependent on Bible writings or seers long dead. She did not believe in a creed-bound religion more than she would allow the roots of a plant to become pot-bound.

Thus Lucretia, a Quaker, is ranked by historians as a Transcendentalist and a prominent Unitarian. The position is made tenable by the fact that not Transcendentalism, Unitarianism, nor genuine Quakerism was defined by a creed.

Transcendentalism, which embraced radical Unitarianism, was a broad, liberal, ever-growing principle rather than a concrete shape. Its adherents were not formally organized. They did not necessarily have well defined aims in common. All who adhered to certain general principles in literature, philosophy, or religion, were called Transcendentalists, although they, themselves, did not adopt the name until it had been fixed upon them by popular opinion.

Transcendental philosophy is a highly important factor in American thought. In the nebulæ of the movement constellations of men developed a national culture that no longer stood with its back to the forests and its eyes upon distant lands, whence formerly had come all things worth while. An American scholarship, letters, and religion came into being. There was less stress in current talk of building townships and sailing ships. The labors of ancestors had given descendants time to pause and think. Pious souls repeated the saw, "Satan finds mischief for idle hands!"

Transcendentalism inspired philanthropy. It stimulated enthusiasm for the anti-slavery cause, it led a movement against capital punishment, it was everywhere on the side of the weak and oppressed, the laborer, and the blind. It exalted humanity over institutions. It was a refreshing oasis in the sterile desert of American horse-sense.

Of course, Transcendentalism had its vagaries, its eccentricities, its unintelligible speculations, and its experiment at Brook Farm. These things were more or less bewildering to outsiders who could not understand them and were consequently scandalized or amused.

The materialism of the day, smacking of barnyards and freshly plowed earth, could not plumb Emerson, who had an aristocratic disdain for the common ways of thinking. To the ordinary minded, his teachings were full of peril.

The very name of Transcendentalism became a term of reproach. The old that was in religion commended itself by its venerableness and the solidity of its traditions. The new was vague and formless.

The yeomanry of America, who understood not Emerson or Lucretia, sought a panacea for all political, moral, and social problems. Old intellectual cupboards were cluttered with partially used theological patent medicines guaranteed to cure pains and aches in this world and the next by Congregational salvation, Episcopalian prayer, or Catholic supreme unction. Naturally, the mass of people were disgusted when they found no pharmacopœia in the literature of Transcendentalism.

Tiring of old style Presbyterianism they turned, not to Transcendentalism, but to the Methodist and Baptist persuasions. The Seth Parkers of America took their religion straight, with now and then a dash of burlesque. They had no nose for bouquet or palate for rare wines, and slightly suspected the morality of intellect in religion.

They are a great American tradition, the backbone of the Nation —never the head.

When Emerson first preached his new ideas, statements that have since become the pride of American culture, were met with ridicule an abuse. "What will this babbler say?" was the question asked. His speeches were characterized as "the most amazing nonsense," sheer blasphemy, and the ravings of one who could not put two ideas together. A wag insisted that whatever was unintelligible was most certainly Transcendentalism.

Not much could be expected from the farms and shops of the Nation when so polished an intellect as John Quincy Adams bitingly wrote of Emerson: "After failing in the everyday vocations of a Unitarian preacher and school-master, he starts a new doctrine of transcendentalism, declares all the old revelations superannuated and worn out, and announces the approach of new revelations."

Emerson's "Divinity School Address" offended the Boston Unitarians, the Princeton Calvinists, and the potent "North American Review." There was talk of prosecution for blasphemy.

People doubted Emerson was a Christian. The maternal grandfather of the elder J. Pierpont Morgan maintained that he was a downright atheist. Other critics called him a pantheist, which was sufficient to blast almost any one.

Progress was necessarily slow among a people dedicated to contemplating the questions, "What shall I do to be saved?" and "What ritual best glorifies God?" The Christianity of adhering to orthodox opinions, observing the Sabbath, and listening to a sufficient number of prayers, hymns, and sermons per week, was not easily challenged.

It remained for Theodore Parker to make Transcendentalism comprehensible to the body of common people.

In the third of the series of epoch-making sermons, which had begun with Channing and been followed by Emerson, Parker delivered a sermon at South Boston, entitled "The Transient and the Permanent in Christianity."

According to the speaker the permanent in Christianity was its moral doctrine and its religious life. The transient was the myth or form—the creed—wrought about it. The permanent element in

THE GREATEST AMERICAN WOMAN

Christianity was contained in the teachings of Jesus rather than the man Jesus, thus affirming Channing's idea that religion was not necessarily salvation. Christ conceived of the Holy Ghost and born of a Virgin Mary added no force to anything Jesus said or did or was. The idea simply made him one of the many mythological beings who form the hub of many religions.

Jesus as a human being and not Savior encouraged men to think virtue possible and to do good deeds on earth, whereas Christ as a divine Savior inclined men to rely too greatly on church membership and "the blood of Jesus" for salvation with little thought of mundane progress.

The teachings of Jesus, explained Parker, stood on their intrinsic merits and needed no miraculous confirmation. They would stand as firm even though it were proved that Jesus never lived.

The sermon had taken simply the transcendental principle of the "Divinity School Address" and given it concrete application. By elaboration and illustration Parker had brought directly before the popular mind what had hithertofore mostly attracted scholars and theologians.

Lucretia wrote of Parker's sermon that it was an elaborate work on the Old Testament and that it exposed many errors and false prophecies, and cleared some mysteries which had taxed the veneration of the believer.

Lucretia was amused to observe how, since Parker had come out in denial of the authority of the Bible and the supernatural origin of Christianity, certain advocates of orthodoxy were beginning to regard the formerly abjured Channing as quite orthodox, whom once they had castigated as a heretic. Compared with Parker, Channing had become eminently respectable. "So true is Theodore Parker's remark, that 'the heresy of one age is the sound faith and orthodoxy of the next.'"

Lucretia was disappointed that Parker's boldness was driving some of the Unitarians back to the "weak and beggarly" elements of old style theology. She regretted the information that Professor Norton of Harvard had been so alarmed at the spread of the new criticism (in which he had taken part) that he was prepared to disclaim his own investigations, or to doubt the expediency of circulating them for the time being.

Lucretia looked upon Parker's preaching as a step of great progress. When she wrote Quaker friends in Ireland she asked if the Bostonian's writings had permeated that far, and if Quakers there were prepared for the "advanced step." She rather doubted that they were.

She hoped her sister Martha would get Parker's "Transient and Permanent in Christianity." It was a beautiful production, she thought; "the sentiments so just, and yet so horrifying to orthodoxy." She had read a review of the sermon which did Parker injustice, "as all such pious notices do, by making him say what he had not said."

A nephew studying for Episcopalian ordination read the same review and another by his "good bishop Onderdonk." The student expressed the opinion that he never had perused "a stranger production" than Parker's, professing to be a sermon by a Christian pastor. The sermon denied "every possible groundwork of Scripture and antiquity" and was "a lamentable exhibition of the absurdities" which the human mind could believe "when it deserted Catholic principles."

The Quaker aunt thought her nephew's letter betrayed sentiments, in her opinion, "much darker" than those he was reviewing. What "lamentable absurdities those are involved in, who bind themselves to church theologies! . . . . The truth is, that all orthodox sects have modified their faith or their creeds, with the advance of rational principles of religion; and now that a large class of Unitarians are moving forward and leaving the fathers of that reformation behind, these in turn are raising the cry of 'heresy,' which dying orthodoxy seizes as a straw whereon it may rest its expiring hope."

The cry that Parker denied "every possible groundwork of Scripture and antiquity," Lucretia considered of slight importance. "Our veneration is trained to pay homage to ancient usage, rather than to truth, which is older than all."

"The more we seek truth," declared Lucretia, "the more we shall discover that we owe much of our present belief to traditions. We need to be shocked; Christendom needs to be shocked."

"We need non-conformity in our age, and I believe it will come. . . ."

She looked about her and saw the world weighted with creeds which, because it was assumed that they were of divine origin, were highly praised. Clergymen in good faith had so long assumed the

59

perfection and beauty of theology that they had come to think only
an infidel could dispute the creeds.

The Quaker woman of Philadelphia perceived a striking similarity
between modern and ancient idolatry. She illustrated it with the story
how Jesus in his day had found the Jews borne down by unmeaning
ceremonies and useless forms and sacrifices, adapted by Moses and
others, to fit the needs of a people in a low condition.

Jesus had attacked those ancient superstitions.

Lucretia believed Christianity itself had acquired superstitions, perhaps useful in the ignorant past, but which in the light of increased
knowledge were as much idolatry as the practices discountenanced by
Jesus.

Radical as was Lucretia, she did not pull down the temple to
repair the pillar. She warned her congregation there had been gross
impositions too long practiced upon the credulous, but now that skepticism as to the theology of the schools had become somewhat a duty,
she cautioned free-thinkers not to go to the other extreme and fail
to award the Scriptures "all the beautiful and blessed instruction" they
contained. "I have for some years accustomed myself," she explained,
"to read and examine them as I would any other book, as nearly as
early education and veneration would permit. I have now no difficulty
in deciding upon the human and ignorant origin of such parts as conflict with the known and eternal laws of Deity in the physical creation, be the claim to the miraculous ever so high, and the assumption
of the pathetic and God-inspired ever so strong. Still less, if possible,
do I waver, when any violation of the divine and eternal law of right,
such as murder in any of its forms, slavery in any of its degrees, or
priestcraft in its various phases, as palmed upon the religious world,
is declared to be 'Thus saith the Lord.' It is impossible by any theological ingenuity to reconcile the moral codes of the Old and New
Testaments, as proceeding from Him who is 'without variableness or
shadow of turning.'"

Lucretia was concerned more with the rights and liberties of struggling mankind than any horror of Sabbath desecration, with human
freedom than the doctrine of transubstantiation, with fair wages than
proof of the Trinity, with world peace than formal prayer.

She admitted that "reluctance to shock even the religious *prejudices* of those who yet scarcely dared think for themselves" made her

hesitate to declare views which conflicted with prevailing opinions in Christendom, yet she could not keep silent about the unhappy effect of systematized divinity on mind and character, its tendency to lower the estimate of practical righteousness and to substitute the belief that mere adherence to Christ's name was sufficient to gain everlasting life.

In her opinion the true test of the worth of a man was not belief, but conduct; not the faith he called his own or the prayers he recited, but the life he lived. Religion was a tree the fruit whereof was morality, and it mattered not if God was one, three, or a host; much less man's opinion on the matter.

Repudiating the sting of "heresy" everywhere raised against radicals, Lucretia maintained that "We are not to be regarded as denying the Scriptures, because we have not so read them, and so learned Christianity, as have many of the authors of the theological opinions of the day. . . . . Women in particular have pinned their faith to minister's sleeves. They dare not rely on their own God-given powers of discernment."

"The veneration of believers has been strengthened by their not being allowed to think. They have been afraid to exercise the test of enlightened reason which God has given them, lest they be called infidels. . . . . "

"I care not for charges of verbal infidelity; the infidelity I should dread, is to be faithless to the right, to moral principle, to the divine impulses of the soul, to a confidence in the possible realization of the millennium now."

Referring to the influence of superstition even in enlightened circles, Lucretia once told an audience of an incident abroad. She said: "When in England, I saw one of the Egyptian idols in the British Museum. Some one of our company said, 'Well, they don't admit that they worship such ugly images as this; they look through and beyond this to one Great Supreme Power.' 'They were scarcely more idolatrous,' I answered, 'than our Quaker friends when they read their Bible with such reverence last evening.' They brought it out with great solemnity, and laid it on the lap of one who was to read it, and he bowed before it, and then opened it and read it in what we Friends call the preaching tone. The passages read were those that had no particular bearing upon the lives and conduct of those then present, nor upon the present occasion which had brought us together; but it was 'the Bible' and 'Scripture,' and a chapter of it must be read in order, and in a solemn voice. I said to the friend who was pointing out this idol to me in the Museum, that the worship of that image was like the worship of the Bible as we had observed it the evening before. To me *that* was the worship of an idol."

While Lucretia believed it to be the duty of seekers after truth to purge religion of its dross, yet no one believed more firmly than she in the right of every person to his own form of worship. The word "tolerant" she never used, explaining that to admit tolerance of another's belief was to express superiority. Nor did she *grant* another a point of doctrine. Everybody had a *right* to his belief, to be respected, not granted. "Let us ever be willing to treat one another kindly, though we may differ from each other; and though we may not be prepared to receive some ideas which may be presented, let us always endeavor to strengthen one another to do that which is regarded as right."

In a day when churches suffered hardening of the arteries, Lucretia made it her duty to preach everywhere an ever-growing religion that would expand or modify, as knowledge increased. "That which is the production of one generation, and adapted to their wants, may not be needed or suited to another," she said.

There is no particular name for Lucretia's religion and she never gave it any name or cared to analyze it to see into what category it mainly qualified. It was a cheerful, kindly, practical sort of religion, as good on Monday as Sunday, and active in good works. An Irish friend thought her an humanitarian, and she replied that "the distinctions among Christian professors are found, on an analysis, to be but hairbreadth, and it is puzzling to bear in mind the distinctive points in their creeds."

In this connection she could not be said to have been a keen logician. Perhaps she was too practical to reason in the theological circle that inevitably comes back to ignorance—the point of commencement.

Guided by no succession of sign posts staked by church authorities. her sermons touched little upon what this or that prophet of old had said; there was completely lacking any attempt to dissect and amplify isolated passages of the Bible, or to reconcile its conflicting verses. She was not a legalist. She was never the cramped theologian worrying about the plausibility of the miraculous conception. Her sermons were outpourings of the Inner Light, the voice of an eloquent soul. Her spirit soared with the stars while her feet firmly trod the earth. She early preached what has since become known as the social gospel. She stressed the practical parts of the Bible, and deplored the zeal for preaching up a religion that was to do nothing until the millennium.

An influence in her religious life was James Mott, Sr., the old gentleman who had, with good intent, encouraged the younger James to become a teacher at Nine Partners.

Many of the teachings of Lucretia in her long ministry have the ring of these early writings of the grandfather who loved "plain teaching" that was calculated to lead the hearers "to practical religion." He wished there was more such preaching instead of so much speculation and divining into subjects beyond human investigations, and endeavorment to explain mysteries that would ever remain mysteries, while man was clothed with mortality.

The wise and simple advice of this gentleman, "our grandfather," as Lucretia called him in her letters, continued after Lucretia became a minister. The full extent of his influence cannot be judged, for while much he advised may be seen in Lucretia's teachings throughout life, they may largely have been inspiriting rather than formative. His ideas were, in the final analysis, the gist of unadulterated Quakerism. At least the old gentleman kept his granddaughter's feet in the path of George Fox and William Penn.

A stalwart disciple of the former, yet James Mott, Sr., cautioned Lucretia not to accept as truth everything she heard from the ministers and elders of her sect. "If what is said accords with our judgment," tutored the old gentleman in a letter to James, "let us carefully put it in practice; if it does not, let us lay it aside, and pursue what is clearly manifested: thus we shall surely know what is necessary for us to know. I very much wish that thou and thy Lucretia may in all you do, feel justified, your own minds perfectly satisfied, let others say or think what they may. Peace within will support much pressure from without."

Critics question whether reliance on the Inner Light is sufficient to guide young or ignorant persons, but the fact may not be disputed that Quakers of all ranks have led exceptionally moral lives and their doctrine, unscientific and mystical as it may be argued, has been sufficient to maintain for them as high an average (to speak restrain-edly) as that of any church led by an inspired book.

Another influence in the formative period of Lucretia's life as a preacher was the man who Jove-like hurled the thunderbolts of dissension into Quaker ranks, the "great and good Elias Hicks."

CHAPTER V

The Hicksite Schism

As early as the opening month of 1819 Lucretia broached to James Mott, Sr., the subject of this man of dissension, wondering what "our grandfather" thought of Hicks' views upon certain matters of dispute—"many Friends this way not being prepared to unite with him altogether," explained she.

On another matter also she sought advice. The propriety of the Quaker rule of Discipline that compelled the disownment of members marrying outside the Society had aroused her attention. She wrote the elders' circle, pleading, "Cannot you enlightened ones set us a good example by making some improvement in the Discipline relative to outgoings in marriage?"

She explained how two daughters of a poor woman preacher had been disowned for marrying wealthy "gentiles." It was, commented Lucretia, a "trying case."

In his answer the sage grandfather wondered with Quaker bluntness if "that sterling virtue, charity" was not getting a "little out of date" among some members of the Society. "I freely own," he admitted, "I am not enlightened enough to form a rule 'relative to outgoings in marriage.' . . . . It is something that calls as loudly for that wisdom which is from above, as any article in the Discipline. It is wrong now, but how to make it right, wiser heads than mine are required."

The heads were not forthcoming, and the Society fuddled along in a growing mood of intolerance. Progressive Friends were powerless to guide the footsteps of the majority who were possessed of that strength which comes to the bigoted who know what they want and are bothered by no problem of trying to protect the rights of any minority.

James and Lucretia worried about "outgoings in marriage," but they also had problems of a more personal portent. Within the year Lucretia had been forced out of her position in the Pine Street School, "a young woman having been engaged by the committee to take her place." Youth was not the new teacher's sole attribute of superiority, for about six weeks afterwards Lucretia gave birth to a second daughter, Maria.

The few dollars Lucretia had been able to earn were sorely missed now that there was another babe in the family.

Business was so bad that James at times would become quite "down cellar." On one occasion his cheerful wife solicited the grandfather if he had "anything to bring out of his 'treasury, either new or old,'" of an encouraging nature to produce it for James' benefit.

"Happy is the man," moaned the husband, "who has a good farm clear of debt, and therewith content, and does not know how to write his name!" Such a person escaped the anxieties of mercantile life when perhaps the hard-wrought earnings of anxious days and sleepless nights would be swept away in an hour of reverse. "I say let those who have been brought up in the country, stay there. . . . . "

Having expressed himself in true mercantile fashion, James (who was born on a farm) entered the commission business. It was a case of promoting one's self downstairs from a steady salaried position because of unemployment.

Optimistically the Quaker grandfather from his rural retreat at Skaneateles, New York, (naively imbued with the belief that a business man in a great city must of necessity be a Crœsus) cautioned the merchant novitiate to be on his guard that he did not misuse his surplus profits.

Unfounded were the grandfather's fears of squandered increment. Hard winters and stagnant trade was the story of Philadelphia in the first quarter of the century. The Revolution was over. The city of Carpenter's Hall, once capitol of the mighty, was no longer gay and prosperous. The triumph of political and social power was no longer hers. The allurements of an inflated currency were reaping their harvest. The Embargo Act and the second war with England had ruined Philadelphia's trade on the seas. Where once wharves had milled with toiling manhood, ships rotted at their moorings, and grass grew between planks that had been holy-stoned by the tread of stevedores. Mechanics paraded the streets of the city in quest of food.

Lucretia and some Quaker women organized a society for the relief of the poor. Akin to a "Fragment Society" to which grandmother Mott had been a member, Lucretia wrote her for "information thou mayst judge useful to us . . . . and if it is not asking too much, I should like to have a copy of your constitution. We expect to begin in a very small way; not because the objects of charity are few, for the sufferings of the poor were never greater here than at the present time; but our power of relief is so limited, that an attempt is almost discouraging; we are, however, going to try what can be done. James is engaged this week at the soup-house; they have handed out to many, who have heretofore been in comfortable circumstances."

James, a short time before so mournful, adds, "I have within a few weeks thought I should like to be rich, not to hoard it up, but to relieve the necessities of my suffering fellow-creatures; for many there are in our city, who are in want of food to sustain life. I have sometimes felt deterred from visiting them, for want of ability to give much relief; for what is more affecting, or more humbling, than to see helpless children crying around an' emaciated mother for bread? . . . . It had, however, one effect which may be useful, to make me number my blessings and be thankful that I have food and raiment. As this comes to be the case, a disposition that I have sometimes felt of repining my lot, will be done away with; and that it may be, I do at such seasons much desire."

This relief of the poor of Philadelphia in the winter of 1820 is the first public philanthropy on record of this noted couple.

Organized charity did not meet Lucretia's approval. She was at times discouraged about the continuation of the Fragment Society, being convinced that with her limited means she could easily do all in her power to relieve the necessities of others without associating in a society, the conversation of whose members at its several meetings had been not very interesting, instructive, or pertinent to matters in point, being given, charged the twenty-seven-year-old philanthropist, too much to "what is called gossip."

In a short autobiographical sketch, Lucretia later summed up the difficulties of these early years with the philosophical conclusion that "these trials in early life were not without their good effect in disciplining the mind, and leading it to set a just estimate on worldly pleasures."

The decade between 1820 and 1830 were years largely spent at home. Another son, likewise named Thomas, arrived in 1823. Lucretia kept no wet nurse, though the fortunes of business permitted the employment of one servant. She was mucn occupied with trying to balance the budget, then better known as making both ends meet.

It was during this period of life that she devoted much time to reading and reflection. The period of motherhood was the era of mental incubation.

The woman studied with absorbing interest the writings of William Penn. Possessing a folio copy of the works of this liberal prophet, she would lay the ponderous volume open at the foot of her bed; then, drawing a chair near, with her babe at her breast she would attentively read the passages that attracted her attention till they were stored in her memory, never to be forgotten. In public discourses throughout life she constantly made use of them to illustrate, or confirm, the views she advanced.

Her familiarity with venerated authorities served her in good stead in contests with critics, and she was uniformly able to disarm opponents with their own weapons.

On one occasion she was visited by two women Elders of the Twelfth Street Meeting who, after sitting some minutes in silence with her, stated that Friends had sometimes been unable to unite fully with her in her opinions. Particular objection had been aroused of an expression used by her at meeting the previous Sunday; they could not exactly remember the sentence, but it was something about the "notions of Christ" (and must have been sinful). Lucretia repeated the entire sentence from memory. "Men are to be judged by their likeness to Christ, rather than by their notions of Christ," asking if that was the objectionable phrase. On their admitting it was she quietly informed them that it was a quotation from their honored William Penn. The Friends sat in silence a few minutes, but the spirit was blighted. They arose and went their way, satisfied that what had been said was right. It had the sanction of time and the prestige of a revered name.

Common in days when books were scarce, Lucretia's reading was thorough rather than wide. Books were not skimmed; they were digested. "Southey's Life of Wesley, with the Rise and Progress of Methodism" came to her attention. She found it an interesting book, though some supernatural parts she did not favor. She wrote of Southey that "he appears as much attached to the doctrines of the Episcopal Church, as some of us Quakers are to ours."

These years of study plotted the chart of life. More and more Lucretia was leaning towards the views of Elias Hicks. Opinions formulated in germination were destined to carry her beyond the boundaries, not only of accepted Quaker thought, but that of the religious and moral world outside her sect.

She was rushing fast into that state of mind which was to make her a woman whom the orthodox would fear to introduce to their children lest she contaminate them with heretical ideas.

Hicks, the carpel of Quakerism, visited Philadelphia and went his way confident that he had never performed a journey so much to his "peace" and the contentment of his friends. But the Elders of Philadelphia thought otherwise. Waiting until the preacher had safely quitted the city, they pursued him with a letter in which they charged in substance that he had denied the divinity of Jesus Christ.

Hicks appears to have separated the elements of Jesus and Christ. He believed that Christ, the Eternal Word, was truly God; that Jesus, the son of Mary, was truly man, his divinity consisting of the indwelling of the Eternal Word in him.

This interpretation of Jesus Christ was acceptable to many Christians a half century later, but in the "twenties" the good people of Philadelphia shuddered.

They not only shuddered, they prepared to do a little weeding.

Their peace of mind was not soothed when Hicks, in a sermon, declared that "not all the books ever written, nor all the miracles recorded in the Scriptures, nor all other external evidence of what kind soever, has ever revealed God (who is an eternal invisible Spirit) to any one of the children of men. Heaven is not a fixed place above, nor hell below, but both are states of the soul. The blood of Christ shed upon the cross has no more power to cleanse us from sin than the blood of bullocks and rams poured out on Jewish altars could cleanse that people from their sins. We must know Christ within us to save us from sin; men depend so much on the crucifixion that they deem not the light within."

Hicks denied that God had sent Jesus into the world as his only begotten son to die for the salvation of man, by the act of death.

These doctrines gave rise to great excitement, and extended abroad. Militant Quaker missionaries crossed the ocean to put down the rebellion. Lucretia tells that on one occasion when she was present, an English Quakeress, in preaching salvation by the blood of Jesus, spoke with more than usual unction and enthusiasm. As soon as she had finished, a profound hush fell upon the meeting. What answer to a doctrine so long established could be given? Not one person stirred when slowly rose Elias Hicks, and removing his hat, uttered in deep inspired tones, "Friends, to the Christ that never was crucified; to the Christ that never was slain; to the Christ that cannot die, I commend you," referring to his concept that Christ is an inward, ever-present spiritual monitor for the guidance of man.

It is a peculiar fact that until the closing years of his long life Hicks was held in general esteem, and there appears no sign in his writings of any change of opinion or departure in his teachings. These facts suggest that the fierce conflict which arose in the seventh decade of his life is not to be attributed entirely to his denial of the divinity of Christ, or his doubts about the miraculous conception, or his disbelief in the personality of the devil, or his opinion that the story of the Fall of Man was an allegory, unless it is believed that the members of the sect had just become conscious of the full meaning of his teachings.

That many Quakers *had* become conscious of the import of his views may be gathered by their horrified recoil. Adjectives were not spared to describe the man whom once Quakers had revered as a mighty prophet in Zion. Hicks was regarded as "an emissary from the bottomless pit," and denounced as "a Tom Paine masquerading as a Quaker."

It is the opinion of Quaker historians that objections to Hicks arose partly out of his resistance to the growing tendency of Quakers to join with the Protestant sects in Bible societies and other "worldly" enterprises.

Elias Hicks was an outspoken opponent of Bible and missionary societies. He thought their methods and underlying ideas repugnant to the practices of primitive Quakerism. Idolatrous worship of the Bible had been discountenanced by the Fathers, and it was only in late years that he had observed the growth of the practice of reading the Scriptures aloud in Quaker families. An increasing reliance on the authority of the letter of the Bible, and less in the consciousness of the Inner Light, distressed him. He feared a return to the Protestant ranks from whence George Fox had so loudly seceded nearly two hundred years before.

The warrior stood in the position of one who advocated a liberal way of religious thought by a turning back to ancient Quaker ways.

The Society of Friends has been always a paradox, but never more so than during these years of controversy. On the one side stood Hicks fostering a "liberal" movement that looked back to old principles. Opposed to him were arrayed "progressive" friends who thought Quakerism too narrow in its adherence to the Inner Light (its broadest feature), and wished to keep abreast of the times by going backward to the rigidity of the old evangelical creeds.

That the doctrines of Quakerism had hardened in the flight of the centuries since Fox had come out of Leicestershire was only too evident to lovers of the "Inner Light."

Lucretia was distressed that the worship of precedent had become plainly evident. The society had contracted its tolerance into defined channels. It had built a fence about its members and wished not one of them to explore beyond its hallowed confines.

Friends were cautioned not to mingle with worldly people, they were disowned for violation of many rules of conduct, they were admonished to affect the "thee" and "thou" of Quaker speech as diligently as any Catholic adherent said his rosary, and they wore clothes as distinctly a uniform as the cassock of the monk.

The peculiar langauge, the singsong address, the wearing of hats in courts of law, were all in contrast with the deep spirituality of the society. They exemplify man's inescapable desire to force all his fellow-beings into the same narrow mold.

More and more as the infant years of the nineteenth century lengthened into maturity, the unpaid ministers and elders of the sect of Friends assumed the arbitrary powers which George Fox had assailed in the hireling priesthood.

The Elders snooped, cautioned, lectured, and reprimanded, and made life unbearable to the mass of members, especially the young. Thousands of "birth-right" children turned to other faiths because of the fostering of these harsh and narrow rules. The moral standards of the society were not only too high for the spiritual development of many persons, but its control of the details of daily life had become hardly endurable. The unemotional service of the church was not able to compete successfully with the picturesque antics of clergymen of newly popularized faiths. Gradually the society,

71

deprived of a natural source of increase, dwindled away, and split by schisms it today numbers a few adherents in the great picture of religion.

Lucretia watched with anxiety the growing assumptions of power on the part of ministers and elders, and their attempt to enforce uniformity of opinion. For this, if no other reason, she would have been in sympathy with Elias Hicks and the liberal faction. She perceived also in the teachings of Elias, opinions in alignment with those of George Fox, William Penn, and other founder Friends.

Lucretia accepted the instructions of Elias Hicks, not because they were his principles, however great she deemed him, but because she thought them true. More especially her great soul embraced the man's loftiest ideals—for be he considered radical or reactionary in regard to evangelism, he stood in advance of the minds of his day in the advocacy of woman's rights, anti-slavery, and the promotion of peace.

The matron who was to become the greatest woman preacher in America was now in her early thirties, and had been a minister a half dozen years. Yet she took no outstanding part in the gathering storm that was to split the Quaker ranks in twain. She had begun young as a "preaching sister," but duties in the home had prevented any precocious advance towards national prominence.

Two years after the birth of Thomas, another daughter was born and named for Lucretia's sister Elizabeth. The children of the family numbered four. Anna, the eldest, was thirteen, Maria seven, and Thomas two.

Occupied in the home, Lucretia left religious affairs largely to her husband. Only did she attempt to meet the situation in the society, indirectly, by stressing the fact that Quakerism was not concerned with theological disputations.

Neither she nor James would discuss controversial doctrines, though they both bore their testimony against whatever had a tendency to interfere with the right of private judgment and individual opinion. They feared if the Elders were allowed to prevail, the society would soon have articles of faith to which its ministers would be obliged to subscribe; the essential element in Quakerism would be dead, and any excuse for the society's separate existence at end.

"Of what consequence is it," opined James, "if he [Hicks] should differ from some of us in minor points, mere matters of opinion, in which he may be correct, and we incorrect."

"I think there is a spirit of persecution about," James concluded, and "I cannot remain neutral in my feelings, nor altogether in my words and actions, yet I most sincerely desire to be preserved from this spirit in thought, word, or deed that the uninterrupted harmony that has prevailed in our society in this city may not be broken or impaired."

Lucretia was pleased "to observe a disposition to prevail among a large majority to hear and judge for themselves. We have been much in his company," she wrote of Elias Hicks, "and find him the same consistent, exemplary man that he was many years ago; and I believe the criterion still remains, that 'the tree is known by its fruit.' We had a very pleasant visit from him, and dined in company with him at Dr. Moore's, who has had independence enough to remain his fast friend."

In his last letter to his grandchildren before death, the elder James Mott sensed the coming schism and gave sage advice, expressing the wish "that we might be preserved from so unprofitably spending our time in perplexities about speculative opinion upon incomprehensible subjects, to the neglect of clearly manifested duty. . . . . Stand open," he advised, "to hear and obey the inward calls of duty, but shut your ears to what this, or that, party would whisper into them. Let party business alone, meddle not with it, but endeavor quietly to repose yourselves where safety is. 'To your tents, O Israel!' —God is your tent."

The old gentleman's death removed a strong influence from the life of Lucretia Mott. The name of the kindly ancient is all but forgotten, yet his spirit, through Lucretia, was to exercise a potent effect upon thousands of persons yet unborn.

His advice encouraged the granddaughter to adhere to her policy not to become embroiled over matters of doctrinal difference. She remained aloof from participation in scenes of discord at Quarterly Meetings which brought no credit to the reputations of many of the actors.

She dreaded the Yearly Meeting of 1825. But the convocation passed without the expected earthquake. Efforts for temporary harmony proved so successful that Lucretia in an intimate letter was able

to report more about the conduct of her children than details of insti-
tutional debate.

The children did pretty well, she thought, though more exposed
to the air "by running out" while at meeting than she liked. . . . .
Thomas was still poorly, very fretful, and required patient attention
. . . . she was writing this with her babe in her arms (born that
year) . . . . she wished her correspondent could see "what a lovely,
fat, little pet" she was . . . . her father already flattered himself
that the infant looked pleased when he took it . . . . if it had
measles, they were very light, a slight eruption, but no fever. . . . .

In 1828 the anticipated schism shook the society to its foundations. After years of smoldering fire, evasions, flare-ups, soothings,
and averted gazes, the opposing factions openly admitted their differences and their inability to any longer work together.

In the civil war which ensued families were divided, congregations
thrown into commotion, and suits at law fomented between rival factions of the church for possession of its property. Quakers showed
themselves very human in courts of law, and not the less human in
after years by blaming lawyers for the spectacle of Quaker testifying
against Quaker. Public interest in the sect was much heightened by all
this, but internal harmony was wrecked for years to come.

In the reorganization of the society each faction presumed to call
itself the Society of Friends. The secessionists were derisively dubbed
"Hicksites" by those who remained in the fold. The latter called
themselves "orthodox," a deceiving appellation when it is remembered that the Hicksite seceders were more truly in accord with
primitive Quakerism.

The separation sharply divides the history of the society in
America. It was likewise a turning point in Lucretia's life.

When it became evident that free speech was no longer to be
tolerated in the orthodox society, James was ready immediately to
cast his allegiance with the Hicksite faction, but Lucretia was loath
to decide. She was finally swayed by the arbitrary conduct of the
elders of the old society, and the thought that by moving into the new
society she might be able to wield an influence in promoting flexibility
in the Code of Discipline.

With hesitating steps the sweet-faced woman of thirty-five years
left the shelter of the society she had loved so well. It seemed "almost
like death" to be shut out of old meeting houses where once she had

been so welcome, and to see cold averted looks from those whose confidence she formerly had enjoyed.

No sooner was the schism complete, and the ranks of the Hicksites filled, than Lucretia observed an inclination on the part of the leaders of the new party to instigate measures of policy marked more by a desire to uphold new sectarian purposes than to advance the principles of liberty so ably propounded by them at the time of secession. The "liberals" were now as zealous to uphold their doctrines against counter-revolution as once they had been to promote their own views when they, in turn, had been radicals.

Loving the affection of friends, Lucretia discovered with sorrow that the schism not only estranged her from attachments in the old party, but that her failure to sympathize with illiberal members in the new group met with unfriendly admonitions.

She was able to effect very little in the way of liberalizing the Code of Discipline.

Disappointments and persecutions followed Lucretia's transfer to the Hicksite party like scavengers of the sea the wake of a vessel, but never in years when orthodox Quakers left the room upon her entry and Hicksite Quakers failed to extend her the customary hospitalities of their sect, did she feel that she had done wrong in making the change. Yet could she have seen the immediate future she might have hesitated long before leaving the older branch to move so short a distance.

In the personal feuds that followed the rift, James and Lucretia took no active part. The fact that Lucretia's much loved sister Elizabeth felt best satisfied to remain with her husband's family in the old society was a trial to both sisters, but the separation did not lead to estrangement in the families concerned.

The parents of James also held to the old faith, but in this case with so much feeling that it alienated them temporarily from their son. For nearly half a century intercourse between the families of James and his uncle Richard Mott was discontinued. A bowing acquaintance with James' and Lucretia's son was established by Richard's grandson who, late in Lucretia's life, took his little daughter (thereafter a prominent Quaker historian) to visit "Cousin Lucretia" that she might cherish the memory of the great Quaker woman who, by that time, had become a leader of social thought in America.

CHAPTER VI

Black Bondage

A reason why Lucretia took no great participation in the Hicksite schism was the birth of baby Martha in 1828. There were meals to be prepared and dishes to be washed, and elder children to get off to school, one little tot to be scrubbed and fed, and Martha to be nursed.

Writes Lucretia, "I never had so many cares pressing upon me." Martha was more troublesome than the others united, although Lucretia admitted she sometimes had three of them in bed with her by daylight in the morning.

Martha was Lucretia's last child. Anna was sixteen years of age. The time was drawing near when the mother would be able to arrange her domestic duties so as to enter larger fields of labor, and to peer beyond the cramped confines of the local Quaker meeting.

The alert little woman, busy with household exactions and the duties of the Quaker ministry, little realized as she moved blithely about the house the drama she was to play ere long upon the Nation's forum.

The cynosure of the day was the babe that cooed in its cradle. The rumble of drums, the crash of arms, were all unheard. Had anyone asked her of slavery, her answer would of necessity have been rather vague.

She was opposed to slavery perhaps largely because Quaker tradition imposed that duty upon sectarians. She was still in the process of mental growth and more accustomed to accept things as they were, than she was in later life.

The subject of slavery had come to her attention as early as 1815 when information had been received that a gentleman of South Carolina had willed slaves to the Philadelphia Meeting of Friends in order that they might be manumitted, something which could not legally be done in the South except under repressive conditions. The request had involved, James had thought, "considerations of no small magnitude to civil society."

Undecided in his own mind what the Meeting should do, the husband had suggested Friends would have to act with great caution and circumspection. "I cannot help believing that much depends upon this case as regards the future situation of the blacks in the Southern States," had been his warning.

Lucretia's introduction to actual slavery came three years later when she accompanied Sarah Zane, a minister in the Society of Friends, in a religious visitation to Virginia. Her first sight of slaves at labor came, by coincidence, near Harper's Ferry, where forty-one years later John Brown was to be hanged on a scaffold, while his wife sought asylum in Lucretia's home.

Recording her first glimpse of slavery Lucretia acknowledged the sight of the poor negroes had been indeed affecting, though she had been told their condition in that neighborhood was rendered less deplorable by kind treatment from their masters.

Slavery does not appear to have made a deep impression upon her at this time if one is to judge the contents of Lucretia's few extant letters of this period. The woman's composure may be attributed in part to the fact that writing was always an effort to her and she was curiously lacking in that perception of outward things which in most persons is an incentive to narration.

When Elias Hicks had suggested the economic boycott of produce raised by slave labor as a discouragement of black bondage, she had not followed him at first. Then one day, in the quiet of Quaker meeting, the conviction had come to her that she should thenceforth refrain from the use of goods produced by slave labor.

Her mind reverted to school days at Nine Partners when recitations depicting the horrors of the Middle Passage had maintained an honored place in the school curriculum. Clarkson's stirring sentiments rang again in memory's ears as she recalled them piped in juvenile voices during weekly declamations.

She had been not unprepared for the revelation, yet the conviction of it, when it came at last, was drenching in its intensity. She knew it meant sacrifice of comfort and money, that it would necessitate the use of shoddy materials embarrassing to a person of her position in Quaker society.

Since that day Lucretia had followed earnestly in the home as closely as possible the rigorous doctrine promulgated by Elias Hicks.

She continued to do so until the proclamation of freedom in 1863 made it no longer obligatory.

So far as possible she purchased supplies from free-labor stores, one of them known by the not so modest title of "Lydia White's Requited Labor Grocery and Dry-Goods Store." In this and similar shops cotton, rice, sugar, and other Southern-type merchandise were sold under certified guarantees that slaves had had no hand in its production.

It was a hardship to use non-slave goods, and there was a difficulty in obtaining the rarified products. A grocer in Philadelphia once offered a premium of ten dollars above the market price for five casks of rice "clean of the taint of slavery."

Unfortunately for Lucretia free sugar was not always unadulterated, and free calicoes could seldom be called pretty even by enthusiasts of human freedom. Free candies were an outrage in the confectioner's trade. The last struck the children.

A birthday party was given by one of the younger Motts. The usual popular candies with mottoes, wrapped in bright colored papers, were distributed among the anxious guests. Imagine the grief of the little ones when, upon opening the packages, they found in place of silly couplets, the virtuous free-store proprietor had printed anti-slavery sentiments on the candies, such as:

> If slavery comes by color, which God gave,
> Fashion may change, and you become the slave.

Another one read as follows:

> 'Tis not expedient the slaves to free?
> Do what is right—that is expediency.

Needless to say the budding generation found it difficult at times to comprehend the principle involved. But those who were engaged in the war to extirpate slavery were upheld by an enthusiasm and devotion that derision could not laugh down nor persecution dismay.

The line of demarcation between principle and fanaticism has been always vaguely definable.

Though things were "honest" in the home, neither Lucretia nor James had been completely satisfied. They had been distressed by the fact that James was established in the cotton commission business, a profitable trade which necessitated the handling of Southern merchandise.

LUCRETIA MOTT, SOCIAL PIONEER

It was contrary to Lucretia's nature to ask her husband to give up the business for her sake, yet she had endeavored to persuade James to come to his own determination to quit the enterprise. In this she had had the support of her husband's mother, who had reminded her son of the Quaker intolerance of slavery and had cautioned him not to let love of money dull the prinicples of morality.

James was not a man to shirk any step which duty demanded, but he had a cautious disposition and was slow to form convictions. Father of a family, he had found the prospect no easy task to abandon a business that was increasingly prosperous after years of pecuniary struggle, to face again the toil and doubtful financial rewards of a new and unfamiliar vocation. He knew the business had little direct connection with slavery, and that it was held in good esteem by many people of anti-slavery instincts. The issue of slavery was not much discussed, and he found it hard to convince himself that he should attempt to stem the current of custom by so puny an individual effort.

After a struggle of five years, conscience triumphed. James quitted the cotton business and entered the wool business, in which he was to remain with varying success until his retirement from business twenty-two years later, with a moderate competency.

A friend writing of this long struggle says of him: "This was one of those spiritual crises which never leave a man exactly as they find him, but always touch his moral vision to brighten, or to dim it."

The change left the family "quite unsettled with regard to the future," Lucretia admitted, "but both were prepared to bear the consequences, and were happy in the final freedom.

The embarkation of her husband in an uncertain field of business endeavor, the addition of the fifth baby, and the petty persecutions of a religious schism, came all at once. They might have overwhelmed a less courageous woman than Lucretia Mott.

It was the severe mental discipline of the Quaker Separation that widened her spiritual vision, and made her thrive in adversity. Obliged for the first time to judge for herself upon a vital issue, and to abide by that decision at sacrifice, she underwent a mental and moral growth that enriched her life. Breaking away from narrow viewpoints she became less idolatrous of authority than ever before, and developed confidence in her own opinions. She perceived there were forests beyond the enclosed gardens of sectarianism and extended fields of labor wherein workers were needed.

The millions of down-trodden slaves in the land being the greatest sufferers, the most oppressed class of all, she felt called upon to plead the cause of Abolitionism and to do all in her power to attain its end.

She resolved she would preach against slavery, and this she did so early as 1829 on several occasions in the colored church at Philadelphia, antedating thereby the activities of William Lloyd Garrison.

If there be any humanitarian movement in modern history in which the church can be said to have taken an early and leading part, it was the participation of the Quakers in the movement to abolish slavery; a movement, however, more individual than official.

That many Quakers did not favor the agitation was only too soon pressed upon Lucretia's attention. Not that Quakerdom accorded in the satisfying excuse that the African was created by an all-providing God to serve the economic necessities of the white man. The society's objection to abolitionism lay in its dislike of any sort of disturbance which had a tendency to ruffle the calm currents of existence.

Quakers saw in the South a civilization of chivalry, honor, grace, and beauty—a pearl of scintillating brightness—laid out as a jeweler displays a stone on a background of black fabric for the world to admire. The followers of William Fox did not admire, but when the anti-slavery agitation aroused a storm of criticism, many of them took care not to denounce.

The reform of slavery was not popular when Lucretia began preaching it in the little colored church at Philadelphia.

The turn of the first quarter of the century found the issue of anti-slavery in the doldrums. Slavery, flanked on one side by the Bible and the other by the Constitution, earned the respect of all law-abiding citizens. It had the status of a vested institution. It was the economic life blood of the South, the bone and marrow of Northern industrialism.

People who spoke of upsetting this firmly entrenched system of exploitation, deified by the priests of the church and sanctified by the Fathers of the Constitution, were not considered the best class of persons. Good citizens, in popular opinion, are never opposed to anything which tends to upset the established order of things, or to imperil hard-earned fortunes. The teacher of new and unwelcome truths, the champion of abstract principles, is not befriended by the popular drift of thought.

The horrors and inhumanities of the slave trade and the injustice of holding human beings in bondage were nearly everywhere gazed upon with supine complacency.

It was current philosophy south of Mason and Dixon's line that only when man was bred in ease, with servants at his beck and call, could he acquire the grace, the genial hospitality, the virtues that marked the gentleman.

Slavery was manure applied to the root of the magnolia. Without the sweating labor of dark people, the fair flower of Southern chivalry could not bloom so fragrantly.

Always there had been remonstrators against American slavery. In colonial Massachusetts, Justice Sewall had published the first pamphlet in Anglo-America against the iniquities of the custom. In Pennsylvania, Quakers and Mennonites had expressed unfavorable opinions on the subject before the close of the seventeenth century.

The torch of freedom lit in the new world by Puritan and Quaker burned long, but not steadily. There were times when it flickered precariously and all but went out.

By the opening of the nineteenth century the clear flame had become a smudge. New England, which had taken the lead against human bondage, had had her economic bloodstream poisoned by the toxin of slavery as certainly as manufactured cloth was in demand. Boston, the center of mercantile influence, believed that the stability of her wealth depended on the continued existence of "King Cotton." It was not the slave trade of shipowners and shipmasters but the rumble of cotton mills that dulled New England conscience.

A moral issue had become entangled in the mesh of profits.

It was Lucretia's opinion that Northerners and Southerners, alike, were responsible for the shame of slavery. Hand in hand men from the two sections of the country had contributed to the maintenance of the power that was to fall in civil war.

Many people saw in slavery an abomination in the eyes of Christianity and free institutions, but few were strong enough to overlook the expediency of economics and still fewer were willing, as was Lucretia, to brook the unpopularity of criticism. Others thought it

was not right for the North, because it had no slaves, to interfere
with the South; the happiness of the negro being ignored.

There were few Lucretias to deny the sophistries of business and
law.

The American Revolution, with its wide diffusion of the doctrine
of man's equality, had given impetus to thoughts concerning the status
of black bondage. But with the coming of peace the energies of the
Nation had been given over to an unsurpassed physical expansion
which left little time for reflections of a metaphysical sort. The
philosophies of the French School waned in the minds of a hustling
people busy making the wilderness blossom with cornstalks.

In the South grew a sentiment against slavery, but it drew nour-
ishment largely from Quaker soil. Many notable Southerners of the
plantation class have been of late years put forward as no great advocates of slavery, but not one of them was noteworthy in lifetime for
any appreciable effort to free the blacks, to his own discomfort.

Individual Quakers, for the most part small farmers, attempted
to manumit slaves, but this was made difficult by legislation passed by
the planter class, in control of lawmaking, to prohibit the freeing of
slaves except for meritorious conduct. Cruel as may seem this attitude, it contained a large element of necessity and caution. Free
negroes were an economic and social menace in a land of bondage.

It was during the era between 1800 and 1830 that the American
Colonization Society took root in the soil of philanthropy, and died
with scarce a bud.

This organization called to its ranks high-minded men who hoped
in some rational way to solve the problem of slavery. It was not a
Quaker enterprise, and Lucretia was not interested in its workings.

Decades later she wrote that it was revolting to her moral sense
when she heard Dr. Tyng at a Colonization meeting say, that with all
the cruelties of the slave-trade, the horrors of the middle passage, and
the evils of slavery in this country, he was prepared to say that slavery
and the slave-trade would yet be a blessing to Africa. At that time
Liberia was held up as a great evangelizer. It was smugly argued
that had it not been for slavery in America, millions of negroes never
would have known the name of Christ.

The purposes of the society seem not to have been widely understood by most of its Abolition adherents, for its policy was exclusively
directed to the colonization of *free* persons of color, that is, manumit-

ted slaves. Henry Clay at a pre-organization meeting took occasion to describe the design as a noble one to "rid our country of a useless and pernicious, if not dangerous, portion of its population. . . . . Of all classes of our population, the most vicious is that of the free colored people. Contaminated themselves, they extend their vices to all around them. They are the most corrupt, abandoned, and depraved."

A member of the Colonization Society in a memorial to Congress explained that free negroes were "a mildew on our fields, a scourge to our backs, and a stain on our escutcheon." A writer in the "African Repository," the mouthpiece of the Colonizationers, exclaimed: "How important that we hasten to clear our land of our black population! What right, I demand, have the children of Africa to a home in a white man's country? Let Africans rise to empire; but let it be under the shade of their native palms. Let the Atlantic billow heave its high and everlasting barrier between their country and ours."

Strangely enough Clay and his associates, in advocating that these dangerous characters be deported to Africa to spread "the arts of civilized life, and the possible redemption from ignorance and barbarism of a benighted quarter of the globe," perceived nothing incongruous in what they proposed. Without arts, without science or a knowledge of government, these forlorn and allegedly immoral men and women were to be pitch-forked into the wilds of Africa, there to establish an empire to the glory of God and the Christian religion.

Politicians and philanthropists seldom are endowed with a touch of humor.

Opponents of the Colonization Society cited statistics to show the organization could not take care of the increase in slaves, let alone the bulk, and that ardent supporters who argued that by this method of Abolitionism slavery would eventually disappear from western shores were woefully deficient in mathematics.

Whittier issued statistics (surprising in a poet) which attempted to show that, during the society's first sixteen years of existence while one million human beings in slavery had died, the number of slaves in the United States had increased more than half a million, in which time the society had shipped 613 manumitted slaves out of the country!

A modern historian, friendly to the American Colonization Society, can only say of this organization that its success should not be measured solely by the number of shiploads of negroes taken out of America; that it played a part in the program of preserving national unity.

It was a patriotic, not an Abolition society.

The Colonization Society gave good people, mainly uninformed people, an opportunity to do a benevolent deed and at the same time remedy a social evil, so they thought, by doing nothing very drastic. Immediate Abolitionists, of Lucretia's ilk, refused to be deceived.

They watched ladies' colonization societies and children's colonization societies spring up side by side with missionary and tract societies, sewing circles, and revivalistic meetings. A general enthusiasm permeated the Nation; North and South were united in the unholy cause, and a cloud of sanctity lay over the land.

All the pious Sabbath schools of America and all the pious frauds of philanthropy were unable to put over Colonization; or ministers who saw in the society a providential means of sending the Gospel to Africa without going there themselves.

The opening of the rice and cotton fields of the Far South gave impetus to the cause of slavery just as it was becoming economically neutral in the northern tier of Southern States.

The domestic slave trade boomed.

Lucretia in religious journeyings through Maryland, Washington, Virginia, and Kentucky saw some of the centers of this flourishing traffic in human beings. At Baltimore, Wheeling, and Louisville great warehouses stood like stockyards. The early cattle barons of America dealt in human flesh. Male adult negroes were marched through city streets, faces southward, arms manacled, followed by a heterogeneous straggle of women and children. Leather-skinned Americans with droopy mustaches stained by tobacco juice drove them along with the impersonal detachment of stockmen driving home a herd of cows.

From an editor's chair an impecunious printer saw the genteel Colonization Society bustling around as it accomplished the deportation of a handful of negroes amidst an oratorical burst of Roman candles. He saw the rice swamps of the lowlands opening their muddy maws to engulf a steady stream of negro field hands. He saw renewed activity in Maryland and Virginia in the breeding of human beings to feed this voracious monster. Like ants, a black surge of man-power moved unceasingly along the roads of the South to the swamplands. The apathy of the Nation tended to fasten slavery permanently on the country as an incurable evil.

If slavery was to be rooted out, heroic measures were necessary. Gentle suasion had stirred but a ripple of interest. The time had come when the rights of slaves as human beings should be measured by moral principles and not the expediencies of economics, law, religion, or social custom. A mortifying leg is cured by surgery, not smelling salts.

In his opinion a race of men too long had been denied the rights of person. Slavery was wrong, hence every slave had the right to instant freedom. In 1829 the young printer pointed his trumpet to his lips, and raised his banner on the battlement of immediate emancipation, painful, brutal, costly though it be. The South heard the horn of Joshua before the walls of Jericho, and trembled on its bulwarks of church and Constitution. William Lloyd Garrison had entered the lists.

Under his guidance Abolitionism shifted its base from colonization to immediate emancipation, and the course of history was changed. Heretofore Abolitionism had been an innocuous affair in a holy atmosphere of great names. Washington and Madison, this and that soldier and statesman, had expressed his genteel dislike, but now it was as though the parlor socialist of polite social intercourse had become a raving communist.

The few Southern gentlemen who had been distressed by the evils of slavery were solidified in a united front to defend their economic interests.

It was easy, they thought, for the Abolitionists to come down from the North like wind off the frozen waters of the Arctic to freeze the hot blood of the South with theories which augured economic doom. Abolitionists had no slaves. Their lives, culture, homes, and the fortunes of their loved ones were not inseparably entangled in the throes of the institution that had thriven so many years as a respectable phenomenon. Was not the slaveholder's mother a Christian and his father a pillar in the parish church? How then to charge slavery was immoral?

In the North the conservative element drew away from Garrison as though a man was among them shouting "unclean." Solid, respectable business men, selectmen in the government and deacons in the church, saw in Garrison another starry-eyed youth who had fallen prey to those half-baked notions to which young men without means are susceptible unless early inoculated with a steady position in a counting room, where the reforming ardor may be snuffed by drab association with unimaginative minds.

Henry Ward Beecher, who later joined the anti-slavery cause when it had become popular, voiced the sense of the Nation when he pointed out to his congregation that the road to financial success and eminent respectability did not lie along paths that deviated from the normal. "Let a man be a mechanic, lawyer, physician, a merchant, or what he will, he will find that he must conform to those by whom he is surrounded. . . . . Men are accountable for their *feelings* and their *opinions* as their conduct."

This was a good practical dissertation that substantial business men were used to hear, and they went home encouraged with the thought that as long as sane, level-headed men like Henry Ward Beecher lived, the Nation was safe for dividends, notwithstanding its Garrisons, Jeffersons, and Lucretia Motts.

CHAPTER VII

THE BLACK MAN'S FOURTH OF JULY

The historic anti-slavery convention of 1833, held in the city of Philadelphia, marked Lucretia's first prominent appearance in the national anti-slavery drama.

The convention was called by William Lloyd Garrison for the purpose of organizing a national society predicated on the doctrine of immediate emancipation. Already Garrison had found that the apathy of years could not be broken without sacrifice. Three years previously he had been convicted of libel and confined in a Baltimore jail. Released—a humble, penniless, almost unknown youth, with a national drama fermenting his soul—the first woman to reach out the hand of friendship had been Lucretia Mott.

Garrison had hoped to renew his campaign against slavery at Boston within the shadows of Bunker Hill, but meeting with many discouragements, he turned to Philadelphia as the rallying place for the opponents of slavery.

An odd five dozen delegates filed into the Adelphi Building on Fifth Street below Walnut the morning that was organized the American Anti-Slavery Society. From the convention hall was to go forth a cause that was to convulse the Nation. Thunder was to come and the land was to be filled with showers of oratory, the hail of adjectives, and the rumblings of infuriated language. The subject of immediate emancipation was to be forced into the Nation's conscience in an irritatingly persistent manner.

At the height of tumult men were to glean the contents of the Bible for what the great Jehovah had said to the children of Israel centuries past. Dusty law books were to be tilted off library shelves that the words of the framers of the Constitution in regard to slavery might be read. Never in America was there to be such a revival of learning in religion and law, and never was the country to be so given over to lawlessness and an unchristian spirit as in the dark days preceding the Civil War.

But all was quiet in Adelphi Hall where, on an eminence at the west end of the auditorium, sat Beriah Green, the presiding officer, former president of Western Reserve College, a fresh-faced, sandy-haired, rather common looking man, who had the reputation of being an able and eloquent speaker. Flanking him on either side were the secretaries of the convention, Lewis Tappan, co-founder of the "Journal of Commerce," and John Greenleaf Whittier. Tappan, who was a descendant of Peter Folger, of Nantucket, was a handsome, intellectual looking man in the prime of life, a merchant who was not afraid to take his stand in an unpopular movement. When he spoke his modulated voice rang firm with hope and confidence.

The poet who acted as his associate was in many respects his antithesis. Whittier was a young man, boasting no more than twenty-six years. He had none of the calculating poise of the merchant. His eager soul trembled with the ardour of a Quaker bent on reform. He had left his secluded farm at Haverhill and the quiet life his gentle soul demanded and ventured forth into the world of acrimony. On the red-hot forge of a burning soul his pen was to forge in clanging words inspired poems for the freedom of a race.

Sitting sedately in his chair the poet observed that the delegates in the convention hall were mainly men of scant years, some in middle life, few far beyond that period. Nearly all were plainly dressed, with the idea of comfort rather than elegance. An atmosphere of earnestness prevailed that was surcharged with expectancy, for the delegates knew at that any moment a brawling mob might break into Adelphi Hall and put their convention to an end.

On the floor Whittier glimpsed a circulating flow of men, Garrison, prematurely bald; Samuel J. May, large hearted, tender, and loving; slight, eager Thomas Shipley; gaunt, swarthy Lindley Coates; portly Doctor Bartholomew Fussell, beloved physician, weaving his way among sparer frames; and James Mott, sombrely earnest.

Some of the delegates were clergymen, others Quakers, and there was a sprinkling of college professors, including Elizur Wright who already had lost a post for his bold advocacy of freedom. The names of the delegates were soon to be known in every hamlet, village and town. But largely now they were obscure figures wielding little political power or influence, or possessed of fame of any sort outside sectarian circles.

Whittier's glance reached the balcony. There he saw Lucretia, quietly knitting, with three other women guests. The young secre-

tary was enraptured with the lively matron whose acquaintance he
shortly before had made. He described her appearance that day as
a woman "singularly beautiful in feature and expression . . . . with
a face beneath her plain cap as finely intellectual as that of Madame
Roland."

The reflections of the secretary, the attention of the woman to her
knitting, were interrupted by a tap of the gavel. The convention was
prepared to organize. It was thought expedient to secure the services
of some citizen of Philadelphia of high social standing to preside over
its permanent deliberations. The problem would have been solved
had Benjamin Franklin been alive, but he had gone to his rest these
forty-three years. Accordingly the delegates made search in vain for
a titled civilian or celebrated doctor of divinity to hold before the
radicals the shield of a noted name. A committee, with Whittier as
a member, was sent to interview Robert Vaux and Thomas Wistar, of
flowering Wistaria fame, both gentlemen of impeccable social standing.

The committeemen were received by these gentlemen with the
perfect courtesy of old school dignity. They were bowed out of cool
homes with a politeness equaled only by that received by the senior
Pickwick and his unprepossessing companions. As doors blotted out
respectable figures of distinguished worthies, Whittier and his associate could not refrain a smile as they contemplated the small inducement their proffer held to men of prominence and wealth.

The information, returned to the convention that no philanthropic
gentleman could be found in the city willing to lend his name to an
anti-slavery convention, cooled a number of otherwise ardent hearts.
The delegates beheld themselves a small band of unknown men
embarking upon an enterprise calculated to attack an entrenched institution representing millions of dollars in property. What could they
accomplish without the luster of names and money? How foolish
were they to think themselves a collective David going forth to slay
Goliath.

A youngishly middle-aged matron in the gallery sensed the crisis.
With eyes luminous with excitement, Lucretia rose from her seat and
addressed the chair, uttering words described as "brief, timely, well-
chosen, and weighty" in "a clear, sweet voice, the charm of which I
have never forgotten," narrated Whittier. She reminded her hark-
eners that "right principles are stronger than great names. If our
principles are right," she urged, "why should we be cowards? Why

should we wait for those who never have had the courage to maintain the inalienable rights of the slave?" Amidst cries of "go on" she
resumed her seat and picked up her knitting. Not another word was
uttered on the floor in favor of delay. A new spirit animated the
house, and the convention was saved.

The delegates proceeded to organize. The task of preparing the
paper which was to propound the ideals of the new movement was
left to Garrison, a fit choice, for Garrison was not only the father of
the convention but the man who was making the idea of immediate
emancipation a living doctrine.

The following morning Whittier and Samuel May hurried through
gray December streets and climbed stairs that led to the little attic
of a colored friend, where they found Garrison weary, but triumphant,
writing the last sentence of the Declaration by the light of a lamp,
after a night of unceasing labor.

The draft which he read contained sentiments such as these:

"We shall organize anti-slavery societies, if possible, in every city,
town and village in our land.

"We shall send forth agents to lift up the voice of remonstrance,
of warning, of entreaty and rebuke.

"We shall aim at a purification of the churches from all participation in the guilt of slavery.

"We shall encourage the labor of freemen over that of the slaves
by giving preference to their production; and

"We shall spare no exertions nor means to bring the whole Nation
to speedy repentance."

The manifesto rejected "the use of all carnal weapons for deliv-
erance from bondage" and opposed also compensation to slaveholders,
the thought being that compensation, if any, should go to the slaves.
These words summarized better than any before or since, the gist of
the abolition movement subscribed to by Garrison, May, Whittier,
Lucretia, and others of the pacifist, or non-resistant, school.

Only minor changes were made in the document after it reached
the floor. It was the wording of a phrase that brought Lucretia again
before the convention. A constant attendant and careful listener, she
suggested the transposition of phrases in a sentence. The session
being officially under way the action of a woman arising in public to
address a convention of men in the year 1833 was unique. A number
of delegates turned in their chairs to peer at the woman whose voice

came down to them so clear, determined, yet graceful. One gentleman was so startled to hear a woman make intelligent use of the word "transpose" that the picture of Lucretia at the moment, dressed in the plain but not inelegant garb of a Friend, remained with him through life. He thought the woman singularly beautiful.

Before coming to her point Lucretia apologized for what might be regarded as an intrusion. Beriah Green assured her that what she might say would be very acceptable. As a quasi-public character she had greater reputation than many of the men on the floor; so the delegates paid her respectful attention. After the woman had spoken the chairman expressed the hope that "the lady" would not hesitate to give further expression to anything that might occur to her during the course of the proceedings.

Small wonder people thought Beriah Green a radical!

The Quakeress in the gallery made a third suggestion. Then it was announced that the document, which promised the freedom of a race, was ready for signature. The delegates came forward with gravity. As James Mott stood, pen in hand, awaiting his turn to sign the Declaration, Thomas Shipley warned him to consider well what he was about to do; a merchant was apt to suffer financial detriment in an unpopular cause more than a farmer. Lucretia overheard these cautionary remarks and impulsively commanded her husband: "James, put down thy name."

James joined in the quiet smile that rippled 'round.

It did not occur to Lucretia that she too should be allowed to sign the Declaration in the adoption of which she had played a not insignificant part. At the close of the last day the convention passed a resolution without dissent:

Resolved, That the thanks of the Convention be presented to our female friends for the deep interest they have maintained in the cause of anti-slavery, during the long and fatiguing sessions of this Convention.

Samuel J. May commented on this vote in his reminiscences, writing that he would never forget "the wise, the impressive, the animating words" spoken in the convention "by dear Lucretia Mott." But with this last recollection would be forever associated the mortifying fact that the *"men* were then so blind, so obtuse" that they did not recognize the women guests as members of the convention and insist upon their subscribing their names to the Declaration of Sentiments and Purposes.

CHAPTER VIII

THE FEMALE SOCIETY

Enthused by scenes she had witnessed at the formation of the male anti-slavery society, Lucretia resolved to form a society of women. Immediately following the adjournment of the bigger convention, a group of intimates gathered in the little schoolhouse of one of their number and organized the Philadelphia Female Anti-Slavery Society.

So inexperienced were the organizers that not one in the group felt qualified to take the chair. Lucretia confessed she had no clear idea of the meaning of preambles, resolutions, or "votings." In Quaker circles a vote was never taken, the clerk endeavoring to obtain what was called the "sense of the meeting." The first time Lucretia had witnessed a vote taken was at a convention of colored people.

The women found it necessary to call a man to the chair, and the man called to wrestle with preambles and "votings" was James McCrummel, an educated negro. Under the guidance of this member of a despised race, a constitution for a white woman's club was adopted and signed by eighteen members who, because of sex, had had less education than a energetic free negro.

Lucretia was the society's first secretary. She held the office of president during most of the society's existence. While the women listened to the secretary's glowing plans they little realized the years of labor that stretched before them—the campaign that was to be carried on steadfastly for thirty-six years—and it was well that they did not for they were stronger in the hopes of early victory.

With sanguine expectations the members of the society turned to the churches of the city for support, and abrupt was the blow they received. Ecclesiastical influences were violently opposed to a female anti-slavery society. Applications to local church bodies for the use of meeting rooms were frequently refused. One exception was held in honorable remembrance, and that was the church of the Covenanters in Cherry Street.

The brazen conduct of females forming a society did not accord with standards of Christian humility and repression, long established as womanly prerogatives. It was an almost unheard of thing for females to belong to a society not officered by males under the church's patronizing wing. The clergy saw in the new attitude of women not only "acts of flagrant sedition against God," but a definite challenge to their almost plenary power in churches patronized largely by weaker vessels.

Women had become anti-slavery pioneers when the overwhelming membership of the priesthood was concerned with theological differences more than the sufferings of enslaved humanity. Women were to sew and clothe and feed the negro on his way to Canada while clergymen huddled in churches and wrung their hands, forecasting the doom of the American home and the good old traditions of the fathers and mothers.

When it was learned that Lucretia had become an impressive speaker against slavery, that Lydia Maria Child had ruined a promising literary career by deliberately writing the first anti-slavery work in America of book length, and in particular that Sarah and Angelina Grimke had addressed "promiscuous audiences" of men and women, the General Association of Orthodox Congregational Ministers of Massachusetts, in 1837, issued a tirade against women who preached the brotherhood of man.

Women had gone far enough. Too far!

More in accordance with clerical ideals was the conduct of Henry Ward Beecher's pious sister who, when she wished to preach a sermon on woman's rights, did so through the voice of her brother, who read her words from the pulpit where it was thought a woman ought not stand.

Many an anti-slavery clergyman found intolerable the thought of equality in his own home, though in ringing words he preached equality of manhood on Southern plantations. The traditions of patriarch and family, baron and wife, and the "monkery" of St. Paul, were too strongly fixed to be disregarded by Northern abolition clerics. It was well enough to score tradition with abstract theories applicable to someone else, but when the principle was brought home, agitators found tradition insurmountable.

Despite the handicap of sex, the members of the Philadelphia Female Anti-Slavery Society spread their "infidelity" both North and South, preaching freedom for negroes and themselves, with pro-slavery opposition before them and anti-slavery enmity behind them and in the Quaker camp.

Alas! The flaming evangelical zeal that had characterized the Quakers in early days had degenerated into a respectable passivity. Early Friends had been fanatical in their emotional zeal to preach the "Light." They had hooted magistrates, disrupted sermons in meetinghouses of other faiths; hysterical women had "testified before the Lord" naked in the streets, but now members of the society were exhorted by officers in authority to "keep in the quiet," and not to join anti-slavery societies. Even in so good a cause as human liberty, Friends were warned not to associate with "gentiles," as Lucretia dryly expressed it.

It was in relation to the religious society which Lucretia loved that she strikingly demonstrated her genius for adherence to fundamental principles. Her attitude involved many discriminations as to what practices of her sect she could conscientiously break and what of its rules were, in her opinion, fundamental truths which she felt impelled to obey as a Christian. Early she cleaved to the right of private judgment against the dogmas of authority.

She assumed the stand that the principles of the Quaker Society permitted her to participate with other sectarians in moral reform, therefore she quietly defied the pleadings of members of her church who would have her adopt the policies of the "do nothing" clique. Under her guidance and that of warm friends, notably Mary Grew and Sarah Pugh, the female anti-slavery society maintained a useful existence for many years.

Its activities were ambitious. It published an address to the women of Pennsylvania, bringing to their attention the claims of the slave, and urged them to sign petitions for emancipation. It memorialized Congress for the abolition of slavery in the District of Columbia and the territories of the United States. It established a school for colored children which was partially sustained by its treasury, and there was a standing committee appointed to visit other schools for colored children in the city. Aiding the forlorn waifs of these institutions, and those of the colored orphanage, were among Lucretia's favorite duties.

The society arranged a course of scientific lectures, particularly inviting the colored people of Philadelphia to attend, perhaps the first instance in the United States of colored people being summoned to an intellectual feast in company with whites.

Important as were these enterprises, they were of secondary value to the work of direct appeal to the Nation's conscience in behalf of the merits of immediate and unconditional emancipation. Realizing that the several anti-slavery papers published by the larger societies were the most powerful instrumentalities in the creation of that public sentiment essential to the overthrow of slavery, the women expended a considerable portion of the society's funds in the direct circulation of "The Liberator," "The Pennsylvania Freeman," and "The National Anti-Slavery Standard."

James, receiving a donation of money from a Nantucket Friend for the Female Society, acknowledged the gift in a letter to the donor:

This little band (for few they are in number, and small in means,) still persevere in their efforts to aid in undoing the heavy burdens of the oppressed slave, and are encouraged to do so in the faith that their work is not in vain, or their labor for naught, notwithstanding the violent and unsparing denunciations heaped upon them by the pro-slavery portion of our citizens, among whom are some who call themselves Friends.

An interesting chapter in the society's history was its series of annual fairs, interesting not only as an institution but because of the attitude of Quaker members. When first the suggestion was made that a fair be held to replenish funds, the reaction was one of coolness. Friends looked upon fairs with suspicion. They questioned the moral influence of selling useless and vain trinkets at prices in excess of their value to purchasers who knew not what to do with them after they were bought. It was with hesitation that anti-slavery women brought themselves to this method of raising money.

Lucretia was won to the idea, feeling that the cause was a worthy one and that the prejudice of Friends was another repression which, while meritorious as a rule, had worth while exceptions.

The annual fairs inaugurated at Philadelphia became in time a Pennsylvania institution. The social attraction of these assemblies induced young persons to mingle in them, and thus were brought within the circle of anti-slavery influence laborers who might not otherwise have been converted. This in itself Lucretia considered an excellent reason why the fairs should be continued.

The money raised by the Female Society in various ways amounted, in all, to about $35,000, a remarkable sum in its day to be gathered by a small band of outcast women.

In all phases of anti-slavery work Lucretia took active part. She writes that it was her practice to supply herself with reformatory papers whenever she went from home and to scatter them abroad. Thousands of papers were thus distributed, including pamphlets and publications sent her by English and Irish friends. "We never suffer a moral paper to be torn or wasted," she said, adding humorously, "There are political productions enough to supply the world with waste paper. Part of my preaching of anti-slavery is the divine mission of scattering tracts."

She was not only a leader in the Female Society, but was the recognized leader of her sex in the main current of the movement. She was the early, the outstanding leader, the most constant worker, and perhaps the most gifted all-round speaker among anti-slavery women. Never hired as a lecturer, she gave many discourses in Quaker meetinghouses as a part of religious or reformatory talks, and also spoke at local and general anti-slavery conventions free of charge.

A true Quaker, she spoke extemporaneously, seldom making notes before hand. When bantered by a non-Quaker acquaintance that she should arrange dates for lectures ahead of time when Quakers were supposed to speak only as the "spirit moved," she quaintly retorted with a twinkle in her eye that customarily the spirit told her several days ahead when she was going to speak.

Bearing in mind her acknowledged ability as an orator, one is astounded to read her admission in old age that she always had considered public speaking a "cross," but had performed her gift for public service as a duty, making every effort to "walk worthy the vocation" and to use her skill only in behalf of noble causes.

Sharply in contrast with her abilities as a speaker were her inferior talents as a writer. Words found ready utterance from her only in the excitement of speech or conversation. Whenever possible she placed the burden of writing on James. She especially shrank from correspondence with persons not her "own folk" in years when she knew every sentiment would be isolated and twisted by enemies to her disadvantage.

Critics claimed that her speeches impressed one less logically when read in quiet than when heard in the presence of her magnetic personality. Lucretia's literary defects were most bluntly pointed out by Mrs. Sarah Josepha Hale, a woman much opposed to Abolitionism and woman's rights.

Mrs. Hale's criticisms were, in the main, those of the average man and woman of her day, though in some respects she herself was in advance of her times and would have been more so had her thinking not been so deeply cached in the narrow chasm of religion.

Mrs. Hale was many years editor of Godey's "Lady's Book." In the midst of one of the most colorful periods of American history, while the country seethed with intellectual rebellion, the lady editor fed the female reading public with sentimental novels and Sabbath school homilies, never forgetting that she was a perfect lady in the overstuffed Victorian sense.

Nothing more sharply differentiates the characters of critic and subject than to say that while Lucretia Mott was preaching human rights, Mrs. Hale was campaigning for the completion of Bunker Hill Monument, memorializing the Presidents of the United States that Thanksgiving Day be made a national festival, and resuscitating the movement to preserve Mt. Vernon as a national shrine.

Lucretia cared little for monuments and holidays. Of what avail was Bunker Hill Monument erected in the name of liberty when women did not own their clothes and had no legal right to the custody of their children—unless they were bastards! In the shadow of Bunker Hill, the use of Faneuil Hall was long denied the Abolitionists, while through the length and breadth of the land pro-slavery advocates mobbed anti-slavery agents, burnt their halls, and destroyed their literature. Three million slaves toiled in the land boastful of freedom and the Continental Congress.

Mrs. Hale's greatest book is her monumental tome entitled "Woman's Record, or Sketches of All Distinguished Women, from the Creation to A. D. 1858." The title is comprehensive and the text fulfills the promise, save only that the author did not see fit to include, even in later editions, the names of Lucy Stone, Elizabeth Cady Stanton, or Susan B. Anthony in her mausoleum of embalmed ladies. The omission of these radical leaders of American thought from a collation including so many inconsequential dabblers in poetry is strikingly significant.

Included in the book, however, is a biography of Lucretia, and therein the author seizes the opportunity to give her subject a most astounding rebuke in what purports to be a sedate book of facts.

Says Sarah Josepha Hale of Mrs. Mott, in part:

As a preacher among her own order—the Hicksite or Unitarian Quakers—she is more widely celebrated than any other, of either sex, in the United States. She has a natural gift of speech; her sermons *sound* better than they read, because her persuasive manner prevents the listener from noticing the fallacies of her reasoning, so easily detected in her printed productions.

The fallacies "so easily detected" were opinions wherein Lucretia failed to agree with her critic in interpreting the Scriptures. The Bible that has confused so many minds, broken Christendom into a multitude of sects and caused not a few first-class massacres, Mrs Hale had no trouble in fathoming to her utmost contentment. The Bible clearly shows woman's subserviency to man, explained Mrs. Hale, and she would not change a single idea in the book to please any modern fancy as, she accused, was being attempted by women who preached Abolitionism.

But Mrs. Hale was unconsciously inconsistent. She had one exception of her own. She admitted King Solomon had low ideas concerning marriage and lived in a manner not in conformity with the best traditions of the American home. It was clear to her that God had used Solomon as the medium of many of His best thoughts, but it was equally clear, as revealed to the prim editress of Godey's "Lady's Book" that He had no intention that Solomon's seven hundred wives and three hundred concubines should be accepted as a divine example of home life.

Especially was Mrs. Hale opposed to the foolish "wrangling" of "misguided women" over woman's rights, although no woman in the country materially profited so much as she by labors in a field of endeavor practically monopolized by men. The editress was so prejudiced in her opinions that whenever Elizabeth Oakes Smith, a dear and intimate friend, would go to Philadelphia, Mrs. Hale would refuse to call upon her if she spoke on woman's rights while in the city. On such occasions Mrs. Smith, like many another bold spirit, found encouragement in the home of Lucretia Mott.

In a desperate effort to prevent the spread of heresy Mrs. Hale rehearses, in the general preface to "Woman's Record," the great scheme of things as God intended, beginning with Creation and working down to the misdemeanors of Elizabeth Cady Stanton, Susan B. Anthony, and Lucretia Mott. The old scene in the Garden of Eden is revisualized with all the ancient properties, including apple and snake. The author enlarges how every step of Creation from matter to man has been in the ascending scale. "Woman was the crown of all—the *last,* and must therefore have been the best."

If there was one thing Mrs. Hale was certain of, it was that woman (while subservient to man and the bringer of sin into the world) was his moral superior "in the finer and more delicate qualities"; and the medium whereby vile man was to be redeemed from error.

Having set everybody straight on the St. Hale's version of the Bible, the translator makes the usual challenge that Lucretia's theories of woman's equality, if put into practice, "would disorganize society." And for good measure she adds the prophecy that woman, because of the moral delicacy of her nature, could never hope "to enter the arena of business and public life equally with men"; and this notwithstanding the writer's own extraordinary success as an editress.

The object of the editorial spanking made no reply, but to her defense came the outspoken Elizabeth Cady Stanton, who wrote of Mrs. Hale:

For a woman so thoroughly politic and time-serving, who, unlike the great master she professed to follow, never identified herself with one of the unpopular reforms of her day, whose pen never by any chance slipped outside the prescribed literary line of safety, to cheer the martyrs of truth in her own generation; lamentations from such a source over Lucretia Mott, are presumptuous and profane. . . . . Sarah J. Hale, shuddering over the graves of such women as Harriet Martineau, Frances Wright, Mary Wollstonecraft, George Sand, George Eliot, and Lucretia Mott, might furnish a subject for an artist to represent as "bigotry weeping over the triumph of truth."

Lucretia's occasional reference to the "sickly and sentimental novel and pernicious romance" of the day, and her pleas that women read something more nourishing than the frothy substance published in female journals may have had something to do with Mrs. Hale's spleen, for the latter was perpetrator of more than one anæmic novel which died of malnutrition.

The name of Sarah Josepha Hale lives today because of Godey's books, and Godey's books live because their illustrations, pasted onto lamp shades, make charming bedroom ornaments.

CHAPTER IX

RABID ABOLITIONISTS

Less than a year after the formation of the American Anti-Slavery Society, Garrison passed through the city of Philadelphia and found he was no longer in good repute among Abolitionists.

Philadelphia Quakers had thought Garrison a nice young man with high ideals when Lucretia had introduced him to their circle. At that time Garrison had not fully demonstrated the ardor of his crusading zeal. Since then, the publication at Boston of "The Liberator" had stirred Philadelphia conservatives with apprehension.

Short cropped heads, caged in broad-rimmed hats, were thrown into a tremor as Quakers read the "Liberator's" editorials, dank from the press. Doleful subscribers opened the sheet and were overwhelmed with moral strictures, rebukes, and arguments calculated to cauterize the rotten flesh of slavery. Columns of print belched fiery rocks into startled faces. Sentences gushed like volcanic lava. The unpretentious little sheet was charged with the destiny of a race and was one day to shake to its foundations the mightiest republic on the globe.

The body of anti-slavery, so neatly laid out by the Colonization Society, shuddered like a person emerging from a cataleptic fit. The volume of business conducted by the post office department increased. Not a mail from the South but carried hundreds of threatening letters and arguments bristling with references to the Christian religion and the supreme law of the land.

A woman there was at Philadelphia who greeted Garrison with old-time warmth. Lucretia knew that Garrison's utterances were no mad stream of passion. She comprehended that his editorials were composed of words carefully chosen with the understanding that nothing but a ruffian shake would arouse the Nation to the contemplation of its sin. The editor of the "Liberator" accepted the premise that a vested institution entrenched behind millions of dollars' worth of property cannot be attacked with the dignity with which it can be defended; that it takes an earthquake of reform to move one foot of institution.

Garrison was asked if he did not think Abolitionism would prosper better if he made use of less fiery language. Lucretia thrilled when she learned his retort: "Do *the slaves* think my language too severe or misapplied? Do that husband and wife, that mother and daughter, who have just been separated for life, by sale on the auction-block, think my denunciation of the man who inflicts that wrong too severe?" She sympathized with the editor when he said he had need to be all on fire, for he had mountains of ice about him to melt.

It greatly disappointed the unswerving Quakeress that Garrison was constrained during his visit to address the colored people in two of their churches. He would have had a public meeting, informs Lucretia, "had he met with more encouragement from our timid Philadᵃ abolitionists. He was also discouraged in the desire he felt to say a few words to our young men on the evening of their forming themselves into a society—at their request he took no part—they thinking the feeling here, of opposition to his zeal and ardent measures in the cause, was such, that it would be rather a disadvantage. . . . . It appears to me important that he should have the countenance and support of his friends. . . . . "

Timid people bore hard on Lucretia's patience. She knew there had been anti-slavery people in America before the immediate Emancipationists, most of them gentle, kindly and patient men, and they had been brushed aside or trampled under foot.

Years her friend, the meek Benjamin Lundy, had given his strength and money and the comforts of life to promote the cause of *gradual* emancipation. By kind words and religious texts he had sought to create in the South a public opinion in favor of manumission. Politely he had requested plantation owners to free their blacks and to colonize them in Haiti and Mexico, but to little avail. He had spoken at house-raisings, militia musterings and wherever he could find an audience, and had expended much energy.

True, anti-slavery societies had sprung up like mushrooms. Of 130 societies in the United States enrolling 6,625 members in 1827, 106 societies had been in the slaveholding states, but nearly all these societies had recruited membership from the Quaker and non-slave owning classes.

Lucretia could not overlook the fact that critics who opposed the doctrine of *immediate* emancipation were persons primarily not concerned with the success of Abolitionism. Some were openly pro-slavery. Many feared the safety of the Union, others desired non-interference with business, especially a business which supported so many deserving employees in Northern cotton mills and the Southern domestic slave trade. Religionists feared the infidelity of a reform that did not respect creeds. The pulpit prattled about the mild influence of Christianity and the soft melting power of the Sun of Righteousness as a means of dissolving the iron fetters of slavery, but forbade Abolitionists from lecturing in churches.

Daniel Webster was one who believed that the immediate emancipationists should not be too brutally hasty . . . . the world had not been made in a day. . . . . Slavery could not be abolished over night. . . . . What, demanded the great orator in sonorous voice, were 2,000 years in history? Negroes in rice swamps and cotton fields thought 2,000 years a long stretch of time. And so would have Webster, awaiting payment of a lawyer's fee.

A modern school of historians maintains that the anti-slavery agitation was fundamentally an economic conflict between yeomen farmers and free white labor in the North on the one side and plantation lords and exploited black labor in the South on the other.

Whatever the value of the economic assertion, and it has merit, it can scarcely be denied that the anti-slavery agitators of the 'thirties, 'forties, and 'fifties never recruited the mill workers or the bulk of the free farmers of the North. The vast horde of Irish immigrants that poured into the country prior to the Civil War were extremely apathetic towards Abolitionism. Freedom for the slaves would have encouraged many negro laborers to have emigrated North, where they would have competed with the Irish in unskilled pursuits.

Political economy, however, did influence the surge of settlers into the new Western States, many of whom had been non-slave owning whites in the South, obliged to emigrate because of social pride and their inability to compete with slave owning planters, but it is difficult to discover an economic motive in the activities of leaders such as Lucretia Mott, Benjamin Lundy, Elias Hicks, William Lloyd Garrison, or Wendell Phillips, the men and woman who initiated and kept alive the anti-slavery agitation.

Economically these people had nothing to gain by the abolition of slavery. Some, like Lucretia, suffered pecuniary losses and social ostracism, for conscience's sake. They were inspired by emotionalism and religion, not dollars or cents.

Lucretia was persecuted because she was a Garrisonian Abolitionist, because she advocated the immediate and unconditional emancipation of slaves in preference to colonization or the genteel wringing of hands. She demanded *now* what others put off vaguely into the future. She was, therefore, considered a menace to the community. Almost any reformer is who get down to brass tacks.

Gradual Emancipationists, on the contrary, were too innocuous to stir hatred. They were looked upon as soft-hearted (and perhaps soft-headed) humanitarians who should be treated with a pitying sneer behind their backs as not fitted for the rigors of this world. But they did no harm.

Lucretia opined the surgery of immediate emancipation was just. Regulating her own life in all things by principle, she exacted the same high moral standard of others, and saw no wrong in it.

John Quincy Adams called on Benjamin Lundy and walked with him to the house of Lundy's friend, James Mott, where the visitors found a tea in progress and a large party of men and women, all of the Society of Friends. "I had free conversation with them between ten and eleven o'clock, upon slavery, the abolition of slavery, and other topics; of all which the only exceptional part," adds the guest with true Adams' introspection, "was the undue proportion of talking assumed by me, and the indiscretion and vanity in which I indulged myself. Lucretia Mott, the mistress of the house, wife of James Mott, is a native of the island of Nantucket, and had heard of my visit there last September. She is sensible and lively, and an Abolitionist of the most intrepid school."

Six years later the historian Bancroft went to the house of Thomas Earle, the Anti-Masonic candidate for Vice-President of the United States, and there found, among others, Lucretia Mott, whom he had long been curious to see, and whom he found was rather a different person from any he had seen before—"womanly and yet full of zeal: a complete Abolitionist: and a thorough woman's rights advocate." He stayed an hour.

Though "a complete Abolitionist" of "the most intrepid school," never did Lucretia indulge in abusive criticism of Southern slaveholders. She did not toss the lie, hurl recriminations or, with heated adjectives, whip the emotions of her listeners. Her appeals were directed neither to lust nor prejudice, but to the higher qualities of justice and mercy. She was a reformer, not a psychopath. Her arguments were spiritual rather than emotional.

Clear in thought, calm and dispassionate in speech, her presence on the platform was marked by an earnestness and simplicity which made more powerful the occasional touch of humor or sarcasm or outburst of eloquent indignation which peppered her discourses. So persuasive was her manner that opinions received with hisses from another speaker, when repeated by her lips, were often applauded; a fact which afforded her colleagues considerable amusement.

Yet she never temporized. She stood boldly in support of a principle in the presence of foe or friend. She spoke frankly against sugar-coated references to the "naturalness" of Southern belief in slavery. She wanted none of that said she, believing the attitude was a salve to the slaveowner's conscience, the very conscience to which she made her appeal.

Nor was she convinced of the genuineness of the defense of victimization, raised by Southern farmers, in the face of the interstate slave trade and bitter opposition to gradual emancipation. Let plantation lords lose money and they soon would find a way to relieve themselves of the incubus of slavery, notwithstanding the tangle of circumstances.

Lucretia thought slavery wrong and that no ingenious pleading, no talk of expediency, could make it right. The Constitution of the United States did not make it right, nor the Bible, nor St. Paul, nor the specious reasonings of Big Business.

Isolated from the atmosphere of the institution the Quakeress saw sharply focused the evils of the system and not clearly enough the difficulties that confronted the slaveowner who, conversely, suffered a similar distortion of perspective whenever he contemplated the Abolitionist.

What the Southerner saw in his hand mirror was a different reflection than that delineated by the "Liberator's" type. In his own image the Southern master perceived a peaceful, law-abiding, Christian gentleman, trying to make an honest living, attending church regularly, and paying taxes without protest.

Lucretia thought that many persons had become so inured to slavery as not to discern its sinfulness. "It has been said that 'no one in his inmost heart ever believed slavery to be right.' We know there is this instinct in man, else it would never have been proclaimed that all men are born equal, and endowed by their Creator with the inalienable right to life, liberty, and the pursuit of happiness. Many have so seared their minds that the light of the glorious gospel, which is the image of God, does not and cannot shine in upon them."

Southerners who heard garbled reports of Lucretia's speeches regarded her as "the modern Borgia, the planner of wars and murders." Surprised indeed was one who saw her for the first time and ejaculated in astonishment, "Why, she looks like a saint. I believe she is one of the saints of God."

The slaveholder knew the Abolitionist by hearsay; and this was never flattering. He was firmly convinced that preaching freedom for the slave was incitation to rebellion and bloodshed. The haunting dread of negro uprisings ever brooded in his mind. On great farms and plantations, in vast numbers the planters and their families were surrounded by members of an ignorant and untutored race, descendants of men and women not long removed from the jungles of Africa. Short wonder the master looked upon the Abolitionist with horror, and cried out murder!

Demands were made that legislators in the free states suppress Abolition societies by law and that it be made a penal offense to publish or distribute newspapers and tracts having to do with "insurrection and revolt," that is, the abolition of slavery. Every petty postmaster in the South became a self-appointed censor of the mails. Hysteria so far developed that reform was seen in the light of treason, and free speech was throttled in the name of patriotism. It could hardly be expected that gentlemen should remain calm while measures were being taken to destroy the most of their property.

It is difficult now for many persons to conceive the extent of hostility towards Abolitionists. The Nation which feverishly had addressed Lafayette in his visit to America, and which had hailed the birth of the French Republic with joy, whose people had sung the "Marseillaise" in the streets and worn the red bonnet, was heartily opposed to freedom for negroes in its midst.

Today, the leaders of the Abolition movement rank in history among the Nation's great men and women. Statues, paintings, and memorials perpetuate their fame and are found in public halls and libraries throughout the land.

But in 1833 the money changers of Boston's financial district denounced them as mischievous men and women; while Southerners called them "infidels and Jacobins," and referred to Boston as the Paris of the Abolition Revolution. Abolitionists were children uttering strings of nonsense, "representatives of Beelzebub's heart," and "horrid monsters." They were "professional lunatics." Henry Clay alluded to their doctrine as "a visionary dogma which holds that negro slaves cannot be the subject of property." This was so ridiculous to the great compromiser that he did not consider it necessary for him to "dwell long with this speculative abstraction."

Whittier described life as a constant rowing hard against the stream of popular prejudice and hatred. One of Lucretia's associates in the Female Anti-Slavery Society wrote that the "young generation would probably find it difficult to conceive of the savage form of opposition to the Abolitionists, which prevailed during many years. In these perilous periods, Mrs. Mott proved her fidelity to her principles of non-resistance, as well as her anti-slavery faith." She would never give "her consent that the protection of the police should be asked for the maintenance of our rights."

Anti-slavery advocates were scourged and ridden on rails in the land of free speech, and not infrequently tarred and feathered. Lovejoy was murdered in Illinois and Torrey died in jail. At Concord Whittier was pelted with mud and stone. In the city of Boston—the cradle of liberty and the seat of American culture—a large group of citizens dragged Garrison through the streets by a rope.

Pennsylvania conservatives asked for a law to make punishable "idlers . . . . prowling through the country calling themselves Abolitionists without any visible means of support, stirring up discord and dissension among the people."

James Gordon Bennett urged the merchants and men of property of New York "to frown down the meetings of these mad people," if they would save themselves. "What business," he enquired in his paper, "have all the religious lunatics of the free states to gather in this commercial city for purposes which, if carried into effect, will ruin and destroy its prosperity?"

He beseeched his readers to "go on Tuesday morning to the Tabernacle, and there look at the black and white brethren and sisters, fraternizing, slobbering over each other, speaking, praying, singing, blaspheming and cursing the Constitution of our glorious Union, and then say whether these things shall go forth to the South and the world as the feeling of the great city of New York."

The customary calumnies of physical distortion had free play. Country tavernkeepers, village patriarchs, and crackerbox philosophers—the classes which held more contemporary sway over the minds of men than Ralph Waldo Emerson—congregated at meeting places and took up the hue and cry.

Some of the ablest minds of the Nation and many of its leading poets and writers (which added nothing to respectability) gave the anti-slavery cause their support. Not a few were splendid specimens of physical humanhood; in appearance, refinement, and knowledge of polite life unequaled in the Nation.

Of course the anti-slavery cause attracted to its phalanxes crank as well as brilliant minds. It was not without justification that Maria Weston Chapman—high nosed and cameo profiled—once surveyed a convention hall and remarked, "The good Lord uses instruments for His purpose I would not touch with a fifty-foot pole."

It would be difficult to deny that many rank and file Abolitionists were persons loud, excitable, and argumentative, and forever harping about slavery. The spirit of social reform is a transference of the religious instinct. Agnostic of the practical benefits of religion, the reformer goes out zealously to attain the millennium on earth rather than in heaven. In his fervor he becomes a monomaniac. He is as astringent in his thinking as the pious fanatic who surrounds himself with Bible, tracts, and sacred pictures, and is accomplished in no other subject of conversation. Yet much good has been accomplished by iron-minded people spurred on with the omnipotence of being possessors of "the truth." Intolerance and ignorance are the parents of a vast deal of human progress.

Abolitionists ranted about the Lord and morality in a way that would now be thought revolting to good taste, but they were religious fanatics no more than slaveholders who laid on lustily text for text with Garrison. Mainly, the Abolitionists were sincere and well meaning persons; the objection to them was that they spoke more frankly than was pleasant to the ear, whereupon the ear took refuge in gentility.

LUCRETIA MOTT, SOCIAL PIONEER

Like all anti-slavery agitators Lucretia not infrequently found herself in the vortex of a rough and tumble mob, but a firm and fearless manner was always her protection, plus the fact that, despite the starchy primness of the Quaker costume, she was essentially feminine.

On one occasion she visited Delaware on a religious mission in company with Daniel Neall and wife. Rumors that the trio were dangerous and incendiary characters preceded them. At Smyrna, Delaware, Lucretia was listened to quietly, but stones were thrown at her carriage when she returned to her lodgings in company with her party. This was interpreted by the Abolitionists to be an act expressive of displeasure rather than an illustration of Southern hospitality for the purpose of accelerating their horses into speedier locomotion.

After tea Lucretia sat with her host in conversation when a man appeared at the door explaining that Mr. Neall was wanted to "answer for his disorganizing doctrines." It was plain to the elderly gentleman that the better element was at work. He permitted himself to be led away by the argument of superior numbers.

Fearing violence might be his fate, the dauntless Lucretia harnessed a carriage and set after in pursuit. Neall was overtaken on the highway. Lucretia drove along while she reasoned with his captors on the injustice of maltreating an inoffensive old man for remarks made by her at a lecture. Her appeals seemed in vain. The crowd, tiring of the argument, carried Neall off into darkness where he was lost sight of, eventually returning to his friends after a moderate application of tar and feathers.

"No mob could remain a mob where she went," was Emerson's comment after he heard the story from Lucretia's lips, and we are told by the same authority that she told it "exceedingly well." Emerson adds of her, "She brings domesticity and common sense, and that propriety which every man loves, directly into this hurly-burly, and makes every bully ashamed. Her courage is no merit, one almost says, where triumph is so sure."

Upon one occasion an Abolition meeting in New York was broken up by rowdies. Some of the speakers were roughly handled by the crowd. In the height of tumult, as everybody was attempting to leave the hall, Lucretia requested the gentleman who was escorting her to leave her and help some ladies who were showing visible signs of fear.

"But who will take care of you?" queried the escort.

"This man," answered the frail Quakeress, laying a hand on an arm of one of the roughest looking hooligans. Taken aback at such unsolicited confidence the mobster responded by conducting Lucretia to a place of safety. Her friends said afterwards she had the best protector in the hall!

The following day, entering a restaurant near the place of disturbance, Lucretia recognized the leader of the mob at one of the tables. Going over to him she sat down and engaged him in conversation. As the rowdy left the room, he paused to ask a gentleman by the door the identity of the strange lady, and being told, remarked: "Well, she's a good, sensible woman."

Even in her home town Lucretia was not safe. The escaped slave, Douglass, once made the statement that Philadelphia was a city remarkable for the depth and bitterness of its hatred of the Abolition cause.

Philadelphia was a mob city by tradition. Generations of citizens had roamed its streets armed with stones, spreading the seeds of good citizenship, arson, true religion, and one hundred per cent. patriotism.

Abolitionists who came together and made speeches, though they did not destroy property or mob orphan asylums, were dangerous fanatics; they talked vaguely of a moral law higher than theology or the Constitution, which was ridiculous. Whenever they convened, riot and rapine followed their wake. True, the riots were the efforts of pro-slavery men, but this was begging the question. It was obvious to the sane mind, if Abolitionists were not allowed to gather, the law abiding element in the population would not be tempted to commit acts of violence.

Whatever the angle of observation—law, theology, or good government—the Abolition movement was a menace. The police were feeble in numbers. It was, therefore, a matter that demanded the prompt attention of the best citizens. Gentlemen of property, men of the utmost respectability, the piety and patriotism of the city, worked hand in hand with the drunken and profane, in preserving order.

After an uncommon reign of terror in Philadelphia, an acquaintance engaged Lucretia in conversation at a social gathering. Without giving weight to the fact that the recent disorders had been instigated by the pro-slavery faction of the city, the acquaintance strongly denounced the impolicy of the Abolitionists, especially the women. Much better, he urged, it would be if the ladies would carry on their reform work in the quiet of the Quaker meeting. Being much excited in the course of his remarks he became insulting. Lucretia was tempted to reply in kind, but patiently reasoned with him until at last, becoming indignant herself, as she could in a quiet way, she arose and left her friend, casting the remark across her shawled shoulder: "All I have to say to thee in parting is, 'Get thee behind me, Satan.' "

CHAPTER X

VICEGERENTS OF THE LORD

The infidelity of the anti-slavery movement consists in this
simple thing, that it has outstripped the churches of the land
in the practical application of Christianity to the wants,
wrongs, and oppressions of our own age and our own country.

REVEREND SAMUEL J. MAY.

There were brilliant exceptions to the charge that church and
clergy were the bulwarks of slavery, and many noble men of the cloth
were local and national leaders in the cause of anti-slavery. Nevertheless, the mighty power, the ruling influence of church and pulpit
was on the side of the oppressor throughout the Nation. The church
was slavery's organized hope. Slave breeding, slave hunting, and
slave holding, found its hundreds of apologists each Sabbath morn.
The attitude of the church in this momentous reform, as in war,
woman's rights, and other social questions of the day, raised the
issue whether the church was the moral leader of men or a follower of
established opinions.

Considering the power of the church in the early nineteenth century, it is possible that had religion presented an united front to
slavery it could have revolutionized public sentiment on the subject
and hastened the hour of the shackles' fall.

The American church, like the Southern slaveholder and the
Northern industrialist, was trapped in an economic pitfall from which
it had not strength to emerge. Bishops and priests, deacons and
elders, and Sabbath school superintendents, all derived livelihood
from the proceeds of slavery, directly or circuitously.

"Did not the love of power abide to such an extent among us,
there would be an instinctive revolt against slavery and wrong doing,"
was Lucretia's shrewd comment as she perceived the attitude toward
slavery rise and fall with the value of the dollar.

The Sabbath jingle of coins in collection plates accelerated clergymen to the premise that slavery was approved by the Bible patriarchs,
and that it was consequently the Christian's duty (especially that of
the minister who must be a leader in good works) to hold slaves in
order to win souls for Christ.

No class of Southern society more vehemently defended slavery than the clergy. The pastors were members of the professional fringe, owning perhaps one or two slaves apiece, which toadied to the plantation lords. They shone in the reflected glories of feudalism and the medieval church. They had the learning and the leisure to refute the arguments of the Abolitionists—to their own satisfaction and that of their congregations who footed the bills. The press groaned with the large volume of disquisitions that issued from reverend pens. Slavery became a divine trust.

Who could deny that Noah, intoxicated with wine, laid down in his tent and that Ham saw his father's nakedness and informed his brothers Shem and Japheth, who prudishly took a garment and laid it upon both their shoulders and went backwards into the tent and covered their father's nakedness? And when Noah awoke from his stupor what did he do, when he heard of Ham's conduct, but curse, not Ham, but Canaan the son of Ham (in most fatherly fashion), crying out that Canaan should be "a servant" unto his brethren.

It was this curse that descended to the negro and made slavery a Christian system in harmony with the laws of God in a land of freedom. Surely anyone could see the logic of the argument—and those who could not were heretics!

The hypothesis of the curse required four factors of proof: (1) that the negro is descended from Canaan, (2) that the curse was actually uttered as related, (3) that it announced personal slavery for more than 4,000 years on the descendants of Canaan, and (4) that Noah's curse was authorized by God.

The adherents of anti-slavery argued that neither the Bible nor science had proved that the negro was a descendant of Canaan, and that there was no evidence supporting propositions "three" and "four." It was clerical opinion that slavery afforded the negro an admirable opportunity to practice the Biblical virtue of faithfulness to master. If you are punished unjustly, declaimed good Bishop Meade (genealogist de luxe to the First Families of Virginia and author of a book of sermons for masters and slaves defining the duties of each) it is your obligation to bear it patiently; God Almighty requires that you shall.

Of course this instruction was for negro consumption; if a white man was abused, his honor as a conduit of cavalier blood demanded that he rise up and vindicate himself with less Christian humility than was allowed the inferior African.

The doctrine of submission by negroes was not the doctrine Virginian clergymen taught the American subjects of George III in Revolutionary days when all men were born free and equal, and had rights. British aristocrats had not then believed in democracy, and Southern gentlemen had rebelled with powder and ball. But a slave with the courage to strike for himself was looked upon as a loathsome creature rebellious to God and ungrateful to the master who fed and clothed him. It was inconceivable there could be a black George Washington.

On every side Lucretia was met with pro-slavery arguments: the reverend founder of the Campbellites said it would be, in his most calm and deliberate judgment, a sin against every dispensation of religion—Patriarchal, Jewish, and Christian—to suppose that the relationship of master and servant was, in its very nature, a sin against God and man. "I could as soon become a Socialist, or Free Thinker, or a skeptic, as say or think that it is immoral or unchristian to hold a bond-servant in any case whatever. . . . . I therefore dare not, with my Bible in my hand," concluded the Reverend Alexander Campbell, "join in the Anti-Slavery crusade against the relation of master and slave. . . . . "

The Presbytery of South Carolina referred reverently to the "days of those good old slaveholders and patriarchs, Abraham, Isaac, and Jacob," and others "now in the kingdom of heaven," and spoke lovingly of St. Paul, who sent a runaway home to his master Philemon, and wrote a fraternal letter to the slaveholder.

From South Carolina spoke the Reverend C. J. Postell that slavery was the "Lord's doings, and marvellous in our eyes!"

Sympathy for the slave was called "the Epidemic of the Nineteenth Century," because it ignored the beautiful assertion that God in His wisdom had relieved the negro slave of the great burden of thinking for himself. Pro-slavery churchmen in the North opined that Abolitionism was false and wrong because it destroyed "ancient landmarks" and obliterated "old paths," forgetting they would not have been Protestant clergymen in a democratic state had they followed old paths.

Sentiment in the religious North was not as uniform as in the South. Many pastors remained aloof from any discussion of the subject on the ground that a political institution should not be assailed in a land where church and state were separate. This especially was the attitude of the Episcopal and Catholic churches. Clerics who from earliest times had assumed judgment of moral, and often political issues, prudently discovered that God's kingdom was of heaven and not of this world, especially the cotton plantations and rice swamps thereof.

It was the logical argument of the hierarchy that the business of the Roman Church was to save souls (and souls could be saved as well in, as out, of slavery). The church reserved its interest in public morals till the twentieth century, when the embattled priesthood was to take a stand on the length of women's skirts and against the spread of birth control information.

Although the churches failed to assume leadership in the crusade, the Abolitionists were convinced that the reform could be effectively aided by the institution which denied them the Christian name. They made it a point to raise the question of slavery at seminaries, in the pulpit, and at all religious assemblies.

In Quaker circles Lucretia was actively spurred by the lack of "unity" everywhere discernible whenever she mentioned the subject of Abolitionism. It was a labor she carried on many years in the face of constant and bitter opposition.

Clergymen—including Quaker preaching brethren—who had slept benignly upon the subject of slavery, until the clarion call of the Garrisonians had awakened them from an almost Rip Van Winklean slumber, displayed the peevishness of men aroused from bed in the darkness of morning. They castigated the Abolitionists, they slammed church doors in their faces, and called them names.

The customary great dust was kicked up to frighten away the timid and the lukewarm. The attempt of Lucretia and other Abolitionists to arouse church communicants to a sense of moral duty was interpreted by pro-slavery and neutral clergymen as an anti-religious demonstration. The Abolitionists were very bad children who were trying to disrupt the established order of things by throwing rocks through the windows of heaven. In the stampede of horrified religionists the question of slavery was lost sight of by persons who might otherwise have taken active part in the anti-slavery agitation had it not been for granular substance in the eye which blinded them to the issue. Reverend leaders pointed out that Lucretia was not Calvinistic on sprinkling, salvation, and the divinity of Jesus, and was in all probability an agent of Satan.

Lucretia refused to pine away. She continued to lift her voice in public, and wasted no time in self-defense. She early learnt the lesson not to allow herself to be deflected from the main issue by irrelevant considerations. Wrangling whether or not the Bible taught slavery was a controversy she largely ignored. She early arrived at the opinion that disputations on the subject drew off attention from the actual point in debate and made a theological hair-splitting contest of a vital social reform. She had little faith in the literal translation of a book so full of imagery and parables as the Bible, and written years after the chronicled events. She chose rather to seek guidance in the Bible's broad sentiments of mercy and justice as a book of human experience and thought.

Said she:

We should bear our testimony against the nefarious claim of the right of property in man; and the worst of this is, that we should hear this institution claimed as sanctioned by the Bible. It is the grossest perversion of the Bible, and yet many ministers have thus turned over its pages unworthily, to find testimonies in favor of slavery. "Woe unto him that useth his neighbor's service without wages, and giveth him not for his work." This is what we should quote.

Upon another occasion she made this utterance:

And what do we ask now? That slavery be held up in every congregation, and before all sects, as a greater sin than erroneous thinking; a greater sin than Sabbath breaking. If any one of you are seen on Sabbath day with your thimble on, performing some piece of needlework, the feelings of your neighbors are shocked on beholding the sight; and yet these very people may be indifferent to great sins, regarding them with comparative unconcern, and even complacency. This is what I mean in saying that the standard of religious observance is placed higher than the standard of goodness, of uprightness, and of human freedom. To some, the sin of slaveholding is not so horrifying as certain deviations from established observances. While the sticklers for these gather together and exhibit great marks of piety, in some instances they are guilty of small acts of unkindness, of meanness and oppression toward their neighbors.

One of the evils of slavery, ignored by complacent "sticklers" for established observances, was adultery. The marriage institution was alleged by the church to be of divine origin and within its embracing care. The vows of Hymen were the boasted foundation of the American home. Yet among four million slaves at time of emancipation probably not one legal marriage had existed in all their ancestral generations in Christendom. The laws of the slave states prohibited legal marriage among negroes because otherwise it would have interfered with the sale and division of families.

An ecclesiastical body which undertook to consider the delicate problem whether, in cases of involuntary separation of slaves, the parties were free to co-habitate with others, rendered a decision that was a peculiar conglomeration of specious reasoning, deviation from Christian principles, and truckling to economic privilege. It held that separation of quasi-married couples by sale was in fact civil death, that to hold otherwise would be to expose the slaves to sexual hardship and censure from masters who might wish them to reproduce. In addition, slaves would be open to censure from their churches for refusal to perform the divine duty of obeying their masters' commands—even in so secular a function as sexual intercourse. With a magnificent gesture the church gave its blessing to fornication in black America and proceeded to be shocked at the Mormons.

Slavery was adultery sanctified by the church! This charge openly made by Abolitionists was replied to with storms of personal abuse, but never satisfactorily answered.

Tract societies especially were detested by Abolitionists. These organizations published solemn testimonies against the immoralities of tobacco chewing and novel reading and card playing, horse racing and theatre going, but in the degradation of promiscuous intercourse among negroes they saw no sin on which to take action. Everywhere they were busy promoting what they termed "vital goodness and sound morality," but in their opinion it was no violation of sound morality to sanction a system of slavery where marriage was unknown at law, where the mother was not legally secure for one hour in the possession of her babe, and where a slave who struck any white person might be lawfully killed on the spot.

Zealous and influential officers of tract societies detected no fundamental immorality in an institution that kept slaves illiterate so that they might not become unruly. It may be suspected that they found compensation in the fact that an illiterate slave could never fall victim to the pernicious habit of reading novels. Lucretia acknowledged the efficacy of illiteracy, saying: "It is impossible to hold any Nation to slavery when their minds shall be enlightened sufficiently to appreciate the blessings of Liberty."

Distant kinsmen, Levi and Allison Coffin, were compelled to close their Bible schools in North Carolina, and in South Carolina the thanks of a mass meeting were voted the "Reverend gentlemen" of Charlestown who had so promptly and so effectually responded to public sentiment by suspending their schools in which the free colored population was being taught. This was deemed "a patriotic action, worthy of praise, and proper to be imitated by other teachers of similar schools throughout the State."

Religious papers of "high moral tone," which refused to publish liquor, cigar, theatrical, and other "irreligious advertisements," likewise generally declined as unsuitable for their columns stirring anti-slavery sentiments sent them by Lucretia, who had clipped them from Abolition papers.

The opinions of radicals never defiled the pages of the Simon-pure "Friends' Intelligencer." "As the reading of most of *our* monks and nuns," explained Lucretia, referring to sectarian Quakers, "is confined to such accredited periodicals," the spread of reform was slow. "You have little idea how ignorant both classes of Quakers [Orthodox and Hicksite] are of our reformatory journals."

The attitude of the slaveholding church was broadly caricatured by a fugitive slave who entertained Abolition audiences with a mock sermon purported to be delivered by a pro-slavery minister from the text, "Servants, obey your masters." This was closed customarily by the singing of a parody on a hymn entitled "Christian Union," then very popular in the Southland; the last sentence of each verse being stressed with the sonorous enthusiasm of stout burlesque. Several verses ran as follows:

> Come, saints and sinners, hear me tell
> How pious priests whip Jack and Nell,
> And women buy and children sell,
> Then preach all sinners down to hell,
> And sing of heavenly union.

LUCRETIA MOTT, SOCIAL PIONEER

They'll church you if you sip a dram,
And damn you if you steal a lamb,
Yet rob old Tony, Doll and Sam
Of human rights and bread and ham,
Kidnapper's heavenly union.

They'll crack old Tony on the skull,
And preach and roar like Bashan bull,
Or braying ass, of mischief full,
Then seize old Jacob by the wool
And pull for heavenly union.

CHAPTER XI

DISCORD

At the age of forty-seven Lucretia was elected a delegate by the American Anti-Slavery Society to attend a proposed world's anti-slavery convention to be held in the city of London.

Behind the appointment lay considerable history. For several years the proposition had been advanced by members of the society that slavery was a political as well as moral issue, and that Abolitionists should be elected to office to accomplish the overthrow of the institution supported by law. Two men in particular—James G. Birney and Henry B. Stanton—favored the formation of an anti-slavery political party with National, State and local tickets.

Opposed to this faction was Garrison, who denied the practicability of a small group of idealists becoming sufficiently strong to effect political change. He cited the elector's distaste of "throwing away" his vote. He feared that political activity by Abolitionists would invite a swarm of intruders into anti-slavery ranks for the purpose of using the organization as a stepping stone to political preferment.

But mainly differences of opinion in the Abolition ranks had been over the participation of women at public meetings. A group of anti-slavery clergymen not only belittled Garrisonian ideals of reform by education and non-participation in politics, but were active against women whom they felt had been responsible for bringing Quaker-like concepts into the anti-slavery agitation.

Added to these insoluble ingredients had been Garrison's inclination to perceive in every idea opposed to his own the handiwork of Satan, the master artisan. Garrison had gone about correcting and rebuking alike friend or foe who had not seen with him eye to eye. Scarcely an institution, sacred or profane, but he had attacked in a manner that had brought down ill-repute upon all Abolitionists, alike. He had rebuked the church . . . . he had rebuked the Constitution . . . . he had rebuked the politicians . . . . and had spoken against those who saw danger "of shape resolving into chaos" because ladies spoke in public.

Respectable members of Abolition societies—conservative in all things, but anti-slavery—did not appreciate being tarred by the Garrisonian brush. It was bad enough to be scorned as an Abolitionist without being suspected of numerous heterodoxies.

The woman question was made an issue at the meeting of the American Anti-Slavery Society of 1840. Some one had had the temerity to suggest Miss Abby Kelly for membership on the business committee.

Up had jumped members of that committee—Tappan, Phelps, and Charles W. Denison—to announce their refusal to serve with Miss Kelly, not because the lady lacked ability or suffered a contagious disease, but solely because she was a woman. The gentlemen did not wish to see Miss Kelly's "feminine bloom" tarnished, or to lessen their own chances of salvation, so they renounced association with her from the floor.

Lucretia took a prominent part in the controversy. Pending the vote of the convention she was amazed to observe a clergyman, who with fervid eloquence had declared it a sin against Scripture for woman to vote anywhere, press through the audience urging every woman who agreed with him to vote against the motion to sustain Miss Kelly's appointment—to vote against the right to vote! When the tally was discovered to be favorable to Miss Kelly, a large minority in the society had moved out, taking with them almost all of the anti-slavery clerics and the majority of the voting Abolitionists.

The seceders formed a new national anti-slavery society. Its members were popularly known as "New Orgs," and those remaining in the original socity, "Old Orgs." Purged of the reactionary element the old society had proceeded to elect Lucretia and two other women to its executive committee, and had chosen as delegates to a proposed world's anti-slavery convention to be held in London, among others, Lucretia who had done so much to uphold the dignity of womanhood, and Charles L. Remond "an accomplished gentleman of mixed blood." By these appointments the old society demonstrated its tolerance of race, sex, and religion, which did nothing to allay popular suspicion of its subversive tendencies.

In addition to these honors, Lucretia was appointed to head a full delegation to England from the Philadelphia Female Anti-Slavery Society; and the "Association of Friends for Promoting the Abolition of Slavery" gave her a certificate signed by prominent Hicksite Quakers. The New England Anti-Slavery Society, a subsidiary to the national Garrisonian organization, likewise appointed a number of women to represent them abroad.

At first Lucretia and James questioned whether they could make the voyage to England because they had suffered recent financial reverses. The destruction by fire of a factory in which James had been part owner had been a serious loss. Lucretia's health at this time was much broken. The likelihood is that she was in her menopause. Her condition at times was so critical that it seemed as if life could not much longer be retained in the frail appearing body. Possessed of a strong constitution, she had been careless of herself and had continually overtaxed her strength. Sometimes it seemed as if the woman's body could not keep pace with her amazing mental activity. It was spiritual vitality which was the sustaining influence of her long life. Each fresh field of endeavor spurred her to renewed exertion.

No mere trip for health tempted her from the quiet of home. Only the thought of a mission to England in behalf of the slaves aroused her. Knowing her rallying power under the stimuli of a loved cause, James consented to her pleadings, and it was agreed that the pair should go. Generous gifts of money furnished part of the necessary finances, and were accepted by the Motts with the humility of persons who could receive as well as give, it being not an uncommon practice among Friends to furnish one another with money to accomplish religious journeyings.

Lucretia thanked one of the donors: "I am far from feeling that my almost wornout efforts [she was to be active forty years longer!] are worthy thy estimate of them;—and yet I would not undervalue any power bestowed for the advocacy of human freedom; and while life and strength enable, my ardent nature prompts me to work on, well rewarded in the evidence that the labor is not in vain. . . . . "

Garrison learned the decision of the faithful pair and with his customary enthusiasm wrote:

I have scarcely room to say how delighted I am to learn that you and James are soon to embark for England, in order to be at the "World's Convention." My heart leaped at the intelligence; for I could not be reconciled to the thought that you were to remain behind. I have only to regret that I shall not be able to go over in the same packet with you both; but duty requires me to be at the annual meeting of the Parent Society, which is pregnant with good or evil to our sacred cause. It will be a trying cause, but I think the right will prevail. A most afflicting change has come over the views of some of our old friends and co-workers; especially in regard to myself personally: whom they seem to hate and despise, more than they once apparently loved and honored. My peace and happiness, however, are derived from God, in whom I live and shall rejoice evermore: therefore, it is, it will ever be, in my estimation, a small thing to be judged of man's judgment.

To George Bradburn, he corresponded:

How glad, how very glad, I am that Lucretia Mott and her husband are going to the Convention! And how sorry, how *very* sorry, I am that I cannot go with them and with you! My dear Bradburn, it is not probable that I shall arrive in season to be at the opening of the Convention; but, I beseech you, *fail not to have women recognized as equal beings in it.* Interchange thoughts with dear Thompson about it. I know he will go for humanity, irrespective of sex.

Lucretia and James made the trip to England on the packet "Roscoe," Huddlestone, master, who was "a quiet commander, and very kind," described Lucretia. Much time was wasted by passengers who searched afar for sails and watched the passing waters, but Lucretia made profitable the hours on board with discussions on slavery in the West Indies with a physician, on theology with a sectarian clergyman, and on politics with Tories and haters of the Irish O'Connell. Tersely she recorded in her diary that she had made "no conversions"; it was "merely bread cast upon the waters."

The passengers debarked at Liverpool, and registered at the Adelphi Hotel, an excellent hostelry with curtained beds and "nightcaps provided for gentlemen!" Setting out for London, Lucretia experienced that startling moment which comes into the life of every person who lives past middle age. While crossing the Mersey in a ferryboat an inquisitive passenger enquired if that "old lady," pointing out Lucretia, had actually come all the way across the Atlantic. The incident merited an entry in the sick woman's journal with exclamation marks.

The journey to London was made by train and coach. The travelers passed places traditionally familiar to Americans, "gazing and admiring" until the coach turned into a dark court in the city where the passengers were discharged at the door of the Saracen's Head

Tavern, made famous by Dickens and its own shortcomings. Out of the rain, they were ushered into a small cloudy room. "And this," ejaculated Lucretia, sadly histrionic, "is London!" Rest was not had until more comfortable lodgings were established at Mark Moore's, No. 6 Queen St. Place, Southwark Bridge, Cheapside, where other Abolitionists had registered, including an anti-woman delegation from America headed by prim James Birney.

The arrival of the female delegation from Pennsylvania relaxed supercilious British brows. Lucretia was introduced as the strongest minded of the American women. Pudgy middle class Britons, who had foreshadowed an apparition of distorted womanhood, were mollified in the physical presence.

Lucretia was welcomed by Joseph Sturge, the man who had planned the world's convention. He endeavored to induce her to submit peaceably to the dictates of the London committee in charge of the convention who, it was evident, had not intention of admitting women delegates.

Quiet but undeviating pressure revealed the admission that Mr. Sturge had received letters about the women from unfriendly Americans. "We endeavored," explained Lucretia, "to show him the inconsistency of excluding female delegates, but we soon found he had . . . . made up his mind to act with our New-Organization, therefore all reasoning was lost upon him and our appeals made in vain."

Sturge was a member of the English Society of Friends. But the Quaker principle of the equality of the sexes had been forgotten when information was relayed to him that Lucretia was "not in unity" with the orthodox faith; that she was a Hicksite rebel. The Englishman was courteous, but he had no heart for a woman who was a Unitarian, perhaps not even a Christian. He had lofty ideals regarding the brotherhood of man, white and black, but narrow vision when mention was made of the sisterhood of woman. Man was the son of God; woman only a misplaced rib.

James G. Birney was the leader of the movement to resume in England the battle against women where it had been left off in America. Ordinarily a calm man, Birney's religious convictions led him to entertain extreme fears of a woman he scarcely knew. This did not prevent his looking upon Lucretia as a female devil disguised in the drab costume of Quaker bonnet and gown. All the way across the ocean the subject of the dangerous Mrs. Mott had been daily expatiated by Mr. Birney from the perspective of law, politics, and theology. Himself a lawyer, politician, and churchman, he was eminently qualified to discuss the subject from every angle except liberality.

His favorite foil in these monologues had been Mrs. Stanton, a woman in whom he had discovered a sad lack of guidance—the prankish and immature bride of Henry Stanton. Daily Mr. Birney had instructed her in right principles, and warned her to keep away from Mrs. Mott. Pacing the ship's deck, he had discoursed at length about the woman who had fanned dissension in America and completely demoralized the anti-slavery ranks; and who was not a good Presbyterian like Mr. Birney. On Lucretia's frail shoulders he had heaped the blame for the schism in the anti-slavery ranks.

Unfortunately for Mr. Birney's reputation as an advocate, Mrs. Stanton was to become a great figure in the woman's movement by the influence of the very lady warned of. Lucretia had been not long in London when she discovered that the machinations of Mr. Birney, the Reverend Nathaniel Colver, and certain orthodox Quakers in America, had been successful in their fabrications. The London Yearly Meeting of Friends disavowed association with the American Hicksite heretic, and warned members of the fold throughout the island to be on their guard. One prominent Quaker admonished Lucretia she must not expect to receive much attention from English Quakery, particularly from such persons as had young people about them, as they feared the dangerous tendencies of her doctrines.

The duty of disclaiming fellowship once performed, Lucretia found a general disposition, with marked exceptions, to show her civility, if not warm friendship. Outside the sacred circle of Quakers and clerics she found her company in much demand. Her reputation as a liberal thinker and a zealous Abolitionist had preceded her across the sea. Harriet Martineau had presented her in print to the British public, and Fredrika Bremer, the celebrated Swedish novelist, had praised her in a book of American travels.

Lucretia found herself in the vortex of the social whirl. To her joy social events were intellectual. She was glad that there was not much catering, as she described it, to "animal appetite"—food and drink.

A pleasant practice in English Abolition circles was the service of tea at committee meetings and the appointment of a chairman to preside over a general conversation after the transaction of formal business. Custom had not included the participation of women, but as several had crossed the Atlantic as delegates, conventionalities were relaxed sufficiently for women to join the circle. Only one English woman availed herself of the privilege at the first meeting. This was Elizabeth Pease, descendant of a Quaker family of high social standing, and niece of Edward Pease, "Father of English Railways."

In the course of an evening Lucretia was induced to give an account of the mob that had tarred Daniel Neall. In narrating the circumstances Lucretia mentioned that the members of the party were traveling with a Minute in the usual custom of Friends, adding parenthetically, "I suppose it is understood here that when I speak of Friends, I do not allude to those in connection with Friends in this country." This careful distinction of Hicksites from orthodox was not enough for Josiah Forster, who did not wish the stigma of Unitarian doctrines to be fastened onto English Quakery.

As soon as Lucretia had finished her story and while the "Oh's" and "Ah's" were circulating, Josiah arose to explain that although Lucretia had stated that she was not in connection with those acknowledged by the English as Friends, yet he felt conscientiously bound to inform those present that she was not a member of *any* Society of Friends.

James came to his wife's defense, recounting briefly the division that had taken place in the Society of Friends in America. He explained that he held a certificate from the Monthly Meeting of the branch to which he belonged and would read it if desired, but that as the anti-slavery convention was not necessarily connected with any sectarian view he had no wish to intrude the subject; still was prepared to meet it then or any other time.

Of more importance to Lucretia than religious classification was the hardening attitude of convention authorities respecting women delegates. Her efforts to mold opinion made small progress, and neither she nor any other woman was given opportunity to appear before the London committee.

At a social function one evening, the official information was brought that it had been definitely decided that women were not to be admitted as delegates to the anti-slavery convention.

On the following day the courteous Mr. Sturge, reinforced with another gentleman, called early on the American ladies to "reconcile" them to their fate. Recalling the formation of the Philadelphia Female Anti-slavery Society, Lucretia suggested the idea of organizing a woman's convention. Mr. Sturge was shocked, and "doubted" if the ladies would be allowed to meet. There was some fear, he said, that religious subjects would be introduced.

The men of the British and Foreign Anti-Slavery Society were not willing to trust the women of England to meet a half dozen of their sex from America, without the overlordship of husbands and fathers. The religious virginity of English womanhood had to be protected by every possible means.

The proposal of a woman's convention died of mulnutrition. Lucretia found little support from English women who waited on their husbands with bated breath. The convention idea was dropped with the comment in her diary that she was "much disappointed to find so little independent action on the part of women." She reported a social gathering as "a stiff company of Anti-Slavery ladies at our lodgings, a poor affair. We find little confidence in woman's action either separately or conjointly with men, except as drudges."

Lucretia occasionally found opportunity to draw blood. At a tea given in the anti-slavery rooms conversation veered to free produce. Someone in the group called on Mrs. Mott to say a few words. Lucretia quietly asked why gentlemen could not say all that was wished to be said, without calling on a rejected woman. The spunky woman, who had been called "spitfire" at school, gave the men a few thrusts and sat down with the request that her husband or Henry Grew speak her opinions for her. Some gentlemen present demanded more. Whereupon she sallied in and "gave a few rubs," as she expressed it, on the exclusion of women; the audience crying "hear! hear!" with hearty British enthusiasm at every blow. The chairman was greatly offended and later informed Lucretia in private that he would have called her to order had she not been a woman.

In the early splendor of a June morning varied knots of delegates from different countries wended their way through the crooked streets of London to Freemasons' Hall in Great Queen Street, Drury Lane, where in a noble room, one of the largest in the city, was that day to be opened the world's first anti-slavery convention.

In vestibules, men and women, like molecules met, broke, and reconvened here and there, discussing the disposition of the women delegates from America. Every strategy had been used by leaders to promote peace and harmony by efforts to induce women delegates to withhold their credentials. Lucretia insisted that the delegates had no discretionary powers in the matter. They had been elected to represent certain societies, and it would be their duty to submit their credentials. The responsibility of rejection must rest on the convention.

By eleven o'clock the spacious hall was filled. A portion of the lower floor opposite the entrance was appropriated to ladies who were admitted as guests. Convention authorities had neatly arranged matters so that the question to be discussed by the convention would not be whether women should be rejected as delegates after taking their seats, but whether they should be admitted in the first place.

Garrisonian Abolitionists were ready to press the combat, though they sensed it would be a losing battle. The cards were stacked, the dice were loaded; though Quaker women did not think of it in such terms. Officers took their chairs. The prominent presence of James G. Birney as a vice-president and H. B. Stanton as a secretary did not strengthen the hopes of the American women.

Famous participants included the Duke of Sussex; Lord Brougham, who has given his name to a carriage; Lord Morpeth, Chief Secretary for Ireland; Guizot, the French minister to St. James; Dr. Lushington; Dr. Bowring; Thomas Campbell, the poet; Sir Eardley Wilmot; Sir C. Buller; the Right Hon. C. P. Villiers, President of the Poor Law Board; and two rising young men, John Bright and William E. Forster.

The meeting was called to order and the venerable Thomas Clarkson, a giant in the movement which had abolished slavery from the British colonies, made an impressive entrance and was received by the audience standing in reverent silence.

Infirm under the toils of eighty-one years, lame, and nearly blind, the sole surviving member of the committee that had begun England's movement for emancipation had arisen from the invalid's couch to address a few words to the audience that had convened from all parts of the world. In deference to his delicate health there was no applause, no cheering; a calmness prevailed. The audience saw personified a name already spoken among them as a great tradition. Even the customary shouts for O'Connell, as the fiery Irish leader entered the hall, were stilled.

Clarkson's address delivered, he withdrew from the hall, and with him went harmony. Young Wendell Phillips arose majestically, his lion-like head tossed for combat, and moved the convention that a committee of five be appointed to prepare a correct list of members with instructions to include in such list the names of all persons bearing credentials from any anti-slavery society. This opened at once the admission of women delegates in a manner abrupt and distressing to lovers of harmony and committeemen who had worked so diligently to sidetrack women.

The patrician lawyer from Boston, in the course of his speech, brought out the fact that the convention's invitation had been addressed to friends of the slave in every Nation and of every clime, and had been interpreted by Massachusetts in its broadest and most liberal sense to include men, women, and negroes. In his own State, he contended, women for several years had been admitted to an equal seat with men at anti-slavery gatherings. "We do not think it just or equitable to that State, nor to America in general, that, after the trouble, the sacrifice, the self-devotion of a part of those who leave their families and kindred and occupations in their own land, to come three thousand miles to attend this World's Convention, they should be refused a place in its deliberations."

Phillips was earnest. His bride was a delegate from Massachusetts. Halting him for an instant at the door of the Convention Hall, she had commanded him not to be "simmy-sammy"; and Phillips aroused was an orator who had few equals.

A member of the London committee took the floor in response to Phillips and explained to the assembly that as soon as the committee had learned the liberal interpretation Americans were giving the first invitation, a second had been issued which limited delegates by implication to "gentlemen" only, as the advocates of women well knew.

A prominent Englishman, Dr. John Bowring, supported Phillips. He refused "to have a World's Convention measured by an English yardstick."

Reverend J. Burnet entreated the convention to be calm. He had great respect for ladies, he assured the delegates, but he felt that an

English interpretation should be put on English phraseology. He referred to the fact that a large number of American Abolitionists thought as did the English. In a touching appeal to the American ladies he asked that they conform to British custom and withdraw their credentials.

A London solicitor by the name of Ashurst directed the convention's attention to the fact that had it attempted to convene in Virginia instead of London, Virginians would have made the analogous argument that the male members had no right to put themselves in opposition to the prejudices of Southern society in respect to slavery, and hence should not meet. Confusion followed this thrust, and many voices wrangled simultaneously. Henry Grew, of Philadelphia, supported Mr. Burnet, and thought the inclusion of women at the convention would be, in the view of many, not only a violation of the customs of England, but of the ordinances of Almighty God.

Things began to look ominous for the ladies, including Mr. Grew's daughter, a delegate-reject from Pennsylvania. English prejudice had been enough; now the women were confronted by the Prophets and the Church. Lucretia knew that this would come. Not a human problem of the century could be discussed without some clergyman purporting to speak God's decision in the premise. Lucretia could answer a jurist or a philanthropist, but when a clergyman wrapped the mantle of divine authority about his opinions, reason had no weight.

The skirmish was over, although arguments continued. Scholarly John Bowring thought the custom of excluding females in England was more honored in the breach than observance, pointing out that the commander-in-chief of the armies and navies of Britain and the ruler of millions of subjects of many races in many climes was a woman—good Queen Victoria (cheers). He referred to the Quaker church which had given women religious prominence. "I look upon this delegation from America as one of the most interesting, the most encouraging, and most delightful symptoms of the times," he said.

The Reverend Elon Galusha rebutted this argument with learning and logic. He explained how Queen Victoria had sent her consort, Prince Albert, to take the chair upon a like occasion, thus showing her sense "of propriety by putting her Head foremost in an assembly of gentlemen"—the head, of course, being the husband and containing the brains.

Just what the Queen would have shown in an assembly of women has to this day remained a mystery. Perhaps the solution was contained in the next remark: "I have no objection," concluded Mr. Galusha, of Perry, New York, "to woman's being the neck to turn the head right, but do not wish to see her assume the place of the head." Many of the women to whom Mr. Galusha assigned the neck in his carving of morals were among those who had early moved the hearts of men against slavery, when husbands spoke only to second their views.

Conscious of this, George Bradburn raised a stentorian voice above the din. Those who could not see, could hear. Mr. Bradburn was somewhat deaf and with the habit of such people he spoke with a roar that was loudly diffused, though but dimly heard by himself. He had been a Universalist minister at Nantucket, and was a member of the Massachusetts Legislature. As a politician and a priest of an unorthodox sect he professed not so great a heavenly dispensation respecting woman's place in the world as did God's duly authorized agents on earth, the Presbyterians.

Half an hour Freemasons' Hall resounded to this man's thundering voice as he bombarded the prejudices of England and the hypocrisies of America. Mr. Bradburn was disgusted by the sanctimonious phrases of his divine brethren, whereby they took away every natural right of woman and substituted in its place fulsome flattery.

There was the rat-tat-tat of prepositions and small words; the thunderous boom of adjectives which shell-like soared in great arcs across the hall to fall into the ranks of the huddled clergy, attendant with a great slaughter of self-esteem. Occasionally Mr. Bradburn's oratorical light infantry rushed the enemy with bayonets of verbs and in hand to hand fighting the clergy line could be seen to waver, break, and retreat in bad order to take up another position on the eminence of an ancient prophet, flanked by St. Paul.

Mr. Phillips, being urged on all sides to withdraw his motion, spoke again, in part asking:

Whether any man can suppose that the delegates from Massachusetts or Pennsylvania can take upon their shoulders the responsibility of withdrawing the list of delegates from your table, which their constituents told them to place there, and whom they sanctified as their fit representatives, because this Convention tells us that it is not ready to meet the ridicule of the morning papers, and to stand up against the customs of England. In America we listen to no such arguments. If we had done so we had never been here as Abolitionists. . . . . When we have submitted to brickbats, and the tar tub and feathers in America, rather than yield to the custom of not admitting colored brethren into our friendship, shall we yield to parallel custom or prejudice against women in Old England . . . . Massachusetts cannot turn aside, or succumb to any prejudices or customs even in the land she looks upon with so much reverence as the land of Wilberforce, of Clarkson, and of O'Connell.

James Gillispie Birney added a word about the dangers of "promiscuous female representation," rolling the phrase unctuously about his tongue. Mr. Birney deprecated the impression made by American speakers that the woman question was settled in America. On the contrary it had led to a split in the anti-slavery ranks and was no more the custom of America than of England. Besides, continued he, with a wide divergence from the point, those who were for the rights of women were also in favor of what was called the "no-human-government" system, that is, non-resistance, the inference of which was anarchy.

The Reverend Mr. Morrison fixed an eye on the American delegation. "Would the American brethren put the Britisher in such a predicament? Why did they insist in keeping up a discussion in which the delicacy, the honor, the respectability of these excellent females who have come from the Western World are concerned?" Reverend Morrison trembled at the thought of discussing the question in the presence of such fragile beings, and was bold to say that were it not for the introduction of woman's rights he believed it would have been impossible for the ladies to have listened to the discussion.

The Reverend Mr. Stout deserted morality long enough to suggest that the convention confirm the list of delegates and not divide on the paltry question of equal rights, thereby suffering the whole tide of benevolence "to be stopped by a straw." "You talk of being men," he challenged, "then be men! Consider what is worthy of your attention." The words fell on deafened ears. Learned Doctors of Divinity raced about the convention hall, Bibles in hand, quoting words of Scripture and waving their fists beneath the noses of disputing brethren who did not know woman's place.

Burnet argued woman's subjection was divinely decreed when Eve was created, and he was willing to show all comers the exact passage.

Exasperated George Bradburn again sprang to his feet. "Prove to me, gentlemen," he cried with tremendous emphasis, "that your Bible sanctions the slavery of woman—the complete subjugation of one-half of the race to the other—and I should feel that the best work I could do for humanity would be to make a grand bonfire of every Bible in the Universe."

Heresy had gone far enough. When the roll was polled it was found that the respectable element had won. An overwhelming majority favored pious feminine virtue. Custom, bigotry, and prejudice had triumphed with the aid of St. Paul and gentlemen who felt that they had God and his angels especially in their care and keeping, and were in agony lest something be said to shock the heavenly hosts.

The conservatism of the clergy had been more than a match for the eloquence of Phillips, the strategy of Ashurst, and the vocal scalping knife of Bradburn. The "delicate ladies" of the Western World, happily for their virtue and the esteem of good men, remained in their places behind the bar and curtain which screened them from the public gaze. The sanctity of the Turkish harem had been transferred to Great Britain.

This sacrifice of human rights by men who had assembled from over all the globe to proclaim universal emancipation was offered in the presence not only of Lucretia Mott, but of such women as Anna Jameson, Amelia Opie, Mary Hewitt, and Elizabeth Fry, more celebrated than any of the men who had argued against them.

The outcome of the issue left Lucretia to sit in silence while speakers inferior in courage, vision, and mentality were allowed to utter what they chose, provided they were of the male sex. An Irish writer in the Dublin "Weekly Herald" described the rejected Lucretia and the place she won in the opinion of spectators:

The middle of the front seat of the ladies' own portion of the hall, was the usual seat of one who was certainly one of the most remarkable women in the whole assembly. Opinions differed materially as to whether Clarkson, Buxton, O'Connell, Garrison, Thompson, Sturge, or Birney were the greatest men, but nobody doubted that Lucretia Mott was the *lioness* of the Convention. She is a thin, petite, dark-complexioned woman, about fifty years of age. She has striking intellectual features, and bright vivacious eyes. This lady has the enviable celebrity of being one of the most undaunted, consistent, able, and indefatigable friends of the slave, being paramount even amongst the female Abolitionists of America.

. . . . We shall not discuss the question here, as to whether it is right for women to take an active and prominent part with their brethren in promoting philanthropic objects; but we shall take the liberty to express our wish, that half the temper, fullness of mind, warmth of heart, distinctness of utterance, facility of elucidation, and vivacity of manners, which distinguished Lucretia Mott, had been the gift of nine-tenths of the gentlemen who raised their voices in the Convention on behalf of the slave, and for our edification.

The writer of the editorial added:

The day we left London after the conclusion of the Convention, we met Lucretia Mott in the Egyptian salon of the British Museum, where her slender figure, animated features, and simple attire, contrasted strangely with the cold and solemn relics of primeval times, by which she was surrounded. We heard her remark on that occasion, that it was hardly reasonable to wonder so much at the idolatry of the Egyptians, seeing that the prostration of mind which prevails in the present day, if not so revolting in its manifestations, is at least as profound.

Unfortunately for Lucretia, two towering figures were absent from the hall during the debate about delegates—William Lloyd Garrison, delayed at sea, and Daniel O'Connell, of whom it has justly been said that wherever humanity sank under the blow of the tyrant there were found the genial heart and clarion voice of Daniel O'Connell sympathizing with the fallen and rebuking the oppressor.

Garrison had been delayed, first, by an important meeting in America. Boarding ship, he was then becalmed off Sandy Hook, ere his voyage had scarcely begun. Long tedious hours the Emanicipationist spent in letter writing and prognostications whether women would be admitted at London. He questioned: "With a young woman placed on the throne of Great Britain, will the philanthropists of that country presume to object to the female delegates of the United States, as members of the Convention, on the ground of their sex? In what assembly, however august or select, is that almost peerless woman, LUCRETIA MOTT, not qualified to take an equal part?"

On the day of the convention's convocation Garrison was on the high seas, four hundred miles off Cape Clear. While the wrangle waxed furious at Freemason's Hall, the delayed delegate was writing. "Today the Convention meets in London. May it lay a broad foundation upon which to build the super structure of Humanity! If it shall exclude from a participation in its proceedings a single human being, on account of complexion, or sex, it will excite the pity and amazement of after ages. I am inclined to think," adds Garrison prophetically, "it will act upon the 'new organization' basis, and while it will not proscribe color, it will make a distinction in sex."

The greatest figure in the Abolition world arrived in London when the convention had but three days more to sit. Lucretia greeted him "with joy and sorrow too," as she expressed it. She told him about the convention's conduct and that the battle had been carried against him before his coming. Impulsively, the new arrival then and there decided upon a typical Garrisonian course of conduct. The members of the British and Foreign Anti-Slavery Society had refused to permit women to sit in their convention, therefore he, Garrison, would not sit with them.

Lucretia reasoned with him on the subject, but the man was obdurate. Demanded he, "Which delegates had the right to reject others? As well might the women get together and reject the men." With these words Garrison climbed the stairs that led to the balcony of the building, wherein the convention had been transferred from Freemason's Hall, and took a chair in the front row where his benign features and shining pate became conspicuous objects to the eyes of the delegates below.

"Haman never looked more blank on seeing Mordecai sitting in the king's gate with his hat on," commented Elizabeth Cady Stanton, than did the London committeemen when Garrison took his place aloft by the side of Lucretia and gazed down upon them with the kindly, inscrutable, patronizing expression for which he was noted.

Garrison had been mobbed, imprisoned, and prosecuted in the courts of America while the philanthropists of England had been playing the rôle of "home guard," and drilling, and making gestures of warfare, and suffering bloodless martyrdom in a land where slavery did not exist; and here was the hero come from the battlefront who deigned to give them no comradely look; he avoided their Arch of Triumph; he refused to play the servile rôle of distinguished guest.

The man had come 3,000 miles by water to speak on the subject nearest his heart, and he chose to share the enforced silence of rejected women. His presence to the delegates as they looked up at him seemed to say:

135

Lucretia Mott is my friend. She, too, has come from the battle-front a wounded and dusty soldier in the holy cause. She has suffered pecuniary loss. She has been ostracized, persecuted from the pulpit, howled at in convention halls, and her home threatened with fire. Now in England you have said she shall not sit with you—you who are a band of raw recruits, unworthy the accolade of a handclasp by a veteran-in-arms.

Although Lucretia sat apart from the delegates, her situation was not one of isolation. She reigned almost as a queen holding court. Famous gentlemen from distant parts were introduced to her. Came Daniel O'Connell, everywhere beloved or hated with equal temperature. The Irishman strode across the hall with the pride of a man who knew that the eyes of the multitude were upon him. He met the sweet-faced Quakeress behind the curtained bar where she sat a center of attraction. He bent low and murmured words of flattery. The woman thanked him, but rejected "complimentary speeches in lieu of robbed rights." O'Connell retired not quite so satisfied.

The frail woman with the fascinating eyes and animated features, whose spirited flow of soft "thee's" and "thou's" was never bitter, charmed O'Connell as many another man had been. He thought over the situation. He saw in it something of his own position—a leader of a despised cause and a despised people. He came back the next day for another visit, a little more humble, a trifle more serious, with no thought to satisfy curiosity, but to discuss principles. He admitted dissatisfaction with opinions formerly held by him.

An agreement was entered into between the pair. Lucretia penned the Irish Liberator a note in which she explained that the rejected delegates from America were desirous "to have the opinion of one of the most distinguished advocates of universal liberty, as to the reasons urged by the majority for their rejection, *viz:* that the admission of women, being contrary to English usage, would subject them to ridicule, and that such recognition of their acknowledged principles would prejudice the cause of human freedom."

The Irishman replied in a long letter wherein he unequivocally placed himself on record as favoring the admission of female delegates, and regretted his absence from the floor during the battle. He avowed his first impression had been strong against woman's admission, "But when I was called on by you to give my personal decision on the subject, I felt it my duty to investigate the grounds of the opinion I had formed; and upon that investigation," he informed her, "I easily discovered that it was founded on no better grounds than an apprehension of the ridicule it might excite if the Convention were to do what is so unusual in England—to admit women to an equal share and right of discussion. I also, without difficulty, recognized that this was an unworthy, and indeed a cowardly motive, and I easily overcame its influence."

The tide of popularity turned swiftly, yet the favor of a great name did not console Lucretia for the opportunity missed to raise her voice in behalf of freedom. Deep in her heart had been gashed a wound which was not to heal and which was to have results momentous in the social and political history of mankind. The men who raised their voices against her were to pass to the grave, many of the more bitter of them unknown to fame, but the seed of woman's rights which they this day had planted in her soul was to change the course of human events greater than did Magna Charta or the Declaration of Independence.

"The 'woman question' has been fairly started, and will be canvassed from the Land's End to John o'Groat's house," exulted Garrison, who was a wild-eyed extremist. "Already, many excellent and noble minds are highly displeased at the decision of the Convention, and denounce it strongly."

Little groups of molecules gathered and broke and gathered again in combinations which friendships had formulated in the course of long and strenuous days of debate during the world's first and last anti-slavery convention.

CHAPTER XII

British Liberals

Visits to England in the 'forties were not lightly undertaken. The voyage by sea was not only slow and dangerous, but arduous and uncomfortable. A number of the American delegates were resolved to see something of the islands before returning home from what would be doubtless their only trip abroad.

After the convention's adjournment Lucretia remained a few days close to London. She attended a meeting at Exeter Hall, presided by the Queen's uncle, and a great tea at the Crown and Anchor. Lucretia informs us that the preparations at the tea were simple, and the company very large, being about four hundred guests. Three tables ran the length of the room and a fourth at right angles at the head. After tea cups were removed, a chairman took charge of the occasion and speakers were called on by name.

The speechmaking was informal; any person wishing to make remarks obtained easy liberty of the chair. Stanton made the first speech and was followed by a Frenchman. Garrison, loudly called for, came next. Irked by convention restraints, he took the opportunity to express himself on numerous points. He dug at English Abolitionists who, going to America, failed to express their sentiments about slavery. He discoursed serenely on the woman question and the conduct of the London committee, launched into the Irish controversy, paid his disrespects to war, and concluded by stressing the need of a universal language. His speech caused no little stir.

He was followed by the governor of Sierra Leone on topics more pleasing to the ear.

An intrepid guest sent up a note to the chairman requesting that Lucretia Mott be called on to make the next speech. No sooner did the chair announce her than Reverend Mr. Scoble, who had had a part in Lucretia's not exposing herself at the convention, tried valiantly to throw himself into the breach. He stood up and begged opportunity to make some explanations about the governor's speech which, he emphasized, was something that was of *importance*. His request for the floor was drowned by cries of "No! No!

138

Mrs. Mott!" The clamor persisting, the woman was obliged to speak. She informed Mr. Scoble that she would occupy very little time.

She chose the boycott of slavery goods as her topic. This was something that weighed on her mind. Arguments at the convention by the Reverend Colver and his satellites on the status of women had aroused little comment in her diary, but her dander had been touched by what she termed "the reasonings of the apostate Colver" and his friends on the subject of abstinence from the use of slave products.

Nathaniel Colver had told the convention how tender he *once* had been on the subject; how he had gathered his little ones about him and explained to them the cruelty and wickedness of such participancy, and such had been the influence of his labors that not one of his children could have been hired to touch a sugar-plum or a cake. Suddenly he discovered that self-denial was not easy, and had given up the restriction.

A gentleman by the name of Crewdson had been encouraged to say that he, too, used to be particular in not using slave produce until he considered that if all should do so, the Manchester mills would stop and the people starve, so forthwith he let fall his testimony, and aided in perpetuating slavery lest his countrymen should have to seek another business.

A third speaker had explained how formerly he had been so zealous as to have the cotton linings taken out of his vests; all at once he found that he might be carried too far, so had sagely concluded to immerse his conscience to the full in slave-gotten goods.

With the memory of these things in mind Lucretia spoke how necessary it was that Abolitionists remain loyal to their principles. When she had finished it was noticeable that the Reverend Mr. Scoble no longer desired further information about the speech of the governor of Sierra Leone.

A noteworthy Abolition party, influenced by the Quaker touch, was held at Tottenham, the estate of William Ball; a formal affair where everything was done in style, including servants in livery. In attendance were writers, leading parliamentarians, diplomats, and philanthropists.

The host had been remarkably kind to Lucretia during the convention. Inviting her to his house he had said that while he wished her to understand that they differed materially on what he considered very important religious points, yet his heart went out to her in much affection. As a favor to women he granted Elizabeth Fry "permission" to pray at the party—an incident of interest because Miss Fry was so much more noted than Mr. Ball. A still less accomplished gentleman, George Stacy, made attempt to block Elizabeth's prayer, but was overruled in the name of courtesy, if not morality.

The activities of Stacy, Scoble, and Josiah Forster, if anything, heightened interest in Lucretia, and everywhere in England she had become either an object of attention or the subject of discussion. The Dutchess of Sutherland and her brother, Lord Morpeth, later Earl of Carlisle, expressed a desire to meet her and the other American Abolitionists—a desire amounting to a command.

Arrangements were made for the introduction to take place at a lawn party to be given at Ham House, home of the rich banker Samuel Gurney, who strangely combined bill discounting with philanthropy. Seven barouches conveyed the Americans to the estate, a pleasant ride of five or six miles through English countryside, where the guests found their destination to be an elegant house set in a beautiful park, with grass as soft as velvet. "A great sensation did we produce," bragged Garrison, "as we paraded through the streets of London. The dinner was magnificent, and all the arrangements on the most liberal and elegant scale."

If youth and beauty did not describe the dominant note of the reception, at least the event was remarkable for the weight of respectability present and the incongruous blendings of fashionable costume with Quaker garb. Perambulating the gardens of Ham, Lucretia perceived the Braithwaits, famous in English Quakery; the Forsters, and many more, some of them members of the English gentry and persons of figure and estate, a surprising number of them connected with the House of Gurney whose greatest member, John Joseph Gurney, was aptly called the Quaker pope.

Lumbering among them was the imposing form of Thomas Fowell Buxton, in a few weeks to be made a baronet, a man powerful, sleek and slow as one of his own brewery horses. A tolerant man, he held membership in the Church of England and lived in harmony with a Quaker wife and was, as may be suspected, a successful politician.

Swirling humanity stopped and the buzz of conversation was sharply stilled as came the important event of the afternoon. "Much fuss," in Lucretia's opinion was made when the Duchess and daughter, accompanied by Lord Morpeth, clattered up in a coach and four with outriders and six servants in livery, amidst dust and the pawing of hoofs and all the ostentation befitting a woman who was daughter of an earl and a duke's wife.

Close to Mrs. Mott, when the noble guests and their accoutrements arrived, stood Samuel Gurney. Trained in the unimaginative routine of the money business he was seized with a momentary panic. "What shall I do with the Duchess?" he panted.

"Give her your arm," suggested Lucretia, "and introduce her to each member of the delegation."

This the banker did, and when the Duchess was presented to Lucretia, a spectator reports that the gracious ease of the noble-woman was fully equaled by that of the simple Quaker lady. Oblivious to all distinctions of rank except goodness, Lucretia talked "freely and wisely" on many topics and manifested not the slightest embarrassment during the marked occasion.

Garrison with his usual enthusiasm related how the Duchess "on parting, shook me cordially by the hand." Lucretia uttered no such brag. If the Duchess was interesting it was for what reposed in heart and mind and not because of what was filed in the archives of the Heralds' College.

It had been hoped my mutual friends that Lucretia would meet the Duchess' daughter, described by Lady Byron as "an uncommon girl" only sixteen years of age; she who later became the Duchess of Argyle. The introduction was effected by Samuel Gurney, who proposed that the girl walk with the American.

Lucretia described: "After all were coupled and arranged, we paraded about the lawn awhile, then stood in a group and heard S. Gurney read a letter from the Marquis of Westminster, on the Convention, British India, the cotton trade, etc., which elicited some remarks that were listened to with attention, though startling in the beginning. . . . . "

Knowing Lucretia's propensity for veiling her own comments with this sort of language, it may be assumed that she took the occasion to express again some of her alarming opinions in regard to the boycott of slave goods.

Fifty guests sat down to the table, a cold collation, except the fish and soup and vegetables. Elizabeth Fry asked a blessing. Conversation was "free and pleasant." When the meal was over the host made a short speech expressing satisfaction at the presence of so many American participants. He was followed by speakers English and American. Lucretia was offered an opportunity to express a few sentiments, but the invitation was declined in deference to some gentlemen present who had had enough female speechmaking for one day.

The affair at Ham House was Lucretia's introduction to the peerage. Heretofore her chief acquaintance had been with the literary and philanthropic classes. These groups were bisected by a number of men influential in government, including Buxton, Morpeth, Charles Pelham Villiers, Dr. John Bowring, and William Edward Forster, the latter afterwards an influence for harmonious Anglo-American relations during the difficult years of the Civil War.

Morpeth was a youngish man of about thirty-eight whose political rise had been fast. His maiden speech in Parliament had been in support of an unpopular motion for the relief of Roman Catholic disabilities. He had also advocated the repeal of Jewish disabilities and put through many Irish reforms. Lucretia was much pleased with the republican manners, urbanity of spirit, unostentatious deportment and intelligent mind of this enlightened nobleman who worked in behalf of subjected races, and bore gracefully the name of the Howards of England. He did more to give it lustre, by breadth of tolerance, than did its admirals with the sword.

Charles Pelham Villiers, Benthamite and friend of Mill the philosopher, Lucretia met at Bowring's house and walked with him and George Bradburn over two miles of English roads.

Bowring, later Sir John, found Lucretia very interesting, and she was his guest upon more than one occasion. The host was a cosmopolite, familiar with twenty languages, a scholar who enjoyed the advantages of personal acquaintance with most of the eminent authors and poets of his time, and who had won fame in diverse walks of life. Like Morpeth he was a defender of oppressed peoples—Maltese, Manxmen, and Irish.

Little wonder he attracted Lucretia's admiration. She called at his seat where once lived Mill the historian, and found the several rooms lined with books and curiosities, its windows overlooking Milton's garden and the house of Jeremy Bentham—historic soil. The master entertained her with anecdotes of Bentham. There was "much talk on war in general" and kindred subjects, for Bowring was the presenter of a petition to the House of Commons for the insertion of arbitration clauses in treaties.

The American Quakeress observed that his family consisted of a "sensible wife" and nine children, "the eldest daughter very clever."

Later she called on the Sage of Chelsea with whom the conversation was not satisfactory. Carlyle was an anti-abolitionist, or rather, she found his sympathies were absorbed in the poor at home, their own poverty and slavery. Lucretia was disappointed in him. Carlyle expressed himself differently. He was "much pleased with the Quaker lady—Mrs. Mott—whose quiet manner had a soothing effect on him."

Another time, "tea'ed" at Bowring's, she met Dwyer, author of popular poems, "old and blind, but very cheerful, and his wife whom he married at seventy"; the very Dwyer who had so amused Charles Lamb; seedy, slovenly, and unsophisticated, but withal so kindly disposed to mankind that once when conversation veered to a notorious criminal who had murdered two families and stirred the horror of all England, he could only say that the criminal "must have been rather an eccentric character."

The evening passed pleasantly with talk of Eastern customs. Lucretia was especially impressed with Bowring's statement, "When Christianity comes recommended by its benevolence as well as its creed, it will recommend itself to all."

Lucretia was happy in changing circles of brilliant men, and a few worth while women. Everywhere she went she was feted by intellectuals not so delicately constructed that they feared to expose themselves to new viewpoints. Liberals who were foremost in movements that were enlightening the kingdom did not find her a dangerous woman, although she had publicly preached in a London church to the horror of Calvinistic clergymen.

Lucretia was visited at her lodgings by Robert Owen, George Thompson, Dr. Hutton the principal Unitarian clergyman of London, and other persons of prominence. In Garrison's words she won " 'golden opinions' on all sides, in spite of the ceaseless efforts of the Orthodox Quakers to obstruct her course."

A noted Londoner, whose company she enjoyed, was William Ashurst of Muswell Hill. Here she dined in company with Harriet Martineau's brother, the world's leading Unitarian, and Dr. Epps the homœopathic physician, and William and Mary Hewitt. Also invited was the Reverend John Keep of co-educational Oberlin College who, as president of the board of trustees, had given the casting vote that had admitted colored students. This had given rise to a scandal among respectable persons who predicted an immediate crop of little mulattoes on the Oberlin campus.

It was "a visit full of interest and delight," described Lucretia, for these were delightful people with inquiring minds, willing to talk on any subject. Epps in particular was interested in a multitude of public questions and incessantly lectured and wrote in connection with parliamentary, religious, and social reforms.

Not until later did he publish his series of lectures on the non-existence of the Devil which ended his usefulness on earth, in the opinion of the orthodox. His command of words, fine sonorous voice, and animated manners made him an interesting table companion, and the vivacious Lucretia was in her element. The Howitts, too, attracted her attention, so completely bound up in each other that jocular friends referred to them as "William and Mary" and maintained that they had been crowned together like their royal prototypes. The minds roved the fields and pastures of philosophy, religion, and sociology. Only a few shied at forests wherein historic devils lurked. One such devil was socialism.

I never felt any special interest in Owen, or his followers [commented Lucretia], "but desired to meet them in a Christian spirit, knowing they would not ultimately prevail, only as they were in the right. Our dear Elizabeth Pease, and some others, quaked with fear, when Owen called on W. L. Garrison, and the other Americans . . . . lest it might give us a bad name; but I regarded no such fears. How could a common observer of heads and countenances tremble for the influence of such a man! The most successful refutation of his visionary scheme is to suffer him to be his own expositor!

The man whose sin was his love for the laboring man, who had relinquished the successful management of cotton mills and the opportunity to wax rich and powerful by the sweat of thousands of underpaid operatives—men, women, and little children—was feared in the best circles of England and America because he denied the right of the few to exploit the many.

Previous to meeting Owen, Lucretia had met his partner, the chemist William Allen, lecturer at Guy's Hospital, called by the Emperor Alexander of Russia a "Model Quaker."

At a tea at Muswell Hill, Lucretia's diary gives no insight of topics discussed except that it was a delightful evening and that she "went into their nice kitchen and buttery." Lucretia never lost contact between the physical and the metaphysical.

She broke bread with James Haughton and his daughters from Ireland. Haughton, she found, wrote on temperance, slavery, British India, peace, capital punishment, sanitary reform, education, and similar questions of the day, and was in general considered a public nuisance. He took prominent part in a series of weekly meetings held at Dublin, where numerous social questions were discussed in such manner that a local newspaper called his school the "antieverythingarians."

An Unitarian, Haughton worked with Daniel O'Connell the Catholic, and for good measure was president of the Vegetarian Society of the United Kingdom. When Lucretia discovered that Haughton's father had been disowned by a Quaker Meeting for countenancing Hannah Barnard, a Nantucket Friend, persecuted in England in 1797 for unsound doctrine, she was much pleased and informed her diary that "she liked to meet with those who have suffered for their liberal views of Christianity." The sin of Hannah Barnard was that she preached that war had never been prosecuted at the command of God.

A name of frequent mention in Lucretia's European diary is that of Lady Byron. It was she who commissioned Lucretia to carry an engraving of Dr. Channing as a mark of grateful regard, explaining, "I say grateful because his writings have done good to more than one of those whom I love best." When Lucretia left London and they parted for the final time, the expressions between the two women were of the kind "not soon forgotten."

Lady Byron had been a regular attendant at the Convention. Side by side in their cloistered pew Lucretia had explained her views on woman to the poet's widow. Once the couple dined with the "opulent Unitarian lady," Elizabeth J. Reid, and there had been "much conversation on housekeeping, neglect of families, and woman's proper sphere; a very pleasant visit." Lucretia's opinions having been very much misrepresented during her stay in England, she made a special point afterwards to call on Lady Byron and more fully explain her position.

She found Lady Byron not only interested in emancipation, but also in common school education. Here was common ground, and the two discussed their mutual interest. Lady Byron invited Lucretia to visit a school in which she was interested, five miles out of London.

"On the way we had much talk about Unitarians," quotes the American. Lady Byron expressed herself as not quite satisfied with any sect, but had often thought Quaker and Unitarian would suit her and that an advantage would arise from visits to other places of worship.

"Her remarks were sensible, and showed dignity of character and Christian simplicity." Her school was to try the experiment of manual labor, and was answering well. The Quakeress was invited to address the pupils and was pleased to have the teacher "express unity" with the discourse. On the return trip the couple made calls, discussed slavery and other topics, and at Amelia Opie's, Lady Byron left Lucretia with a large party of guests, to drink tea and discuss the same topics at greater length.

Amelia Opie was less solemn than Lady Byron. Her waggish face, saucy mouth, and twinkling eyes seemed out of place in the setting of Quaker garb. A dashing woman, she said once that everything she saw the first time disappointed her except Mary Wollstonecraft and the Cumberland Lakes.

Her writings made Walter Scott "cry his eyes out," and Prince Hoar was made so wretched by one of her books that he lay awake all night after reading it. It was not until Mrs. Opie had reached the age of fifty-six, and became a member of the Society of Friends, that she reformed sufficiently to give up the novel writing that so distressed emotional Victorians.

Lucretia gives in her diary an occasional insight of her opinions of some of her acquaintances. The American editor, Nathaniel Peabody Rogers, was one whom she grew to like "better and better." William Ashurst was a man who had "enlarged views" . . . . William Edward Forster she called "a noble young man; I like him very much. He often comes to our lodgings."

In youth Forster had worked twelve hours a day in the mills and spent his evenings studying mathematics and politics, a sort of English

Benjamin Franklin able to find something to do the whole twenty-four hours of the day without resorting to sleep.

William possessed none of Josiah Forster's bigotry, but more of his father's tolerance. The latter, though unalterably opposed to Unitarian sentiments, so much so that he had been sent to America to fight the heresy, when introduced to Lucretia by Sarah Pugh as an "orthodox Quaker" had begged that there might be no allusion to religious differences between them, saying, "Thou touchest me in a tender spot; I remember thee with much affection in Baltimore in 1820."

The more than two weeks of London dinners, teas, and breakfasts passed rapidly in review. Lucretia was ready for a tour of the islands, and the return to America.

CHAPTER XIII

THE TOUR OF THE ISLANDS

Before leaving the city of London, Lucretia had her portrait painted by Benjamin Haydon. The artist had a commission to paint a large picture of the opening scene of the convention in which he was to group the most distinguished personages in attendance from portraits made from life.

Haydon's accounts of the sittings of several of the Abolition leaders are amusing reflections on the characters of subjects and artist. When the zealous Mr. Scoble appeared, Haydon satanically suggested grouping him with a negro. Scoble "sophisticated immediately" on the propriety of placing the negro in the distance "as it would have a much greater effect."

Haydon, too, had his Achilles heel, for he writes: "Lucretia Mott, the leader of the delegate women from America, sat. I found her out to have infidel notions, and resolved at once, narrow minded or not, not to give her the prominent place I first intended. I will reserve that for a beautiful believer in the Divinity of Christ."

The justly famed creator of "Solomon," "Christ's Entry into Jerusalem," "Christ's Agony in the Garden," "The Cruxifixion," and other canvasses, seems not to have absorbed much of the spirit of the subject of his paintings beyond writing two years before death that "the moment I touch a great canvas I think I see my Creator smiling on all my efforts—the moment I do a mean thing for subsistence, I feel as if he had turned his back."

The painting of the anti-slavery convention—Clarkson at the speaker's stand—was hung in the National Portrait Gallery, where any person with good eyes (if not easily discouraged) could have discerned Lucretia in the background, beyond the ringside seats of "beautiful believers." Haydon subsequently painted Lucretia's portrait for the Duchess of Sutherland, his religious scruples being not above a fee.

On the eleventh day of July, Lucretia and her party left London. At Birmingham their train was met by William Boultbee and Father McDonald, a Catholic priest, to whom Lucretia had been introduced in London. She attended that morning what she termed a "Catholic meeting" and heard "McDonald deliver a good practical discourse, with nonsensical forms—a low mass or high mass—and sacrament."

That evening she sat at services conducted by a Unitarian, whom our critic judged good "but in manner not so easy as McDonald, who preaches extempore." The next day she dined with Father McDonald and Hugh Hutton, "a congenial mind." After dinner they went to a soiree under a new chapel built by working men where tea and sandwiches were served 400 guests.

Lucretia visited the cathedral where she met another priest, "an intelligent man, but no reformer like McDonald." He liked old forms, would be quiet to abuses, and submit to the "powers that be." Lucretia opposed his defense of the benefits of costly edifices raised in the name of the Christ born in a manger. A listening stranger "united" with her and expressed a desire to know her name "and where from." Here indeed was bread returning!

At the town hall she heard a lecture on capital punishment, the High Bailiff presiding. Her wish to offer a resolution of thanks was denied because of her sex, but she made a few informal remarks that were cheered—"so much for British usage," she commented laconically. She had learned that she could express opinions unofficially that were denied officially, and that they would be well received.

From Birmingham a hasty trip followed through Manchester and Liverpool into Ireland. Lucretia's diary discloses grateful mention of the generous hospitality of Irish Friends. Ireland was an idyl, an idyl of hospitality in a land of "miserable huts and poor villages, with wretched looking people, mostly barefoot." At Dublin the Motts were joined by Garrison and Rogers. Lucretia walked a mile along the quay to meet them, and passed "the morning delightfully with them at Richard Webb's."

She addressed a meeting at the Royal Exchange in Dublin, where she edified a large assembly of working men and their wives and daughters with a speech on numerous reforms, not omitting the exaltation of the moral and social condition of woman.

"Her clear voice and simple language, and the beauty and benevolence of her sentiments, sent her thoughts home to the hearts of her hearers, who listened with deep attention, and greeted her conclusion with tokens of the most cordial approbation," reported Richard Webb.

Nothing she met in her travels, not even the World's Convention, impressed her so favorably as did the weekly gatherings of reformers and working men at the Exchange, where was exercised a beneficial influence on thousands of fellow beings, despite the fact that the demand for bread in Ireland had almost suspended intellectual cultivation.

Leaving Dublin she breakfasted with the editor of the "Irish Friend" at Belfast, and took a steamboat for Glasgow, where she and James stopped at McFarlane's Temperance House on Argyle Street. If she found Ireland genial, she found Scotland dour. The Hicksite preacher had been given to understand that in Scotland she would receive treatment more gracious than that which had been meted her at London. But Glasgow's bigotry proved worse than any previously encountered.

The specific purpose of the Glasgow journey was to fulfill an invitation to attend the annual meeting of the local Emancipation Society. Rumors of infidelity traveled faster than the tourists, and when Lucretia arrived at the annual meeting she found no place appointed for her on the platform, or opportunity to address the assembly. It was as though this woman of international reputation had been the most humble of spectators.

Small wonder! exclaimed the correspondent of the London "Christian Pioneer," for the assembly was held in the chapel of Dr. Wardlaw, the directors of the society were Quakers and Calvinists, and the American Friend bore about her the taint of heresy. Dr. Wardlaw pushed forward to shake the hand of a colored American, but averted looks were deemed the proper reception of a person who dared to think independently in theology.

One fully prepared for these disgraceful exhibitions of prejudice was George Harris, the Unitarian preacher, known to local Presbyterians as "the devil's chaplain." Harris offered Lucretia the use of his pulpit that the American lecturer might not be silenced in Scotland on the subjects of slavery, education, and a common faith in God. Lucretia set a meeting for quarter past six o'clock on a Sunday evening, whereupon Glasgow Friends put over their customary afternoon meeting till six o'clock in order to prevent any of their fold from wandering into a strange pasture.

A handful of Quakers did more than this. When it was announced that Lucretia Mott, "a minister of the Society of Friends" of Philadelphia would hold a meeting in Glasgow, they issued a disclaimer in a local paper informing the public that they held "no religious fellowship with Lucretia Mott, nor with the body in the United States called Hicksites," to which she belonged, and did not wish to be "in any way identified with, or held responsible for any sentiments" she might utter.

With such splendid advertising, Harris' church was crowded when James stepped forward and opened the meeting with a general statement as to the identity of himself and wife, their object in visiting the country, and their differences in religious opinions from the Quakers of Great Britain. After this introduction Lucretia spoke for nearly two hours, holding "a delighted audience in breathless attention." Her discourse concerned religious tolerance, woman's rights, peace and war, and slavery. Rousing "the best and holiest feeling" of her audience to sympathy with the wrongs of the oppressed, she concluded with "a beautiful and fervid prayer."

Her work at Glasgow done, Lucretia returned to Edinburgh, where she called on George Combe, one of the first intelligences of the age. Two days and a night were spent at Georgia Cottage. "We parted from them all," mourned Lucretia, "with mingled emotions, for we were increasingly attached to them, and they expressed much for us. It is sad that we shall probably meet them no more!"

Another friend, not forgotten, was Harriet Martineau who, upon return from a visit to the United States, had contributed to the "Westminster Review" the article which had introduced to the English public, almost for the first time, the struggle of the Abolitionists in America. Miss Martineau had been elected a delegate by one of the Yankee societies, but ill health had kept her from London. During the persecutions of those summer days she had written sympathetic letters to Lucretia and had commissioned two of her friends, Mrs. Reid and Julia Smith, to look upon Lucretia "with eyes of love," and to take care of her socially.

The authoress had expressed a desire to see Lucretia once more, writing, "Love from my heart I do offer you. Dear friend, it is doubtless a disappointment to us both that we have not met; but if we cannot do so, we can, I hope, bear it cheerfully. Though ill, I suffer little. I should suffer greatly if I thought my friends were uneasy for me. Yet I cannot but grieve for you in the heart sickness which you must have experienced" at the convention's conduct.

After such a letter, Lucretia could not refrain from making a call on the invalid authoress. Walking a mile from the railroad station at Tyne-Mouth she found Harriet in comfortable lodgings, seated at a window overlooking the sea, where she had come the year before prepared to die; and yet performed prodigious quantities of literary work.

The meeting between the American reformer and the English authoress—then no doubt writing "The Hour and the Man"—was cordial and cheerful. Many topics were touched on, the Furness family of Philadelphia, "a favorite theme," and the loss of so many dear friends, "a painful one." Two or three hours passed in pleasant conversation before the invalid was obliged to retire for rest.

The parting from the great writer, like that from Combe, was sad. It was with the thought uppermost in mind that the handclasp and cordial word would never again be exchanged. This was increased by Harriet's belief that she was afflicted with a distemper which would prove fatal—as it did thirty-six years later!

The woman living at the age of thirty-eight, "a prisoner to her couch," suddenly decided to get well by the aid of mesmerism, a means of recovery that excited controversy and provoked Miss Martineau to write "Letters on Mesmerism" to the great offense of some members of her family who did not believe health could—or should —be restored by unethical means.

Comments by Lucretia of sights in the Old World, both before and after her visit to Tyne-Mouth, are interesting disclosures of character. Over hard roads of English countryside, between miles of hedges and shy English houses hidden amidst shrubbery, past forests of oaks where Druids once practiced primitive rites, along the banks of quiet streams reflecting the lazy outlines of millers' wheels that for centuries had ground the farmers' corn, rode Lucretia aloft a stage and discussed reform! Horses rattled her past historic fields and cathedrals that drew a casual glance . . . . quaint cottages and thatched roofs flashed by her eye . . . . there was the rumble of a bridge . . . . the long clatter through the single street of a village, sometimes a mile in length . . . . the surge over the breast of a hill with the breath-catching beauty of a silvery stream winding across the panorama of a distant valley . . . . and Lucretia Mott *wished* someone would tell her what to admire!

Her appreciation of beauty was intellectual. No one was more sensitive to the purity of soul in man or woman or the limpid depths of a great heart, than she. The thunder of Garrison was the roar of a cataract, the sweet gentleness of Emerson was a purling stream, the tolerance of William Penn a pastoral meadow. These she understood, and her heart beat in unison with the music of God's greatest creation, the nobler sentiments of man. She had no room, in the radiance of worship within the Temple of God, to appreciate the beauties of the material world without.

Yet as she rode along she noted that English coachmen were well-dressed, "would be gentlemen" who seldom left their seats, and gave no assistance in changing horses. They were more intelligent than the American breed, who had less delusions of grandeur. And she observed in traveling from Woodstock to Oxford that there were "colleges and churches galore," and between Windsor and London "women in the fields weeding; others, with small children, gathering manure in their aprons and selling it in small quantities." She mentioned how the road was "swept and scraped like our streets," and the walking so good that women might walk five or six miles in the country without dread of fatigue, as she herself occasionally did.

Scotland had "fine roads, and neat cottages" and "farms looking like ours in Chester County," spoiled by "licensed dram houses thick on the road."

A tour of cotton factories interested her because she found the children and women looking better than she had expected, but her ire was aroused by a visit to an institution for decrepit tradesmen known as the *Hospital of the Twelve Brethren*. She found the inmates "dressed up like gentlemen, living in idleness on the labor of others; miscalled charity." Here rotted penniless fishmongers and costermongers and mongers of all sorts in the mellow glow of being past masters of shops. For once the visitor was attracted by furniture rather than humanity. In the pleasant kitchen of the hospital she admired the andirons, and jacks for roasting, the large bellows, pipe box, iron and brass candle sticks and the furniture "like Grandfather Folger's."

The ruins of Warwick Castle at Kenilworth, like the gentlemen ruins at the *House of the Twelve Brethren* had small appeal. There was nothing in a mass of ruins to ameliorate the sufferings of man-

153

kind. They were merely a pile of stone. They pictured the decay of that which was past. Lucretia called them a catch-penny, something to interest the girls of the party, but not for her. She visited Abbotsford. Here the party met the widow of Scott's trusty servant, Tom Purdie, who was very communicative and invited the visitors into her cottage, where she served them some of her newly-baked bread, and water from a silver cup presented by Scott's son, the present Sir Walter. Some six pence were dropped into it, "whereupon," recites Lucretia, "she was loud in praise of Americans, and told us all that the time would admit of."

Lucretia had more sentiment for the children of a slave mother sold down the river to New Orleans than Sir Walter Scott, dead and buried. She commented dryly on the visit to the Chapter House, "full of busts and broken things, wisely kept for such a place." She redeemed herself by recognizing the beauty of ivy climbing over ruined windows, and announced that Melrose by moonlight was exquisite, "so pale and bright."

Touching inscriptions found at the gate of a Jewish cemetery— the heart-throbbing cries of an oppressed people—fired Lucretia's imagination more than castles and graves. While others of the party gazed upon ruins, she transcribed on paper:

> Tribes of the wandering feet, and weary breast,
> We roam the earth around, yet find no rest.
> The wild dove hath her nest, the fox his cave,
> Mankind their country—Israel, but a grave!

James was more observing than his spouse and carefully collected his European impressions in a published book, thereby establishing a precedent for modern travelers who write whilst they run.

Returning to London the Americans enjoyed an early morning drive through the quiet streets of the metropolis. Houses slumbered and stores reposed unopened. At their lodgings the Motts found a pile of accumulated mail, including a copy of the Scotch newspaper containing the disclaimer of Glasglow Friends of any religious association with Lucretia Mott. Deepest cut of all was the signature of William Smeal, a Friend who had entertained Lucretia and spoken kindly to her and assured her that women would not have been rejected had the world's convention been held in Scotland. Lucretia would not bring herself to believe the genuineness of this signature, and charitably hoped it had been affixed by another.

Notwithstanding the disavowal of fellowship by British Quakery in general, "the kindness and courtesy that was abundantly extended to us by some Friends, as well as by many not of that name, will long be remembered with pleasure," wrote kindly Lucretia at the close of her foreign diary. And adds, "My love of approbation was gratified, and the cause of Truth maintained, I trust."

CHAPTER XIV

The Return to America

The memory of the voyage to the far-famed land of England lingered long in Lucretia's memory. The excitement of meeting "enlarged minds," the lively change of scenery and the exhilarating breezes of Atlantic travel, restored Lucretia's health.

The voyage home was pleasant. Very little sick after the third day out, she was up and about ship the greater part of the voyage. Her interest in persons extended into the steerage when she learned that the vessel was carrying a large number of Irish emigrants to America. She asked that she might be allowed to address these men. Word was returned to her that the embryo American politicians in the steerage did not care to attend a religious meeting held by a woman, especially a non-Catholic. This did not daunt her. She requested that the emigrants come together to consider whether they would have a meeting.

This seemed innocuous to the sons of Erin, who were herded onto deck where Lucretia greeted them and explained how different was her idea of a meeting from a church service such as they were accustomed to; she informed them that she had no thought of saying anything derogatory to that service, or of the priests who ministered to them; that her heart was drawn to them in sympathy as they were leaving the land of their fathers to establish new homes in an unfamiliar country. She wanted to address them as to their habits and aims in their everyday life in such a way as to help them in the land of strangers.

Then she asked if they were willing to listen while she gave them an outline of what she wanted to say. Drawn on by silent consent, she delivered the whole of her message. Only the keenest witted of her hearers awoke to the fact, as they went out, that they had listened to the preaching of "the woman priest" after all. This amusing evidence of dove-like guile greatly impressed the master of the vessel, who gave the story circulation.

The return from England found Lucretia anxious to do continued battle for the slave. She had been convinced while abroad that much depended on the activity of women. Men had shown themselves weak in resistance to arguments of expediency and had allowed themselves to be consumed by intestine commotion over religious and sex questions.

In the winter of 1841 she set forth upon one of the many lecture tours that characterized her activities at this period of life, and which took her to the capitols of Delaware, New Jersey, and Pennsylvania, where she plead the cause of the negro before audiences of legislators and their friends.

She took occasion to revisit Smyrna, Delaware, where Daniel Neall had been tarred and feathered. She and James found a large crowd of curious spectators congregated on the piazza of the town's only tavern to greet them as they rode into the village. Many persons and their dogs followed their vehicle to the meetinghouse a short distance through the town, contributing a motley picture as they trudged along behind the carriage driven by the snow-haired James, who peered benignly through spectacles for a glimpse of his destination, his black Quaker coat with upstanding collar contrasting sharply with the gentler tones of costume worn by the sweet-faced woman at his side who sat erect, her forearms crossed primly in her lap, her knitting laid to one side.

The audience at the lecture (though doubtful of Lucretia's good sense) was quiet and orderly, save one man, the leader of the previous ruction, who this time satisfied himself by leaving the hall in ostentatious disapproval when the topic of slavery was touched.

"Truth reigned," commented James of his wife's discourse, "and some 'who came to scoff, remained to pray.'"

But praying was not done on the outside by the unidentified person who removed the linchpin from the carriage, a discovery the Motts were not long in making when they attempted to drive away and one of the wheels started to slide off its axle-tree.

The necessary repair gave the populace time to cluster at the tavern like flies around spilt beer. Small boys and men huddled against the March winds while they watched the Abolitionists in curious silence—peculiar people who had had the audacity to come back and repeat their unjust and unconstitutional doctrine of man's equality.

Abreast the tavern, James hailed the landlord and asked for dinner and feed for the horses, but "mine host" was much agitated. He'd be obliged to them if they would excuse him from giving service

—there was so much excitement—he breathlessly feared the consequences. The Motts drove away. James was pleased to think the fifty or more persons standing in silence about the tavern's door were mortified more than he or Lucretia at the landlord's cowardice.

And so the Abolitionists drove out of the land of Smyrna to the home of a friend, a distance of thirteen miles.

Ostracized by society both polite and impolite, Abolitionists sought the company of each other in their travels. When they came to Philadelphia the habit grew to call at the Mott home. Those who had been delegates to the London convention took especial pleasure in this practice.

Lucretia explained how "we have been from house to house in social parties, when we have talked over many of the scenes through which we passed so pleasantly together. The high-handed measures to which some of us were subjected were placed in the far-distant background, as well as the petty indulgence of the spirit of sectarism; while very near to our view, as well as to our hearts' best feelings, were the great kindness and attention of our many dear friends. It ever affords a delightful retrospect."

There was a binding tie of affection among the band of rejected women. Lucretia regretted that "dear Mary Grew" lived so far from her, "quite in the lower part of the city," as to be unable to meet with her often when friends were present. Sarah Pugh so late as 1878 was to accompany Lucretia, both of them ancient women, to an anniversary meeting of the Woman's Rights Society, thirty-eight years after they had met rebuff at London.

The trip to England resulted, likewise, in lifelong friendships abroad. Decades were to pass during which the delegates from America were not to see those of Britain, yet relations not short of remarkable were kept up by pen and paper. The correspondents were interested in the same things, and their humanitarian lives remained closely knitted however far the physical lives drifted apart. Only death dissolved these friendships mortared by ink and paper.

With the Irish Friends, Richard and Hannah Webb, Lucretia corresponded a third of a century. She opened the letter writing saying:

Here we are at home again, and entering into our every day avocations, just as if we had not been made *somebodies* in our Fatherland. I mean *out* of the Convention! But with all our fault finding of that august assemblage, it was a most interesting two weeks that we were admitted spectators of its doings. I really think I appreciate its proceedings and productions more fully now, than while we were with you, and while the wrong done to dear Wm. L. Garrison and others, was uppermost with us . . . . "

She recalled the "delightful day at the seaside . . . . the walk up Killarney Hills, the prospect from the top, all, all are remembered with dear delight. When will you come here? I cannot convey by expression how much I want to see you again. These dear familiar letters to Sarah Pugh, Abby Kimber, and ourselves, some of which are lying before me, bind you to our hearts as bosom friends."

Richard Webb remained always the dearest of Old World intimates. Garrison called him the "delightful Irish Quaker," and Webb responded genially, writing how he longed to hear from his "noble friends across the herring-pond." So enthused was Webb with the Garrisonian doctrine of non-resistance that he printed a small pamphlet on the subject, "just to raise a little bit of a row, and to set people thinking," he explained.

If Webb was enthusiastic about non-resistance and anti-slavery and other "glorious contagions," Lucretia thought the Irish Friends very backward in religious thought. Even Richard had been conservative to many of her shocking ideas. In course of time she perceived in his letters a growing enlargement of opinion. She playfully gibed him upon one occasion, writing, "Only think, almost seven years ago! You only whispered heresy then."

And she recalled to his memory a scene which took place at his London lodgings, how "your venerable father sat there, looking so grave, as if he had some misgivings as to the propriety of his juxtaposition with heretics of the Hicksite order. I remember, too, his prudential silence when I ventured a little ultraism; and the 'Irish hospitality' with which we were entertained—each one doing so much to minister to our hungry appetites. Again, when in your own social circle in Dublin, I presumed to read a part of what I had written home of your non-commital course in matters of theology, suggesting, as one reason, the fear of your orthodox leaders, the earnestness and openness of countenance with which your brother Thomas ejaculated, 'I'm not afraid,' gave me a sensation of delight. If I forget these things, my memory will forget its office."

As Webb expanded beyond the confines of Irish Quakerism he became restive under the chafings of sect, and wrote Lucretia about withdrawing membership. The woman hastened to persuade him against the move, wishing him to work for progress within the society, rather than without. She had frequently noted, she explained, how persons who were once useful in church societies, after withdrawing from them, became contracted and censorious.

This remark might not apply to all, she admitted. William Lloyd Garrison never was attached to any sect. Sarah Pugh, from the time of the "Separation" in the Quaker society, never felt her interest enlisted on either side but, concluded Lucretia, "I have no fear of her talents rusting from want of use." Despite her arguments, Webb demitted membership after long deliberation, confident it was only a matter of time before Lucretia would do likewise. In this, he was mistaken.

Narrow as had become the opinions of individual Friends, Lucretia kept in mind that it was the maxim of the Fathers that the society should not have articles of faith. The organization was roomy enough to include persons of varied opinions, and so long as she could maintain freedom of expression, she was determined to remain within the fold, to be of service in a day popularly given over to organized religion.

Had the Light gone out, a mighty influence for liberalism would have been lost to the Hicksite Society.

Yet Lucretia was not entirely confident of the value of church societies. She acknowledged evil in them and once wrote Webb that it was a question still unsettled with her whether the various religious organizations, with all their errors, were more productive of good than evil. But, she thought, until one could offer something better in their stead to a people largely governed by religious sentiment and a natural love for association, it required great care how one shook their faith in existing institutions. She thought so when sitting in the colored Methodist meetings, where appeals to emotion called forth loud shoutings; and yet the effect of the religious training received by the communicants, with all its grossness, was wholesome on their lives and conduct.

Was it not so with the Quaker Society? With all the undue stress on externals, and all the preaching up of "quietude," still, the appeal to the inner sense was not made in vain, and many of the fold were foremost in reform and good works.

Another English correspondent was Elizabeth Pease. Elizabeth alluded to some little restraint which she thought had existed in their intercourse in England. Her conscience troubled her, and she explained a certain aloofness on her part to have been actuated by the fear that she might engross too much of Lucretia's time, regarding her as among the "lions of the Convention."

Lucretia belittled the awkwardness of intercourse, and replied to her friend, writing in the first person plural:

. . . . as to the 'lion' part, we felt much more that we were 'counted as sheep for the slaughter.' That feeling, added to the knowledge that many among you were greatly shocked at our supposed heresies, did cause a little restraint in our mingling with you. When we met accidentally at meeting, I felt quite a pity for thee, seeing that thou would be brought into a strait after meeting, whether to speak cordially to us, and thus identify thyself with those who were 'despised and rejected of men,' or to turn from us, and thus do violence to the promptings of thy kind nature. But the more intercourse we had, the more these fears and restraints vanished; and our latter interviews—especially the last, in Liverpool—were all any one could desire. . . . .

While letters of friendship loaded with reformatory arguments sped over and back the Atlantic, American opposition to anti-slavery grew bitter. The South daily became more overbearing in its demands that the mercantile element, and Northerners in general, crush Abolitionism like the head of a serpent wherever it was found. This sentiment found sympathetic reception among Friends in New York, Baltimore, and Philadelphia.

The society disliked the spectacle of one of its prominent members engaged in a controversy which threatened national harmony, and going out into the company of persons not of its faith to agitate questions of reform. Lucretia's participation in anti-Sabbath conventions, non-resistant meetings and anti-slavery rallies, focused undesired attention on the society, which was not appreciated.

Quakers were ready to uphold the argument that slavery was a subject too dangerous to be discussed. They disliked Wendell Phillips' opinion that "if there is anything in the universe that can't stand discussion, let it crack." Quaker dissatisfaction found its greatest strength at meetings for ministers and elders, where the hierarchy openly arrayed itself against Lucretia.

Occurrences at these sessions were sometimes so wholly at variance with Christian charity that Lucretia was more than ever convinced that the purposes for which the meetings were instituted had been lost sight of and that their continued extistence was productive of more harm than good. Candidates for the ministry who favored reform were no longer appointed to office. Lucretia was sometimes almost sick of religious societies, seeing that their nature was "to bark and bite."

Policy did not oblige her to attend all the various classes of meetings of the society, and she accordingly discontinued attendance on certain occasions, finding it "dry work to keep up any form, after the life and power of it have passed away." She generally employed the time thus saved in visiting the colored people of the city at their churches and places of refuge.

In England Lucretia had been persecuted by Abolitionists because she was a Hicksite; in America she was persecuted by Hicksites because she was an Abolitionist. She was seldom, if ever, on the popular side of a dispute, an infallible sign of greatness.

Slandered, ignored, argued and pleaded with, Lucretia's mind became neither embittered nor contracted under the stimuli of opposition. The period between 1840 and 1860 was the prime of her life. From forty-seven to sixty-seven years of age she was at the zenith of her powers. She was to reap honor in her ancient years and to grow beautifully gentle, but never was she more grand, more spiritual or forgiving, than in these years when her religious and moral horizons were expanding beyond the vision of blind men and women not in "unity" with humanitarian ideals.

That many members of the society were not in "unity" became plainly evident as the decades lengthened. Rumors went the Quaker rounds, distorted and biased. Committees, official and otherwise, called on her to question statements attributed to her, which by the time they had reached the committees usually had been so distorted by tongues more active than ears that they were easily repudiated.

Customarily Lucretia did not defend herself against calumnies, convinced that persons who loved her needed no word of hers of explanation, and that those who did not, would be unconvinced no matter what she said.

Fortunately for her mental health her sense of the ludicrous enabled her to receive a certain form of criticism with amusement. Her self-constituted guardians might not have felt so exalted had they heard her accounts to her family of some of their visits. James, however, took them seriously as he saw his wife "crucified" for liberal ideals. "Some hard things have been said about one who is dearer to me than life; but she heeds them not, nor turns aside from her onward path of duty and labor. I have felt sad, but not disheartened, trusting that in the end the evil will be overruled by good."

In company with James, Lucretia late in 1842 accepted the taunts of pro-slavery Northerners who were wont to jeer, "Why don't you preach Abolitionism in the South?" Courageously she went forth to visit the slave states of Maryland and Virginia. Some Friends in Baltimore feared for harmony when they learned that Lucretia intended to visit their Yearly Meeting. One influential Quaker greeted the Phliadelphian with the admonition, "Now, Lucretia, let us have no battle array." She would like the slavery question slurred over in the interests of "quiet." Lucretia's sensitive disposition—the heart so resolute before enemies—felt keenly the thrust from one of whom kindlier treatment had been expected.

Lucretia held two appointed meetings at Baltimore and found considerable good anti-slavery feeling among Quakers, if only members "dared speak out." Complimentary articles appeared in the local newspapers, and one editor reported her sermons. This gave birth to the malicious charge that the editors had been paid to insert the laudatory paragraphs.

In Virginia Lucretia and James traveled three hundred and fifty miles by carriage. The wife held seventeen meetings in eighteen days, attending as well the Quarterly Meeting at Alexandria. Slaveholders were present at most, if not all of her meetings, and heard their peculiar institution plainly handled. The audiences were quiet and respectful, and on the whole Lucretia felt encouraged. The tour afforded her opportunity to converse with slaveholders and their apologists, and she was confirmed in her opinion that slaveholders were more open to reason than many deprecating Quakers of the North who expressed themselves as belonging to the "I-am-as-much-opposed-to-slavery-as-any-one-*but*" category.

Swinging home, the woman stopped off at Washington, where she applied for the use of the Hall of Congress for a lecture, but as this was grantable only on condition that she be silent on slavery, the Unitarian Church proved a more acceptable rostrum. There she lectured to a crowded house, including many members of Congress, who had assembled to hear the famous Quaker woman on the subject that had not yet really stirred the Nation at large. She marveled that the people both there and in Virginia "were so open to hear the truth on the subject of slavery."

Loath to leave Washington without an interview with the chief executive, the Quakeress and her husband visited President Tyler, himself a slaveholder. They could not have expected much in the way of encouragement for they knew that Tyler as a Congressman had advocated the spread of slavery into the new states with the peculiar plea that the diffusion of the slave population over a wide area would weaken the institution and increase the prospect of ultimate emancipation.

The Motts found the President favorable to colonization. James contended that the South could not do without the blacks, and thought they should be left free to choose their locations like other people, without being shipped to a strange land merely because their ancestors had originated there. Tyler asked his guests if they would be willing the negro should go North. Lucretia answered, "Yes—as many as incline to come, but most of them would prefer to remain on the plantations and work for wages."

Reminiscences about discussions on the subject years before in Virginia were indulged in by the President, who volunteered the opinion that the Missouri question and other agitations had put the cause back. Lucretia interjected the hope that it was not too late to resume it.

The polite Tyler professed admiration for the way Friends treated the subject of Abolition; he had lately read an address from the Baltimore Meeting. Lucretia promptly disclaimed any similar reaction on her part saying the address "was calculated to set the slaveholder's conscience too much at ease"—it made more apology for him than he could make for himself. This stirred Tyler to wish he could "hand Mr. Calhoun" over to her! The visit broke up in friendly spirit. The nation's chief magistrate bade Lucretia success in her "benevolent enterprises."

She was not certain whether anti-slavery was embraced therein!

The couple next called on the old statesman John Quincy Adams, still eloquently laboring in Congress after having been President of the United States. They found him much discouraged that anything could be effected in the current Congress, or the next, on slavery. Lucretia came away from Washington convinced that the success of Abolitionism rested not on those in power but on the common people. These heard gladly whenever access could be obtained to their unprejudiced hearts. "I ever have hope of a meeting made up of such."

CHAPTER XV

QUAKER PERSECUTIONS

The trip South did little to strengthen Lucretia's reputation among northern Quakers. To this was added the fact that the Hutchinson family of "sweet singers" was invited by Abolition leaders to participate in a professional capacity at anti-slavery conventions, as part of advertised programs.

This gave opponents within Lucretia's church the opportunity to observe a concrete proof of the evils they had so vigorously predicted must flow as a consequence of her attending conventions not under Quaker dominance. In the rigid Discipline of the Society of Friends, music was catalogued as a "vain sport and pastime," analogous to horse racing and stage plays, unfit for persons whose delight was "in the law of the Lord."

What now would the contumacious preacher do? A small clique of conservatives watched the crisis with peculiar relish. The sentiment opposed to Lucretia had grown to such magnitude that there was not wanting in the society a small group willing to see her silenced by disownment, if sufficient grounds could be discovered, and other means failed to muzzle her.

Lucretia did not approve the invitation of the Hutchinsons to the anti-slavery platform because she knew the act would stir Quaker opposition, and she desired as much as possible to conform to the rules of her society. She was obliged often enough to violate the whimseys of her sect without making an issue of so trivial a matter.

She expressed the opinion that anti-slavery conventions had enough of interest in rational appeals to logic "without descending to excitement to carry on the work." She "would far rather have music confined to those who wish for its beautiful, harmonious, and evanescent influence" in the music room, yet she refused to oppose those who wished it at anti-slavery conventions, nor would she discontinue attendance because of it.

She perceived no harm in music. A few years later she admitted a piano into her parlor for the use of her grandchildren, although she herself never aspired to a more æsthetic appreciation of melody beyond simple favorites such as "John Brown," "Dixie," and "Old Folks at Home." Members of her family were occasionally moved to open smiles at her vain attempts to hum one of these airs, and she would share the amusement, recounting, "My mother used to say to me, when I tried to sing, 'Oh, Lucretia, if thee was as far out of town as thee is out of tune, thee wouldn't get home tonight.'" A legalistic mind might have evaded the question of the Hutchinsons by quibbling the point whether their renditions came actually under the head of music any more than Lucretia's humming.

Many years the Hutchinsons were a phenomenon on public platforms. No matter what the occasion, sad, reformatory, humorous, or martial, they had always an appropriate song. A popular theme was "The Old Granite State," whence they came. At temperance conventions they wailed the "Lament of the Widowed Inebriate" or played "King Alcohol." "The Slave's Appeal" was certain always of applause wherever Abolitionists gathered. Even the cause of better wages for seamstresses had its saga, entitled "The Song of the Shirt."

Lucretia's liberal stand in regard to music was quite apart from that of George F. White, of New York, at this time her chief Quaker antagonist. White was a man of greater intellectual endowment than many of his fellow-preachers in the untrained ministry. He was gifted with a talent for a particular species of declamatory eloquence which readily procured him large audiences wherever he went. A rabid defender of the old order of things, he exerted much influence in the New York Meeting. He participated in the disownment, about this time, of three of the society's outstanding members—giant-hearted Isaac T. Hopper, the father of one of Lucretia's sons-in-law; James S. Gibbons, and Charles Marriott who not long thereafter died from causes aggravated by grief.

Hopper's case is without parallel in the history of the Friends. The specific charge on which he was arraigned was that of being concerned in the support and publication of an Abolition newspaper which had the "tendency to excite discord and disunity" among Friends. In other words, like Lucretia, Hopper was a member of the executive committee of the American Anti-Slavery Society, which published the "Anti-Slavery Standard," a paper for excellence of taste and intellectual calibre perhaps scarcely equaled by any periodical of the day. Its contributors included names noteworthy in American letters.

167

For a time Lucretia seriously considered withdrawing her name from the executive committee, aware that enemies were watching every issue of the "Standard" in order to catch her in some un-Quaker-like corner. She was at a disadvantage in this game because the use of her name was nominal and she had no opportunity to review or alter any article going into the paper. So watchful was the opposition of her movements that she dared not attend a memorial service preached by William H. Furness on the death of Dr. Channing, both personal friends. "I should have liked much to hear him, but—sectarian proscription," she explained.

Her final decision was not to withdraw her name from the "Standard." She did not wish in any way to concede to the enemies of Isaac Hopper, one of the Nation's noted philanthropists.

Nor did she allow the conduct of the New York Meeting to pass without comment, for she bore her testimony against intolerance in every circle. The opportunity came to her at a meeting of the Indian Committee appointed from Four Yearly Meetings of the Hicksite Order. Charles Marriott had been an active member of this committee and Lucretia expressed regret, when his former associates came together, that Marriott should have been deprived of his right to labor in the cause he loved so well.

Heartened by their success in dealing with Hopper, Quaker authorities at New York refused to give notice of Lucretia's intention to speak at their meetinghouse, when she stopped a brief spell in that city on her way home from a New England non-resistance convention. Not ready to bring formal charges against her they contented themselves by writing a letter worded with curious circuitousness which they mailed to a member of the Philadelphia meeting with the hope that its accusations might ripen into official action, without burning their own fingers.

Instead of the document being laid directly before the Philadelphia meeting as its authors had hoped, the one to whom it was directed took the epistle first to Lucretia who, forewarned, was able to reply to it both with spirit and success. Laconically she advised a friend, "They failed to bring action against me."

Failure to depose the woman did not prevent a flood of ministers from outside cities surging into Philadelphia, there to hold forth against her within the gates of her citadel. Whenever a conservative preacher heeded the "call" of the Inner Spirit to go forth and do good, he assured himself that this was God's way of prompting him to go to Philadelphia for the purpose of combating Lucretia's disorganizing principles, for nowhere in the society was there a more active minister than Lucretia preaching the erroneous ideals of human liberty, sex equality, and the abolition of war.

For a time all Quaker roads led to the Cherry Street Meetinghouse, and it seemed to conservatives that the way was lit by the Inner Light; the lamp which in Lucretia's soul threw its glare upon the evils they sought to perpetuate. The Inner Light guided its adherents both "pro" and "con."

Many Quaker visitors to Philadelphia were inspired more with zeal and sincerity than either vision or tolerance.

Lucretia's feelings were not infrequently rubbed as she faced friends in her own meetinghouse and heard abused, not alone causes she revered and their workers, but herself as well. James wrote how "the busy tongue of 'tale-bearing and detraction' is not idle and what may be the result of its poisonous influence upon our society, if it shall continue to be indulged, it is impossible to say; but we must hope for the best, and trust that right action will in the end produce good fruit, whatever may be the effect upon the actor."

Lucretia detailed these persecutions to Nathaniel and Eliza Barney, intimate Nantucket friends, as she did to few persons.

"It may seem strange to you that I should thus write," she apologized upon occasion, "and if I could detect in myself any germ of unkind feeling toward G. F. W. [George F. White], I should hestitate. . . . . "

Another letter contains this admission: "I felt badly on First-day last; but we are now trying not to fret ourselves because of evil doers." Dryly she added, "What a fine school to learn non-resistance in !"

Lucretia did not ask that all Friends countenance the course she pursued. She did not expect everybody to think alike. What she asked was that members who did not agree with her that Quakers should take an active part in the reforms of the day, or who disagreed with the methods of the immediate Abolitionists, should leave her to exercise her individual responsibilities as she saw them.

"And we will plead with them, if they cannot be for us, not to be *against* us; and if they cannot countenance our measures, to pursue as much better as their best judgments may dictate. . . . . " This put the issue squarely before sectarians who, while objecting both to slavery and the methods of Abolitionists, did nothing themselves to alleviate the evils of human bondage.

Even in the excitement of an occasional open clash of arms in Quaker meeting, Lucretia's debating manner was, in the description of a young Friend, always "simple and quiet, her voice never raising above the pitch which is agreeable to the ear; and her statements serious, calm, and moderate." Adds the same informant, "I have known her subjected to bitter personal attack without manifesting the least excitement, or making any retaliation whatever."

Lucretia found encouragement in the knowledge that ministerial opponents in the society, although weighty and influential, were the smallest faction, and not strong enough to carry out the hostile measure of disownment. A large number of younger Friends, while they did not wholly agree with her or were not always prepared to openly sustain her cause, were unwilling to see her cast out. Unable to check the tide of persecution, they gave her a moral support which was a source of comfort and strength to her.

A not unimportant factor militating against Lucretia's disownment was her learned knowledge of the history and principles of her sect, and her keen application of the principles of founder-Friends to the issues of modern day. More than once she was able to pin an opponent to the wooden boards of his ministerial seat with an arrow feathered with the words of Robert Barclay or George Fox himself; the victim left to squirm himself free as the meeting broke up, while the calm, collected, and rather innocent looking victor went forth into the yard to be untrammeled for another week.

In the midst of strenuous years Lucretia lost her mother, aged seventy-three. Not long after this blow Lucretia's only brother, Thomas, was victim of the cholera. Unmindful of the risk of contagion Lucretia went at once to his lodgings when he was stricken ill, and nursed him till death. She had his body taken to her own home. Many friends thought her conduct imprudent, but she explained it thus: "How different people are constituted and affected! I loved to be with Thomas all the time, and to do for him afterward all that I could, in laying him out. I helped lift him into his coffin."

At the time of her mother's death Lucretia was recovering from an attack of pneumonia and, being too weak to leave her bed, had demanded to be carried into her mother's room, where she remained until death claimed its victim. This proved too much for Lucretia's weakened condition, and inflammation of the brain set in. Two weeks she hovered between life and death, very slowly regaining her health. The illness affected her nervous system and she was obliged for a time to avoid much reading and writing.

She resumed her correspondence after a period of two years, during which time she hardly had written her "dear English or Irish friends." In a letter to Elizabeth Pease she referred to the death of the Englishwoman's father. "Thy long continued devotion to thy dear father doubtless renders the stroke doubly trying to thee. In many ways we feel such a loss. The tear will naturally flow at the severance of such a tie; and far be it from me to seek to stay it. I know full well the keenness of the separation between parent and child. My dear mother was taken from us when I could illy bear such a shock. . . . . . But we had to yield her, and resignation to the event has been a hard lesson. I therefore feel less able to preach it to others."

She asked the Webbs: "Who would have thought that six years would pass away before one of our Dublin friends would visit America? We are all growing so old that you ought to lose no time. I had fondly hoped to introduce my dear mother to some of you; but she is gone; alas! Two years have passed since her death, and we still mourn our loss."

The long period of enforced rest restored Lucretia's energy. She renewed her former prominent rôles in the many philanthropic societies in which she held membership. She not only spoke, but was often presiding officer.

She was a welcome visitor to organizations in which she was not a member. The Autumnal Convention of Unitarian Christians held in Philadelphia in 1846 was the scene of an interesting incident. The Reverend William H. Furness, perceiving her in the audience, interrupted proceedings to announce that a member of the Society of Friends was present—Lucretia Mott—and moved that she be invited to take a seat in the convention with leave to speak if she found herself moved to it. No objection raised, the woman took the platform.

Stepping to the front she urged Unitarians to be bold and not to compromise religious progress. She attacked the practice of liberal clergymen who raised an ambiguous phraseology around certain ancient precepts of Christianity for fear of the terrible commotion that would ensue if they should openly discard them.

We are too prone to take our views of Christianity from some of the credulous followers of Christ, lest any departure from the early disciples should fasten upon us the suspicion of unbelief in the Bible. . . . . The importance of free thinking and honest speech cannot be over-estimated. Be not afraid of the reputation of infidels, or the opprobrium of the religious world. . . . . If you have had Channing and Worcester to lead you on, why are you not prepared to carry the work forward, even beyond them?

My heart was made humble and tender when I came into this convention. I saw in the chair Samuel Parkman, of Boston, the son of an old friend of my father. Looking at Calvinistic Boston as it then was, and considering how Channing rose and bore his testimony, and what results followed, we may be encouraged. But let the work advance. Lo! the field is white to harvest. . .

The spectacle of a woman addressing a male audience of ministers of another faith and urging radical clergymen on to ranker heresies was dismissed by a number of newspapers as an "unwarrantable 'lugging in the woman's rights question.'"

Lucretia commented on the occasion in a letter to Webb: "Have you noticed what a step the Unitarian convention took in this city, in graciously permitting a woman to speak? And such a woman! [herself!] That made quite a stir in our Zion, and increased the opposition to that woman, too!'" Needless to add, "Zion" was Lucretia's own church society, the Cherry Street Meeting of Friends.

Persecution reached the Quaker peak the following year. Lucretia made a long journey into the Western States for the purpose of attending various anti-slavery and religious meetings, among others the Quaker Yearly Meetings at Salem, Ohio, and Richmond, Indiana.

Earlier in the year Lucretia had responded to an invitation from Theodore Parker to sit in a "Council of Reformers" at Boston for the purpose of a round-table discussion of the general principles of reform and the best means of its promotion. Leading philanthropists, statesmen, college professors, and men of letters had been willing to listen to the words of the Cherry Street minister; but not the mediocre Quakers of Philadelphia's environs. On more than one occasion James and Lucretia, while attending Friends' meetings in the country, were allowed to resort to taverns for repose, a thing not known in former years when breaches of hospitality like this would not have been permitted under any circumstances.

In the Far West Lucretia found conditions more intolerable than at home. Ohio received her attentively, but the visit to Indiana was marred by examples of party spirit seldom equaled among Friends. On the morrow following the close of the first day's session some elders waited on Lucretia and "desired" her to go home or, if she would not do that, "desired" that she should not speak again.

Jane Price, an "approved minister" of Philadelphia, was witness of the spirit of intolerance that prevailed during the sittings of the Indiana Yearly Meeting. Whereas Jane's lot was cast primarily with members of the reactionary party, she disapproved the persecution which she saw on every hand. Writing her husband she reports: "James and Lucretia have nearly always gone back from meeting to their lodgings, having taken boarding at a Friend's house. There has been a great deal here directed against them. Lucretia has been quite poorly, too, but has attended all the sittings. She and James stepped into the widow Evans' between meetings on Fourth-day morning, where were a good many friends of the evangelical order; a roomful present; Lucretia said little or nothing, merely came in to warm her feet. She was in tears all the while, as she sat in one corner by the fire; just before she went out, I *whispered* to her what had deeply impressed my mind all the while she was in the room: 'The *disciple* is not *above* his Lord, nor the servant above his master.'"

The woman who had been welcomed by parliamentarians and peers of England and the intellectual nobility of America was ostracized by the small farmers and tradesmen of Indiana, and their wives. Not alone because she differed in opinion as to the identity of Jesus Christ, or because she preached against slavery (although these were ordinarily sufficient in themselves), but because of some recent remarks made in Ohio denying the divine sanction of war!

Indisposed for several days, at times suffering acutely from neuralgia, she was seized at the dinner table with an unusually severe attack. Her host, a physician, was asked to prescribe for her, whereupon he turned to her and replied: "Lucretia, I am so deeply afflicted by thy rebellious spirit, that I do not feel that I can prescribe for thee."

With the remark by James, "It is evident, my dear, that we are not wanted here; I think we should feel more comfortable in our

173

own lodgings," the pair left the house together, leaving behind them some devout and pious Christians comfortable in the thought that they had so stoutly upheld the cause of true morality.

In Lucretia's memories of the western journey there was one pleasurable thought. Occasionally she had met with Garrison, who marveled that she had not utterly broken down under the pressure of her public labors. Garrison was always a true friend to her as she was always faithful to him.

The discouragements of the western trip did not turn her course. She continued to meet all demands made upon her in time and money. Richard D. Webb from Ireland sought her assistance in raising funds for the benefit of sufferers of the potato famine. John C. Vaughan called on her for help in reëstablishing Cassius M. Clay's anti-slavery paper, the "True American," suspended because of lack of funds.

In 1852 a sad duty befell her. In that year died Isaac T. Hopper. Because of his disownment Hopper had professed a desire not to be buried in a Quaker cemetery. It was an uncommon thing for a Quaker to be interred in non-sectarian ground. As Lucretia followed the remains of her friend to his ultimate resting place, the novelty of the situation impressed itself upon her mind. At the open grave she spoke the following sentiment that might fittingly have been said of herself, years later: " I have no unity with these costly monuments around me, by which the pride and vanity of man strive to extend themselves beyond the grave. But I like the idea of burial grounds where people of all creeds repose together. It is pleasant to leave the body of our friend here, amid the verdant beauty of nature, and the sweet singing of birds. As he was a fruitful bough, that overhung the wall, it is fitting that he should not be buried within the walls of any sectarian enclosure."

CHAPTER XVI
DOMESTIC LIFE

A house on Arch Street was the city home of Lucretia during the years of her matured fame. Prior to that time she had lived nearly twenty years at a location on Ninth between Race and Vine streets, two blocks from Franklin Square. In this home James and Lucretia had raised their five surviving children, and spent the ascent of their happily married life.

From sources widely scattered it is known that the mistress of these homes was a paragon of housewifely excellence. Although an agitator, and often making trips away from home a few hundred to a thousand miles, few women were more domestic than Lucretia. So busy was she in attendance at free produce, anti-slavery, and Quaker meetings that often her mail would remain unanswered so long as a year for, she explained in apology to a correspondent, she traveled so much that when at home she had to be the more devoted to her family and domestic vocations.

She considered the common duties of a wife a part of her compass of life, though not an exclusive one. Interest in outside activities did not mean abandonment of sphere, but an enrichment of life that gave it both broadness and depth.

Because of participation in numerous philanthropic causes, Lucretia's private life did not escape calumny. Harsh falsehoods were employed to express disapproval of her "going out of woman's sphere." Jealous housewives were certain that Lucretia could not devote so much time as they to housework and have leisure to engage in public activities.

Editors who thought they were possessed of information direct from God relative to woman's place in the home, wrote slashing editorials about the duties of womanhood without knowing the less divinely ascertainable fact that Lucretia Mott was "Mrs." and not "Miss," and had a family of children.

When they learned the details of her life, strangers were amazed that a woman so frail in appearance could accomplish so much at home, and yet attend to many works of charity and reform. The

175

secret lay in her elimination of everything wasteful of minutes and the fact that she was an early riser, thus *making* time to attend to the many objects of her care and attention. The fact that she sewed on Sunday—to the horror of all men good and true—gave her an added day's advantage over the average woman.

Lucretia's power of discrimination between things necessary and unnecessary in religion she applied to home life. She did not permit herself to become lost in the myriad of self-imposed details in which some women seemingly took pride—the thousand and one odds and ends of the haphazard homemaker who brags that a woman's work is never done.

Lucretia was a mystic in nearly all things of life, but not home duties. Within doors nothing was left to the call of the "Inner Light." She might wait for the spirit to tell her when to speak in church, but she never waited for the spirit to prompt her to do the dishes. The routine of household economy was organized with businesslike efficiency, and everything went with clock-like precision.

Lucretia had this to say:

My life in the domestic sphere has passed much as that of other wives and mothers in this country. I have had six children. Not accustomed to resigning them to the care of a nurse, I was much confined during their infancy and childhood. Being fond of reading I omitted much unnecessary stitching and ornamental work in the sewing for my family, so that I might have more time for this indulgence and the improvement of my mind.

Lucretia from girlhood to old age always cut and made her own clothes, and was not known to have varied the style of her dress. She was like Whittier who, when a young man, had measurements for a coat taken by a Philadelphia tailor, and thereafter when a coat began to wear out would write for another to be made without the least variation in measurement or design.

Although Lucretia dressed in the simple costume of the Quaker, she attached no special significance to it as a means of religious grace and never advised others to adopt it. She did not discard the inherited uniform because she did not believe any principle was involved worthy the turmoil such an act would engender. Her liberality sometimes led her to wear articles given her which she would not have chosen for herself.

She was once presented with a shoulder shawl of white Canton crepe bordered with a knotted fringe some four inches deep. This was un-Quakerlike in appearance but, pleased with the kindness of the donor and loath to wound his feelings, she wore it several days, braving the comments it excited among the sisterhood of Friends. Unwilling to raise a storm in the Cherry Street teapot over so small a matter, she finally succumbed to criticism sufficiently to shear the shawl of its fringe as far as the last row of knots. This still remained, jagged and uneven, and anything but ornamental, but she said it seemed a pity to cut the whole off. The family laughed, and she laughed. Thereafter the shawl was worn without regard to its mutilated appearance, and was viewed with satisfaction by bigots who read no lesson in the jagged row of knots.

When in England Lucretia was given a gauze hat by a London hostess with the hope that she would imitate its tasty form and silk cord and thus improve the American style of headgear. Lucretia's plainness of garb had astonished English Quakerdom. Webb had written in an Irish paper how she dressed with the utmost degree of Quaker simplicity known in the islands, "yet we heard that in some points she would have been looked upon as rather 'gay' for a very plain Friend in America, which is almost past our comprehension." The headgear was accepted by Lucretia with qualms for, although no precisian herself, she knew how zealous of the slightest innovation were the American lovers of the peculiar dress.

On the return home the "coal-scoop" bonnet, a little more elevated in the crown and with a few additional plaits in it, was regarded by the Cherry Street saints as an unworthy imitation of the "corrupt customs of the world." Lucretia decided to keep the cap in memory of its owner. She liked to produce it at times, so she said, to astonish "the natives" with its high crown and odd shape. But she ceased to wear it after an episode which took place at Friends' Meeting at Wilmington. She attended this meeting soon after her arrival home from England, wearing the new finery pursuant to the donor's missionary intent. At the close of meeting, one of the elders approached her, saying sweetly, "I am sorry, my dear, to see that thou hast made a change in thy dress. When I saw thee coming in this morning with *that* bonnet on, I could think of nothing but a soldier's jockey-cap!" This closed the hat's career for anything but purposes of private exhibition.

In London, while admiring the gorgeous plumage of some beautiful birds at the Zoölogical Gardens, a gentleman who disapproved of Quaker garb because he disapproved of Lucretia, remarked to her: "You see, Mrs. Mott, our Heavenly Father believes in bright colors. How much it would take from our pleasure, if all the birds were dressed in drab."

"Yes," retorted the woman, "but immortal beings do not depend on their feathers for their attraction. With the infinite variety of the human face and form, of thought, feeling, and affection, we do not need gorgeous apparel to distinguish us. Moreover, if it is fitting that woman should dress in every color of the rainbow, why not man also? Clergymen, with their black clothes and white cravats, are quite as monotonous as Quakers. . . . ."

While this silenced her opponent, it only convinced him that Lucretia was a strong-minded woman, and that strong-minded women did not make pleasant company.

The plainness of Quaker life did not reach so far into the Mott home as to make life unbearable for the younger members of the household. The children had parties and un-Quakerlike good times. Lucretia confided to her sister that "dancing was not exactly in her line," but supposed she ought to be careful what she said, since her daughters and son accepted "invites" to parties where there was dancing, and stayed "far too late in the morning. Such a succession of parties as they are having now, I fear will be dissipating to the moral sense. And then the reading of such a thick two-volume novel as the 'Mysteries of Paris' consumes a midnight hour occasionally. I long sometimes to see them more interested in reading that which would minister to their highest good, but I have ceased to force such reading on them."

Lucretia's letters to members of her family contain intimate references to domestic matters. Even the Webbs in Ireland were told how she found time to darn the stockings, "and attend somewhat to a family numbering from ten to twenty every day; for though all our children, save Martha, the youngest, have married and left us, yet they and their children (nine now) are coming constantly. All being out of the city boarding for the summer, ours is a general rendezvous for the husbands to come to dine, and with other company, not a few, we often count thirty a day, including our own family . . . . it is our pleasure thus to enjoy the fleeting hours."

LUCRETIA MOTT, SOCIAL PIONEER

During a Philadelphia Yearly Meeting week the Motts had "nine or ten Friends lodging" with them and "some forty or fifty at meals, daily."

Lucretia gave her sister a vivid picture of preparations made to handle the many guests during one of the annual fairs:

If I did not iron twelve shirts, like cousin Mary, I had forty other things which I accomplished; for we had a large wash, and hurried to get the ironing away before the people flocked in. Five came just before dinner. I prepared mince for forty pies, doing every part myself, even to meat chopping; picked over some lots of apples, stewed a quantity, chopped some more, and made apple pudding; all of which kept me on my feet till almost two o'c., having to come into the parlor every now and then to receive guests. Now I shall rest, as I sit and write after dinner, with all gone to the Assembly Buildings, save one, a well-intentioned guest, who "thought best to remain and be *agreeable!*"

As part of the efficiency which made large scale hospitality possible, was a practice begun in early days when a large family made personal assistance in housework necessary. This was to help clear away the breakast table, and to wash the silver, china, and glassware belonging to the dining room. Lucretia liked to do this and only reluctantly gave it up when obliged to by the infirmities of age.

Wrote a granddaughter of the practice:

The daughters generally helped; and if guests were staying in the house, as was often the case, they sat near to join in the conversation, and sometimes to help in the work. It was not a disagreeable task; the well-scrubbed little cedar tub, with its steaming water, was placed at one end of the table, and article after article was washed and burnished in a systematic manner from which no deviations were permitted. It was a choice time of the day; plans were announced and discussed; letters read and commented on; public events reviewed; and friends of the family were apt to happen in on their way to business to contribute their items of news to the general liveliness.

After the return from abroad, the tax upon Lucretia's hospitality became very great. She wrote: "Our family party Seventh-day was pleasant; fifteen at dinner, and twenty at tea. I worked like a beaver that morning, so as to be ready to sit down with them early; did my sweeping and dusting, raking the grass plot, etc., made milk biscuit, a plum pudding, and a lemon pudding. Marianna and Martha made cake the day before . . . . "; and then the writer goes on to discuss capital punishment!

On another occasion she informed a correspondent: "I thought I was pretty smart to have the currants squeezed and the jelly made before meeting on Fourth-day morning" (that is, ten o'clock).

Although she employed servants the most of her life, she was obliged to do much work herself in earlier years because of limited means, and in later years because of her vast hospitality. From her mother she learned how to treat servants so as to insure contentment and faithfulness. The old lady had used to say, "I make it a rule never to ask them to do what I know they will not do." She in turn quoted the saying of old black Amy who long lived with Grandmother Folger that she "didn't like to be told to do what she was just going to do." It was one of Lucretia's rules to be willing to do herself any work she asked of another.

Even so, organization and executive ability were not enough. Servants required watching. Lucretia complained how she was obliged to stop letter writing to run out and pull off the clothespins and let down the wet clothes which were blowing to pieces in the high wind; "after all I had said about putting them out in a gale; but if we changed help for such things . . . . other things would be as bad. Mother used to say, 'You only change faults.'"

A servant ill with cholera was nursed through her illness and sent to the country to recuperate. Lucretia hired extra help, but found that, "with our large family there is still much to be done; so this morning I have ironed four dozen pieces, made soft custards, attended to stewing blackberries, and potted some Dutch herring, besides doing all the dusting, and receiving several callers. I was more tired when our family of thirteen gathered at dinner, than since I came home."

In 1850 Lucretia's daughter and family, the Davises, who had lived next door on Ninth Street, removed into the country, where they purchased with Thomas Mott an estate called Oak Farm, outside of Philadelphia. At the same time James bought a spacious house in Arch Street below Twelfth, known in the old system of numbering as "338."

The house being too large for the immediate family, now simmered down to James and Lucretia and their youngest daughter, Martha, arrangements were made that the Edward Davises and

Thomas Motts should make Arch Street their city home in the winter, and in turn take the parents and unmarried sister into the household at Oak Farms during the summer. This community life lasted six "delightful years," on the authority of a member of the family.

"Three-thirty-eight" was a house that looked like many another of its size in the city of monotonous red brick buildings. According to fashion the lower shutters were heavy and solid, painted white. With the fall of night these were left open till bedtime, and passers-by glanced in at the bright, cozy parlor with its animated circle around the evening lamp.

The carpet in the two large square parlors was bright colored and of rather striking design, for Lucretia disliked what she called "dingy carpets." She also disliked the prevailing style of dark, heavily curtained rooms, and when she came into the parlor in the afternoon, she would invariably step quickly across to the windows and draw back the green Venetian blinds to let the sunlight stream in; an action characteristic of her mental makeup.

Through the portals of the Race Street home and "338" came and went an almost steady surge of guests of all stations of prosperity, and every nationality. Sometimes it was a distinguished stranger from across the ocean, sometimes it was the hard working anti-slavery lecturer, the celebrated liberal, or the country Friend in town for a few days, or one of the large family circle who made the house on Arch Street a focus place.

From England came Lord Morpeth expressing a desire to a mutual friend to renew acquaintanceship.

So [reports Lucretia] we went to his lodgings, card in hand, reducing him to a common man, on our Republican principles. He was not at home. He soon returned the call, made himself very agreeable, and accepted an invitation the day following, to breakfast with us. He came each time unattended, walking, as any of our citizens would. We are pleased with the ease with which he accommodates himself to our American and Quaker simplicity. We invited Robert Purvis, Miller McKim, and a few other intelligent Abolitionists to meet him here, and had a delightful time. . . . .

Not long after Morpeth, Lucretia had occasion to announce:

Another Lion has just arrived in the city—Charles Dickens. Our children have a strong desire to see him. I, too, have liked the benevolent tendency of his writings, though I have read very little in them.

I did not expect to seek an interview, or to invite him here, as he was not quite one of our sort. But just now, there was left at our door, his and his wife's card, with a kind letter from our dear friend, E. J. Reid, London, introducing them, and expressing a strong desire that we would make their acquaintance. There is not a woman in London whose draft I would more gladly honor. So now we shall call on them, and our daughters are in high glee.

Then was added the quaint admonition from the woman who thought the great author not "quite one of her sort": "I regret that in Boston and New York the people have been so extravagant in their reception of the man."

More celebrated than either Morpeth or Dickens was the famed Hungarian exile, Louis Kossuth, who visited Philadelphia in 1852 as part of his American itinerary. Everywhere in the Northern States people crowded the streets and madly cheered the man who had faced the cannons of the Emperor Joseph on the battlefields of Hungary.

In every city and hamlet Kossuth was extravagantly hailed as a lover of freedom. Because of his reputation, James Haughton and Richard Webb of Ireland, and William Ashurst of London, had endeavored to convince him before he set sail for America that he should use his great popularity to help uproot slavery. Their plea was that he should assume the position of one who was a leader of freedom for all men in all places. But like Father Mathew, the Irish "Temperance Pope," the Hungarian exile was sponsored by men in the United States who advised a reticent attitude on slavery. Political friends warned him that it would be easier for him to arouse enthusiasm for oppressed European peasants if he made no mention of African slaves in America. These were sane men who knew the American public. The same Congress of the United States which passed the Fugitive Slave Act had passed a joint resolution offering a warship to Kossuth and his fellow officers should they be disposed to profit by that mode of escape from exile.

Everywhere that Kossuth went he lauded America as the asylum of oppressed peoples, the land of happiness and the Declaration of Independence, but always he omitted to make any mention of slavery. With eyes that seemed dreamily distant he failed to observe oppression in the valleys of the foreground while he eulogized the far-off mountain tops of freedom.

LUCRETIA MOTT, SOCIAL PIONEER

The revolutionary leader carried with him to Philadelphia letters of introduction to James and Lucretia Mott. In response to these the Motts called on him and invited him to dine with them. They were anxious to converse with the man who had in such a short time become a symbol of liberty. But Kossuth's advisers warned him that it would be unwise to let word precede him Southward that he had broken bread at the table of an Abolitionist, and that he must call only for an informal chat.

This he did, visiting the Mott residence and making himself agreeable. Lucretia admired him greatly and believed that he was opposed at heart to negro slavery if only he dared unseal his lips. She thought him especially wonderful in his clear perception, and believed "his speeches must do good in this country, if that good be not counterbalanced by the warlike spirit they kindle."

Kossuth's sister also called on the Motts where, in the attractive circle of husband, children, and grandchildren, she fell slave to the charm of Lucretia's "moral superiority." Madame Pulzsky defended her brother's position in regard to slavery, and would not acquiesce to Lucretia's argument that the abolition of slavery should be preached in season and out of season by the defender of the rights of nations; yet she was much impressed by Lucretia's earnestness.

She wrote in her published diary:

I have seldom seen a face more artistically beautiful. . . . . Beholding her, I felt that great ideas and noble purposes must have grown up with her mind, which have a singular power of expression in her very movements. Her language is, like her appearance, peculiar and transparent; and it is only when she touches upon the slavery question that her eye flashes with indignation, and her lips quiver with a hasty impatience, disturbing the placid harmony of her countenance and her conversation. But though she so positively pronounces the views at which she has arrived by self-made inquiry, yet she mildly listens to every objection, and tries to convince by the power of her arguments, untinged by the slightest fanaticism.

Madame Pulzsky left her hostess, regretting that she could not spend hours with her, listening and discussing. Her astonishment was great when, expressing admiration for Lucretia to some gentlemen in the city, one of them exclaimed, "You do not mean to say you have called on that lady?"

"Of course I have," was the Polish woman's answer. "Why should I not? I am most gratified to have done so, and I only regret that the shortness of the time we have to spend here prevents me from often repeating my visit."

"But she is a furious Abolitionist," explained the gentleman. "It will do great harm to Governor Kossuth if you associate with that party."

"I perceive, sir," retorted the visitor, "that you highly estimate Mrs. Mott, as you consider her alone a whole party. But if any friend of Governor Kossuth, even if he himself, converses with a person who has strong opinions against slavery, what harm can there be in that?"

"Your cause will then lose many friends in this city," was the answer.

Such intolerance amazed Madame Pulzsky, who little understood the American practice of hushing the merits of anti-slavery. Her friend attempted to point out to her what mischief the Abolitionists were doing, and how long ago emancipation would have carried in all the states, had the Abolitionists not so violently interfered.

"And besides," continued he, "Mrs. Mott preaches!"

"Well," replied the stubborn and amused foreign lady, "do not many Quaker ladies preach occasionally?"

This fact was admitted, but another gentleman interjected the information that Mrs. Mott was dangerous, as her sermons were powerfully inciting.

"Is she, perhaps, a fighting Quaker, who appeals to the words of the Saviour, that he did not come to send peace on earth, but the sword?"

"I am a fighting Quaker myself," puffed the gentleman, "my forefathers fought in the Revolutionary War; but Mrs. Mott is a Hicksite."

An inquiry as to what were the tenets of the Hicksites that they should inspire such dislike, Madame Pulzsky's only enlightenment was that "they are very bad; they, in fact, believe nothing."

Gerrit Smith, the millionaire philanthropist, once made an historic call at the Mott residence which he frequently described as possible nowhere else in America. In a conversation of an hour his hostess was interrupted half a dozen times with applications for charity. At last, in came the glorious Fanny Kemble, meeting Mrs. Mott in a manner that clearly showed they were warm friends; and soon came Frederick Douglass, the negro fugitive slave. There sat the millionaire philanthropist and political power of New York State, the world-renowned actress, the grandest representative of slavery, and the fearless disciple of Elias Hicks. One doubts if the Quaker city ever unveiled so magnificent a tableau for the brush of an artist.

In the steady stream of visitors, callers, and beggars, were self-invited guests who descended upon the Motts with bag and baggage in a receptive mood for an extended invitation. In most instances the astonished hostess quietly submitted to the infliction, preferring to be bored herself rather than wound others by making them appear unwelcome.

The visit once of a slightly deranged Friend who insisted in trudging the streets with her feet encased in thick yellow moccasins, and her shoulders draped with two shawls, was almost too much for Lucretia's hospitality, and she was inwardly relieved when the apparition decided to transfer her belongings to another house. Lucretia admits that when she left her guest at the door of the friend's house, she "turned quickly down the first street."

A feature of "Three-thirty-eight" was the dining room on the second floor rear. It was a spacious hall, thirty feet long. At its table was always room for one more guest. The unexpected appearance of visitors at meal time caused no flurry. Lucretia was like the old Nantucket neighbor who after greeting some unlooked for visitor quietly whispered to her daughter to "put six more potatoes on."

During the anti-slavery fairs or Yearly Meeting week or when a convention was being held in Philadelphia, the house was thrown open for the convenience of all who cared to come, and the long table in the dining room would then be filled to overflowing.

"What illustrious names! How many stirring sentiments! What echoes of laughter and merriment were heard around the festive board," exclaimed a frequent guest. Here were the stern reformers, as genial a group of "fanatics" as one could find, off duty. Without the shadow of a doubt as to the rightfulness of their causes, they made merry over the bigotry of the church, popular prejudices, conservative fears, absurd laws, and customs hoary with age. They held up in their metaphysical tweezers the representatives of the dead past that

THE GREATEST AMERICAN WOMAN

ever and anon ventured upon their platform. With peals of laughter they chopped into mince meat their assumptions and contradictions. And at the head of the table sat James Mott, maintaining the dignity of his position as host, ever ready to throw in a qualifying word, when the fiery reformers became too intense.

At the other end sat Lucretia, always skilfully managing to make the conversation general. When seated around her board, no two-and-two side talk in monotone was permissible; she insisted that the good things said should be enjoyed by all.

Vivid among the early anti-slavery memories of Aaron Powell was the first glimpse he had of the Mott home at the time of one of the great anti-slavery meetings in Philadelphia. In the capacious dining room sat William Lloyd Garrison, Wendell Phillips, Dr. William H. Furness, Mary Grew, Robert Purvis, and others, and all made to feel quite at ease. "Lovely and beloved as was Lucretia Mott in her public service, she was not less but even more ideal in her home life."

Powell described also a quaint practice:

How in a quiet way, toward the end of the dinner, during the period of the dessert, Lucretia had the earlier dishes, which had been removed and washed, returned to her, to be dried by her own hands, thus herself relieving the heavily taxed kitchen maids, meanwhile bearing her full share with her guests of the most engaging table talk! It was a memorable picture, a complete refutation of the criticism which often used to be made, and which still survives in certain quarters, to the effect that the woman who goes upon the public platform and shares in public service must needs be an inferior housekeeper and home maker.

Another guest described Lucretia's hospitality (without reference to the table) saying:

You can't think what delightful times I am having here as guest in Lucretia Mott's spacious mansion. Oh, the Quaker conveniences! comforts! There is nothing like them. So beautifully neat, too. The whole air of the house and its lovely mistress constantly suggests to me the purity and fragrance of a sweet, fresh-blown rose.

So much for the élite of the Nation whose names fill the biographical shelves of libraries. But no roll can be prepared of the humble and the poor who knew the house on Arch Street as a castle for runaway slaves, or the paradise of the forlorn. In the broad hall stood two roomy chairs, identified by irreverent daughters as the "beggars'

186

chairs," they were in such constant requisition by supplicants of all sorts, "waiting to see Mrs. Mott, miss."

James was sometimes amused to hear the objects of some of the calls. It seemed as though people thought his wife could do anything. "It is true," he commented, "she does do a great deal; no one out of the family knows one-half, and no one *in* the family knows the whole."

At table, black guests and white were treated with equal courtesy. This consideration was not always palatable to friends, but such as did not like it learned to stay away. One young gentleman of excellent family, finding himself expected one day to sit next a colored man at dinner, felt so aggrieved that he resolved to go no more to the house. For some time he managed to keep away, in which determination he was "violently left alone," but the attraction of a daughter proved too strong and he returned, preferring rather to be converted than forgotten, and afterwards became, not only a son-in-law, but an earnest advocate of the equality that had so offended him.

Once the mayor of Philadelphia suggested to Lucretia that women Abolitionists should avoid walking with colored people on the streets. Lucretia replied that the women "had never made a parade," as charged, of walking with colored people, but they would do as they had done before, walk with them as occasion offered, that she had done so repeatedly within the past month, meeting with no insult on the account; it was a principle with Abolition women which they could not yield, to make no distinction of color.

Twenty years of journeyings in controversial reforms, and a too abundant hospitality eventually collected toll from Lucretia's health. In the winter of 1856 it became apparent that the woman of sixty-three years could no longer bear the strain of open house. She wearied of exhausting numbers of guests, and of being called hither and yon as if she were public property, presiding now at this convention and now speaking at another, attending meetings of executive committees, and listening to bickerings, and subjected to persecutions.

She yearned for an hour of uninterrupted solitude, for the day she would not be called incessantly from her duties to attend the front of the house, when those chairs in the hall would not forever be saddled with supplicants, when she would not forever be listening to the tale of some negro beggar, some story of poverty and unhappiness, some request for aid or money.

For the moment she could stand it no longer; she was worn, exhausted, weary: oh, for the peace and quiet and the contentment of rural life, away from the hubbub of the city and that everlasting horde at dinner time. . . . . Would that she and James could read and think without interruption, potter in the garden, and see only invited intimates and hear the voices of kindred spirits.

The family realized that change was imperative if the health of the woman was to be restored, even as it had been in 1840 by a tour abroad. To meet the emergency James decided to uproot everything and remove from the city into the suburbs where the wanderer and the supplicant would not find their way so readily. The aged couple sought an asylum where they could go now that the campaign had become too strenuous for spirits no longer resilient with youth.

"Three-thirty-eight" was sold, and the couple bought as the haven of their descending years a stone farmhouse eight miles out of town on the Old York Road, opposite Oak Farm. This was not done without the mourning and lamentation of members of the family left in the city, daughters and grandchildren, and sister Yarnall—desirable little Elizabeth of childhood.

The old house on Arch Street was endeared by many pleasant associations. When its sale was consummated, a last family reunion was held in the hospitable parlors, where rhymes and poems expressive of humor and sentiment were read. There was much laughter and jollification, but beneath it all flowed a current of sadness.

An original poem was read:

> Who wearied of the world's renown,
> And sought a useful life to crown,
> By selling off his house in town?
> > James Mott.

> Who was it that the sale decreed,
> And urged him on to do the deed,
> And wished to close the terms with speed?
> > Lucretia!

Some sixteen or seventeen other verses closed with:

> Who constantly will ring the bell
> And ask if they will please to tell
> Where Mrs. Mott has gone to dwell?
> > The beggars.

THE COFFIN HOUSE, NANTUCKET

"ROADSIDE," NEAR PHILADELPHIA, HOME OF JAMES AND
LUCRETIA MOTT AFTER 1857

And who persistently will say
"We cannot, cannot go away.
Here in the entry let us stay?"
                    Colored beggars.

Who never, never, nevermore
Will see the "lions" at the door
That they've so often seen before?
                    The neighbors.

And who will miss, for months at least,
That place of rest for man and beast,
From North, and South, and West, and East?
                    Everybody.

When the reading was finished not a few eyes glistened with tears at the thought of losing daily sight of the snow-headed James and the angel grandmother.

The young man and the young matron had gone over the mountains and were looking into the sunset, their years of greatest influence were past. They had labored together much since those early years when, as a newly wedded pair, the depressions of the war of 1812 had made the bridegroom "down cellar" and Lucretia had taught school until within six weeks of the birth of her second daughter.

And what had been accomplished? Slavery was the law of the land, bigotry flourished in religion, and peace was an ideal far removed. But the word had been spoken, and the word had been heard. The churches were opening their doors to anti-slavery agitators, women were demanding rights, peace talk was heard, and the cause of liberal religion had grown. Perhaps Lucretia Mott had not lived in vain. At least she had friends who loved her, and thousands of persons called her benefactress. And James, the merchant who had wanted only enough to be comfortable, "with a little over," had prospered in the marts of trade with the peculiar fortune of the Quaker sect.

CHAPTER XVII

THE SPIRIT OF '48

When Lucretia was refused admission as a delegate to the World's Anti-Slavery Convention at London, she concretely had been brought face to face with the reality of woman's subjection. This denial of the right to participate in the cause dearest to her heart, coming as it did from a convention of men of humanity, was the bitter potion in the cup she was compelled to quaff because of sex. The silent trial of listening to abuse heaped high upon the feminine sex in the name of God, custom, and morality, she bore with unruffled calmness, but the iron of indigation sank deep into her soul, not so much because of affront to her as to womankind, and she was resolved to do something to right the wrong.

It was not chance that drew Lucretia Mott and Elizabeth Cady Stanton into each other's company at the end of the first day's session. A bond of common interest—a belief in the dignity of woman-hood equal to that of manhood—brought the plump young bride to the side of the middle-aged Quakeress when the delegates walked home to their lodgings. A day of wrongs, generations of wrongs, seared their hearts and made nothing the difference of twenty-three years in age. Centuries of Christian humility, long ages of patri-archal and feudal law, only fanned their rebellion toward assumptions of authority on the part of clergymen—gentlemen who denied that an anæsthetic should be administered women in childbirth because the Bible taught that the mothers of men bore children in pain and travail!

The soil out of which sprang the organized woman's movement (like a weed, most persons thought) was the great humanitarian movement of the nineteenth century, the Abolition cause—more especially the plot of churchmen to silence the participation of women in that reform.

Perhaps more than to Lucretia Mott, Elizabeth Cady Stanton, or Susan B. Anthony, modern woman owes a debt of gratitude to the bigotry of clergymen who did so much to awaken the world to the evils of woman's status. Let the religious scruples of Colver and

LUCRETIA MOTT, SOCIAL PIONEER

Torrey and Galusha (who would let Queen Victoria turn the head of the Prince Consort), be never forgotten. These are the fathers of woman's rights, notwithstanding the bar sinister in the coat armor, and the fact that the fathers failed to recognize the legitimacy of their offspring.

At London the cause of woman's rights had come to an issue and beaten about the frail figure of Lucretia Mott. Women before her had spoken of equality, but it was left to her to inspire and encourage and lead organized claims of sex equality. It is an irony of history that the World's Anti-Slavery Convention should stand as a landmark, not for the freedom of the slave, but of woman.

Had the question at the world's convention not come to an issue in the heat of preparation for discussion of slavery, the convention might more have been noteworthy as a monument between an old and new order of feminine rights. Dr. Bowring expressed regret that the "subject was launched with so little . . . . preparation. . . . . But bear up!" he wrote of Lucretia and her associates, "the coming of these women will form an era in the future history of philanthropic daring. They made a *deep* if not a wide impression, and have created apostles if as yet they have not a multitude of followers. The experiment was well worth taking."

When the news of Garrison's act of taking a seat in the balcony was reported to Harriet Martineau, she had responded, "It has done much, I am persuaded. You will live to see a great enlargement of our scope of usefulness, I trust; but, what with the vices of some women and the fears of others, it will be hard work to assert our liberty."

Seers who foresee the inevitable are few in any age. Men who laughed at the simplicity of King Canute, placed the throne of theology on the sands of time and commanded the waters of social progress to recede.

There are often periods in lives of thinking beings when some new book or acquaintance comes to them like an added sun in the heavens, lighting the darkest recesses and chasing every shadow away. "Thus," explained Elizabeth Cady Stanton, "came Lucretia Mott to me, at a period in my young days when all life's problems seemed inextricably tangled; when, like Noah's dove on the waters, my soul found no solid resting-place in the whole world of thought."

THE GREATEST AMERICAN WOMAN

Before meeting Lucretia, Elizabeth had heard a few men of liberal opinions discuss various political, religious, and social theories, but with her first doubt of her father's absolute wisdom, came a distrust of all men's opinions on the character and sphere of woman. She naturally inferred if their judgments were unsound on a question she was sure she *did* understand, they were quite likely to be on those she did not. Hence she had often longed to meet some woman who had sufficient confidence in herself to frame and hold an opinion in the face of opposition; a woman to whom she could talk freely, and be understood. In Lucretia Mott these longings had been answered at last.

She had been prepared in no wise to find Lucretia to her liking. She knew nothing of the merits of the division in the anti-slavery ranks, but as her husband and a kinsman, Gerrit Smith, were on the other side, she supposed Lucretia would not be friendly. Consequently she was embarrassed, as the only lady present representative of the Birney faction, at her first meeting with Lucretia Mott. To her surprise Lucretia received her in a quiet way with cordiality and courtesy, and the bride was seated by her side at dinner.

Mrs. Stanton has given us a picture of that strange meal:

No sooner were the viands fairly dispensed, than several Baptist ministers began to rally the ladies on having set the Abolitionists all by the ears in America, and now proposing to do the same thing in England. I soon found that the pending battle was on woman's rights, and that unwittingly I was by marriage on the wrong side. As I had thought much on this question in regard to the laws, Church action, and social usages, I found myself in full accord with the other ladies. . . . . In spite of constant gentle nudgings by my husband under the table, and the frowns of Mr. Birney opposite, the tantalizing tone of the conversation was too much for me to maintain silence. Calmly and skilfullly Mrs. Mott parried all their attacks, now by her quiet humor turning the laugh on them, and then by her earnestness and dignity silencing their ridicule and sneers. I shall never forget the look of recognition she gave me when she saw by my remarks that I fully comprehended the problem of woman's rights and wrongs. How beautiful she looked to me that day.

The Philadelphia Quakeress opened a strange world of possibilities. To Mrs. Stanton it seemed like vision to eyes of stone and vigor to limbs that had been halt. As the American delegates toured London, the young woman embraced every opportunity to cohere to the side of the Quaker leader.

She found that nothing was too sacred for this marvelous woman to question. To Elizabeth Stanton, reared in the cramped confines of inherited Presbyterianism, it was like meeting a being from a larger planet to find a woman who dared to question the opinions of popes, kings, and parliamentarians with the same freedom she would have criticized an editorial in the London "Times" (perhaps more than an Englishman would dare to do), maintaining no higher authority than her own judgment as a pure-minded woman of education. Elizabeth was awed to learn that her mentor feared neither ministerial frowns in this world nor Christian tortures in the next.

The bride of Henry Stanton, in the happiness of her escape from thraldom, "felt at once a new-born sense of dignity and freedom; it was like suddenly coming into the rays of the noonday sun, after wandering with a rushlight in the caves of the earth."

So enamored was she with the older woman that it was with trepidation that she had confessed that she greatly enjoyed dancing and dramatic performances. The Quakeress gave her a motherly look and replied that she regarded dancing as "a very harmless amusement," and added that the same Evangelical Alliance which so readily had passed a resolution declaring dancing a sin for a church member, had tabled a resolution declaring it a sin for a bishop to hold slaves.

As Lucretia and Elizabeth walked arm in arm down Queen's Street in London they had agreed to call a woman's convention on their return to America as a step towards a general movement for equality. Their resolution to promote a convention did not materialize for eight years. Because Henry Stanton was a "New Org" and the Motts "Old Orgs," Elizabeth and Lucretia did not meet at anti-slavery conventions. The two families went their separate ways engrossed in their own affairs. Lucretia was deep in the Abolition cause and had little time to think of launching a still more radical movement which would make her position even more perilous in her religious society, and perhaps end her usefulness as an Abolition lecturer among the people of her sect.

Sporadic mention of organization was talked of in letters between the women, but no encouragement offering, the idea slumbered until the summer of 1848, when Lucretia journeyed into western New York to attend the Yearly Meeting of Friends at Waterloo. Visiting her sister at Auburn, she learned that Elizabeth Cady Stanton had moved recently to Seneca Falls hard by.

It was arranged the two women should meet again. Perhaps Elizabeth wondered if she would still look with awe and love upon the woman who had won her heart in London, and done so much to give her a sense of importance. Would her mature eye perceive grossness where the girl's had been blinded by the novelty of hearing shocking ideas openly discussed?

At the tea table of a mutual friend the two women came together. Immediately there was a reblending of affection and the spanning of years of separation. Elizabeth yielded again to the spell of the reformer whose fame had grown so fast since 1840.

Lucretia looked upon the younger woman and saw that she was no more an unsophisticated bride with Calvinistic complexes, hoping someone would tell her that girls had a right to go to college or pursue careers. She was a mother, and had grown matronly, but she was still the same Elizabeth with the flashing wit and quick retort.

Elizabeth reminded Lucretia of the day when the Abolitionists "did" the British Museum, and how Lucretia (scant interested in objects of antiquity, but always interested in thoughts which cannot be put into glass cases or catalogued with numbers) had seated herself in an anteroom and talked with Elizabeth while the rest of the party made the rounds of the museum in orthodox fashion; how three hours slipped by and the party returned to surprise the women seated in the same place, having seen nothing but each other, their whole time absorbed in social and religious discussions.

One memory led to another. How, following the exchange of confidences at the British Museum, Elizabeth had attended the Unitarian Church the following Sunday, where for the first time she had listened to a woman preach. She had never heard a woman speak in public, let alone occupy the pulpit, although she had often expressed the idea in private circles (without invitation or appreciation) and been received with a coolness no greater than had she expressed admiration of free love at a meeting of a Presbyterian missionary society. When she had seen Lucretia mount the pulpit and preach as impressively as she had always hoped a woman could—"It was like the realization of an oft-repeated happy dream."

Her heart had warmed to the vivid woman, the spiritual face, the little figure in Quaker costume, the delicate hands that fondled the leaves of the Bible, as much in her sphere as any pulpit-pounding male preaching eternal damnation. How pitiful that good people should ostracize this woman because she held opinions that differed from their own. Incapable of getting outside their prejudices, how small they looked beside Lucretia, to whom form was nothing but substance everything, who wore Quaker clothes because they could be made without fuss, and who considered even dancing a harmless amusement.

The talk at the tea table drifted into channels which had to do with woman's rights. The resolution made in London to call a woman's rights convention was recalled to mind. The youthful Elizabeth was impatient for action. She implored Lucretia to lead the cause that had so many years been germinating in mind and heart.

Feeble in numbers, members of a sex without standing in public affairs, only one of them famed and she with a following limited to free thinkers, liberals, and Quakers, the ladies were determined to organize a woman's convention. Great social reforms, they comprehended, were not customarily originated by wealthy or influential persons, or adopted by large numbers of supporters in the beginning, so they had the courage to launch the woman's rights movement. With them it was not a question so much what was woman's appropriate sphere, or what she might or might not be capable of doing, but whether one class of human beings was to fix for another class of human beings its field of action or mode of enjoying the faculties conferred by Nature's God.

The spirit of the women at the tea table was that of the 'forties wherein the yeast of reform leavened social ideas. In the ferment of the decade, the claim of sex equality was a logical step. Too long the heritage of freedom had been a male perquisite. The blood of Saxon clansmen roving the forest of Germany, and of the haughty barons of Runneymede no longer was to flow for naught in woman's veins.

It was not strange these women should have been inoculated with the virus of the revolution which everywhere in the civilized world was tending to substitute for the divine right of kings, priests, and patricians, the broader right of individual conscience and judgment in matters of life. The age-long battle for freedom wherein the right of the serf to migrate and the peasant to self-government, and the plowman's claim of individual judgment in religion, were logical sequences, was to be extended another step.

But the claim of woman's rights was the step most radical of all because it was a feminine step. Of all heresies advocated by the Garrisonian reformers, the doctrine that women had an equal right to participate in Abolition assemblies had been considered the most ridiculous. Temperance, non-resistance, church reform, were bad enough. It was conceded in popular imagination that a man might conscientiously eat graham bread, or be a "barnburner" in politics, or a deluded victim of nearly any "ism" and still be a patriotic American and a good Christian, but to advocate woman's rights was to be a creature without moral standards and beyond the pale of religion. It was not so presumptuous for a negro or a peasant to assert equality as it was for members of the sex which always had been submissive to man.

How wicked the conservatives of a former generation had thought democracy! A form of government whereby a majority of the ignorant would choose rulers instead of submitting to the wiser choices of Heaven exercised through the strong arm of robber barons; and how wicked had been the separation of church and state and the growth of self-governing religious societies in place of bishops especially anointed by God to exercise a monopoly over the morals and worship of men! The prognostication for each step had been that its ultimate attainment meant the end of morality and true religion.

Woman's rights was the climax!

Time was short. Sunday morning the women met a second time, in Mrs. McClintock's parlor. There the woman's movement was launched in a cup of tea.

The mothers of the movement were handicapped by the fact that they had had no experience in getting up conventions. Lucretia had addressed many audiences, but she confessed her unfamiliarity with the business of a convention. It was humiliating to the women to find that they must resort to the study of masculine speeches and petitions in order to prepare a good form for their own productions. They consoled themselves with the thought that this was because women never had been allowed to take an active part in what always had been considered a masculine prerogative.

Their inexperience was so great that they did not realize that the phraseology of every legal document is based on forms, in many cases hundreds of years old, and that there was not a lawyer living who had ever drawn up a completely original paper of any sort. The women found a batch of peace, temperance, and anti-slavery reports, but a perusal of them convinced the readers that they were altogether too tame "for the inauguration of a rebellion such as the world had never before seen." They at length decided to use in substance the form of the Declaration of Independence with slight modifications, substituting the phrase "all men" for "King George," and in other ways broadening the scope of that paper so as to make it applicable to all humanity and not alone Americans of the male sex.

Perceiving that the patriots of America had had eighteen grievances, a protracted search was made through statute books, church usages, and the customs of society in general to find an equal number of acts of oppression towards women. The ladies knew the grievances existed, but now for the first time they found it necessary to ferret them out and marshal them in presentable shape. With the discovery and announcement of the final "abuse," the women felt that they had enough evidence to go before the tribunal of the world with a good case, and one, indeed, stronger than the "brief" prepared by Thomas Jefferson.

One youthful male assistant could not forbear the opportunity to joke the women that their grievances must indeed be great when they were obliged to resort to books to find them out.

In their own private lives, not one of the four women had experienced the coarser forms of tyranny resulting from unjust laws or association with unscrupulous men, but they felt the wrongs of others, and Lucretia in public life had experienced enough of the handicaps of femininity to know the restraints incidental to sex, as every proud woman should.

The women who called the convention were not sour old maids, childless women, or divorced wives, as the newspapers soon declared them to be with characteristic inaccuracy. Lucretia in particular was happy in marriage with a husband of sufficient ability to have no fear of independence on the part of his wife.

James Mott had twice amassed a competency in trade, one of which he had given up for conscience's sake. His activities in the fields of reform had made him a noteworthy figure in anti-slavery, religious, and similar circles; but because he felt seldom called upon to address audiences he was overshadowed by the genius of his more brilliant wife. Yet he had no need to bolster his self-respect by suppression of the activities of the one whom he loved and admired.

It was written of their old age that he would sit behind Lucretia on the platform and radiate benign satisfaction at every word she uttered. Dr. Charles Gordon Ames once spoke on a platform with Lucretia, and delighted to tell how, after she had criticized some statement of his, James leaned over to him, aside, and whispered placidly, "If she thinks thee is wrong, thee had better look it over again."

Shortly before the day set for the woman's convention James suffered ill health and Lucretia doubted if she would be able to get to the meeting place at Seneca Falls before the morning of the convention. For a while it was thought James would not be able to attend until the second day's session. He especially requested that Mrs. Stanton's "great speech" be reserved until that day.

Lucretia penned Elizabeth a hasty note, in which she expressed fear that the attendance would not be as large as it might otherwise be, owing to the busy labors of harvest. "But it will be a beginning," she thought, "and we hope it will be followed in due time by one of a more general character."

The morning of the appointed day dawned, a day which will figure prominently in the pages of history when historians come to write the story of mankind as a series of social movements rather than wars and tariffs. The migration of women to the Unitarian Church at Seneca Falls was a saga of heroism as romantic as the opening of California or the breaking of the Northwest by pioneers of plow and covered wagon. The one was a picture of economic and political expansion—the lure of adventure and the urge of the stomach—the other a gigantic epic in the upward toiling of the human race from the inequalities of barbarism toward the pinnacles of human justice where principle, and not custom, is right.

In due time the ladies in charge of the program arrived at the church carrying their declaration of rights, resolutions, and bulky volumes of the statutes of New York State, wherein were contained legal outrages against the feminine sex. They found the doors of the church locked. Debate ensued among the sponsors while a crowd of spectators clustered around. At length an embryo professor of Yale College was boosted through a window, and a man unlocked the door to woman's freedom.

As he swung open the portals a buzzing throng pushed in. The little chapel was quickly filled. There was much whispering and rustling noises peculiar to women and children in church. Interest was

TABLET ON BUILDING IN SENECA FALLS, NEW YORK

Now standing on the site of the Wesleyan Chapel, where the first Woman's Rights Convention in the world's history was held, July 19-20, 1848. Lucretia Mott signed the Declaration of Rights. (Her name has been brought out more distinctly in this reproduction of the tablet, which is becoming stained and discolored through oxidation.

as highly pitched as though a professor of phrenology or an evangelist had come to town, perhaps more, since a convention to discuss the social, civil, and religious condition and rights of woman had never before been advertised.

The call for the convention advised that the first day's meeting was to be exclusively for women, that the public generally were "invited to be present on the second day, when Lucretia Mott, of Philadelphia, and other ladies and gentlemen" would address the audience. The decision that men should not be present on opening day was an inconsistent one when it is remembered that the women were objecting to sex disparity.

Notwithstanding the plain wording of the invitation, the women observed a number of men in attendance, and being already in their seats they were allowed to remain if for no better reason than that no way to get rid of them could be thought of.

As the fatal minute for opening the convention approached it was discovered that no woman present felt capable of assuming the responsibility of organizing the audience and presiding over its destinies. A general timidity prevailed. The participants were strangers to Cushing's "Manual of Parliamentary Law." A hasty council was held at the altar. It was decided that man could make himself useful upon even an occasion such as this, and James Mott, tall and solemn in Quaker costume, was drafted to the president's chair. Fortunately for the convention's success, his previous indisposition had not kept him from attendance. Mary McClintock, wife of an influential citizen of the county, was appointed secretary, and the strange convention got under way.

The moving spirit of the convention . . . . we are told [wrote Isabella Beecher Hooker twenty-five years later in a letter to the woman's silver anniversary meeting] was Lucretia Mott, who spoke with her usual eloquence to a large and intelligent audience on the subject of "Reform in General," and, from time to time, during the numerous sessions of the Convention, swayed the assembly by her beautiful and spiritual appeals, and was the first to affix her name to this prophetic and inspired "Declaration of Sentiments," an act which she will tell you today, I trust, has brought to her more joy than, perhaps, any other act of her life.

Elizabeth Cady Stanton, hardly thirty years of age, delivered an address. Martha Wright (Lucretia's sister) read some satirical articles she had published in the daily papers answering diatribes on

woman's sphere. Ansel Bacon, one of the men responsible for passing the married woman's property bill in New York, spoke on that
legislation. Samuel Tillman, student at law, read extracts from the
most exasperating English and American statutes reflecting the law's
tender mercies towards wives in permitting husbands to relieve them
of the care of their property, money, children, and responsibilities of
government.

The Declaration of Independence, revamped as Thomas Jefferson
had never thought of it, was freely discussed by many persons present,
reread, and slightly amended. The declaration and resolutions passed
at this first convention for equal rights demanded all that the most
radical friends of the movement have since claimed; the right to vote,
to share in all political offices, honors, and emoluments, the status of
complete equality in marriage, equal rights in property, wages, and
custody of children on a par with the husband, and the right to make
contracts, to sue and be sued, and to testify in the courts of justice
whence women were barred together with idiots, children, and China-
men. What the women asked, after many centuries, was the right to
be human, and not to be glorified incubators.

The only resolution not unanimously adopted was that which
demanded the electoral franchise. Mrs. Stanton and Frederick Douglass held stoutly for this right. But Quaker Lucretia urged against
the present adoption of the measure on the ground that it was premature, and would make the cause ridiculous at that early date, and
do harm to the advancement of pressing social and economic demands.
Women desired more than suffrage, she contended; but she gave in
when she saw that sentiment was against her.

The convention at Seneca Falls dissolved in a buzz of discussion.
Many a member of the audience left for home with stirrings in head
greater than had gathered there a twelvemonth before. A customary percentage went away disturbed. Some ladies feared men would
laugh at them if they signed petitions for woman's rights, others maintained that they had rights enough, while men said the women already
had too many rights.

As pulpit and press began to thunder, one by one women signa-
tories withdrew their names from the convention's roll. The statesman William H. Seward agreed with Mrs. Stanton that the women
had the argument, but thought custom and prejudice was against
them, and that these were stronger than truth and logic.

CHAPTER XVIII

The Hand that Rocks the Cradle

Emboldened by the sound of their voices in public, the women of the countryside met again at Rochester two weeks after the session at Seneca Falls. There is a left wing to every radical cause. A small group of participants came prepared to elect one of their own sex president. This move was opposed by the founders of the movement who doubted if any woman's timid voice was ready to preside over an audience filled with male hecklers bobbing up to call points of order. The embattled women, however, proceeded to their business in the face of both Lucretia's and Elizabeth's threatened withdrawal.

The convention opened with the quietness of a Quaker meeting. The voices of the president and secretaries could scarcely be heard beyond the first row, until a school teacher volunteered to read the minutes of the previous meeting, and everything went loudly and smoothly. Dull moments were few. An array of gentlemen were present primed with arguments calculated to stop the ungodly foolishness of unsexed females. The obstructionists did not much dispute the right of women to equal pay with men in the business world, but they expressed concern of claims made of equality in the home. The old idea of a divinely ordained household head, and that head in all cases the man, whether wise or foolish, educated or ignorant, sober or drunk, had warm defense.

Male speakers thought the problem one of expediency, and they chose to argue the question on that basis rather than that of justice. A gentleman in the audience asked when two heads disagreed who must decide? There was no lord chancellor to whom to apply, and besides, did not St. Paul strictly enjoin obedience to husbands, and that man should be the head of woman?

Lucretia replied that as a practical matter the problem was not vital. The Society of Friends she cited as an example of a sect which provided no promise of obedience on the part of the wife in the marriage ceremony, and she had never known any difficulty to arise on that account. There was no mode of appeal save appeal to reason.

In some of the meetings of this society women were placed on an equality with men, yet the results so much dreaded had not occurred. Warming to her task, she asked why men, who were so anxious to follow St. Paul as a guide to all social problems which concerned women, rejected his counsels—for did not St. Paul advise men not to marry?

The objections made at Rochester were those she was to hear many years with monotonous repetition. This time they had the virtue of being fresh. Honest men quoted and misquoted the Bible. Fear was expressed that doctrines expressed by Lucretia would be detrimental to business, morality, and law, which in many states since have become recognized practices, Blackstone and St. Paul to the contrary, notwithstanding.

One gentleman especially deprecated woman's occupying the pulpit, this being a male monopoly by many centuries of custom, and hence divinely arranged. Lucretia was stirred. Prohibitions quoted in restraint of women, she replied, were too often obtained from the clergy and not the Bible. Supporting her position by numerous quotations and explanations, she complimented the Rochester church for opening its doors to a woman's convention. She recalled how a few years back the Female Moral Reform Society of Philadelphia had applied for the use of a church in that city in which to hold one of its meetings and had been allowed only to use the basement on condition that no woman should speak at the meeting. This had necessitated the presence of a clergyman who called the meeting to order, and another clergyman who had read the ladies' reports to the society.

Every gentleman who spoke on the Rochester platform was not an obstructionist. William C. Nell read a speech which Lucretia appreciated, but explained she thought too flattering. Unlike many feminists of the century Lucretia was an advocate of equality; she did not contend woman was innately superior to man except as custom had made it necessary for woman to profess a higher code of morals.

It was a bold convention, and not the least daring was Elizabeth's challenge to the audience that if any churchmen were present they should not keep quiet at the convention and then do as their brethren had done at Seneca Falls, use the pulpit throughout the city to denounce the women, from pulpits whence women would not be allowed to reply.

The challenge swept the hall with no response, but the convention had not long adjourned ere a second hail of denunciation descended from the pulpit, and continued many years.

The seed of the woman's movement germinated, not under shining sun and balmy showers, but pressed in unfriendly soil, subjected to the chilling animosities of merchants and the storms of politicians, and wilted down by the glaring heat of reverend gentlemen, all of whom united to prevent the female from speaking in public.

The press likewise beat down its editorials on the women with unsparing ridicule; many of the articles being written, apparently, not only *for* morons, but *by* morons. Precedents, hearsay, and hasty judgments passed as counterfeits of thought.

A steady stream of clergymen marched on and off convention platforms with arguments which meant the perpetual maintenance of prevailing standards. One clergyman claimed superior rights and privileges for men on the ground of "superior intellect"; another because of the "manhood of Christ"—if God had desired the equality of woman He would have given some token of His will through the birth, life, and death of the Savior. Declared an Unitarian editor: "Place woman unbonneted and unshawled before the public gaze, and what becomes of her modesty and her virtue?"

Reverend Byron Sunderland, later chaplain of the United States Senate, preached a sermon, taking for his text, "The woman shall not wear that which pertaineth unto man; neither shall a man put on a woman's garment; for all that do so are an abomination to the Lord thy God." What the good man would have said had he foreseen the day when haberdashers would sell gentlemen's silk underwear in shades of blue and violet, no one can augur.

The vicars of Christ were certain that the woman's movement was a challenge to Christianity. If it were conceded that Christianity was wrong in its attitude that woman was sinful and had brought evil into the world, and was weak in intellect and body, then the whole of Christianity would tumble and the world be thrown into darkness, for if the Bible was admitted wrong in regard to woman's status, then might it not be wrong in every other matter? Christ was denied by anyone who denied the complete efficacy of the Bible, for Christ believed it all; hence the believer in woman's rights, like the Abolitionist, was anti-Christ and the Devil's agent. Lucretia and her associates were vicious women!

All this had the iron of theological reasoning. It was based on the plenary inspiration of the Bible, and no clergyman went behind this assumption. Standing firmly on the premise, the clergy waxed logical, facetious, or vindictive, and customarily carried their congregations with them. Good shepherds herded their sheep and ferreted goats. Few women wished to be goats. The majority preferred to be sheep and to follow the bellwethers of the pulpit.

The religious argument against woman's rights was the one Lucretia tried her best to avoid, although when pressed she was able to hold her own in the exchange of scriptural texts. She related her anti-slavery experiences upon the Bible question; how one party took pains to show the Bible was opposed to slavery while the other quoted paragraphs to prove it had divine origin, "thus wasting their time by bandying Scriptural texts, and interfering with the business of their meetings." Abolitionists, she said, soon learned to confine themselves to their own work of declaring the inherent right of man to himself and his earnings. "It is not to be supposed," she often concluded, "that all the advice given by the apostles to the women of their day is applicable to our own intelligent age; nor is there any passage of Scripture making those texts binding upon us."

The press was prone to greater humor than the pulpit. An attitude assumed by editors not able to differentiate between child-bearing and voting was the allegation that the purpose of the woman's movement was "to seat every lord at the foot of the cradle, and to clothe every woman in her lord's attire," that is, to interchange the sexes.

When Lucretia asked to speak in public, or call a convention, or discuss affairs of state, or vote, it was thought she was violating the "laws of nature." It was believed women in the home would never be able to learn about political science, or study social reforms affecting the Nation, quite so intelligently as men who, in instances not a few, absorbed their opinions with their beer at the corner saloon.

Male electors long had basked in the admiration of wives who believed them statesmen close to the lords of high decision, whereas their associations with rulers consisted of a handshake and a cigar of doubtful ancestry on election day from Michael O'Shaughnessy, "the people's candidate."

The tone of the newspapers Lucretia was compelled to read sound not unfamiliar to modern ears: " 'Progress,' is the grand bubble which is now blown up to a balloon bulk by the windy philosophers of the age," expounded one editor. Papers sneered at the "progressive age." "Great effort is everywhere being made to bring out some new, impracticable, absurd and ridiculous proposition; the greater its absurdity the better."

All were agreed that the women's conventions should openly resolve that the men should wash dishes, scour up, handle the broom, darn stockings, patch breeches, dress up in the latest fashion, wear trinklets, look beautiful, and be as fascinating as "those blessed morsels of humanity whom God gave to preserve that rough animal man, in something like a reasonable civilization."

A few editors pursued different tactics. One professed to see nothing to get excited about in a cause which already had excited him. He thought the women of Seneca Falls and Rochester extremely dull; aside the novelty of their cause they were hardly worth noticing.

A Philadelphia paper appealed to civic patriotism by explaining how girls of other cities wanted to be President of the United States and governors of states, but the girls of Philadelphia (God bless 'em) objected to fighting and holding office. They preferred "the baby-jumper to the study of Coke and Lyttleton, and the ball-room to the Palo Alto Battle." Women, continued the editor, had enough influence over human affairs without being in politics. Mothers, grandmothers, aunts, wives, and sweethearts managed everything. "Men have nothing to do but to listen and obey and to say 'of course, my dear, you will, and of course, my dear, you won't.'"

Horace Greeley astonished himself with the discovery of a great panacea for all feminine dissatisfaction, drunken husbands, poverty, and legal disabilities—it was "a wicker-work cradle and a dimple-cheeked baby."

The New York and London papers called the women "sour old maids." The opprobrious epithet "strong-minded" was applied to woman righters just as the strongest term of contempt that could be used by a Southern slaveholder was "free nigger."

Only one editor had the spirit of prophecy, and this was watered with foreboding. He wrote from down east: "Before the morning of the twentieth century dawns, women will not simply fill your offices of Register of Deeds, but they will occupy seats in your Legislative Halls, on your judicial benches, and in the executive chair of State and Nation. We deprecate it, yet we perceive its inevitability, and await the shock with firmness and composure."

Woman, "the angel of the family altar," as she was portrayed (or betrayed) in the genteel magazines, and woman the creature of Coke and Blackstone, were two different figments of interpretation.

Disapproval of woman's rights was not universal. A small coterie of males rallied around Lucretia and lent the cause lustre, and credit to themselves, although certainly not contemporary honor. Thomas Wentworth Higginson was one of these. Meeting Lucretia for the first time on the woman's platform, he scribbled enthusiastically:

How shall I describe to you Lucretia Mott . . . . the most brilliant eyes. Such a face and such a regal erectness! Nobody else ever stood upright before. She said but little in the meetings, but that so clear and sagacious and wise; and there was such an instinct of her superiority, that she rules like a queen on the platform, and when she looked as if she desired anything we all sprang to see what it might be.

Garrison, of course, became an advocate. He was a congenital "joiner" of cracked movements—anti-slavery, woman's rights, spiritualism, and Graham diet; a combination which united itself in the popular mind as having about equal merit.

Henry B. Blackwell, brother of Dr. Elizabeth Blackwell and husband of Lucy Stone, was another male speaker on the woman's platform who described himself as owing no apology for his stand.

William Henry Channing expressed himself "heart, mind, soul and strength for the Equal Rights of Woman"; and so did James Mott, C. C. Burleigh, Wendell Phillips, and other Abolitionists of the non-resistant school.

The bachelor Whittier did not grace the woman's platform, yet he did not share the misgivings of those who feared that when women voted, their beauty and sentiment would go. In this matter, thought he, "we can trust nature. Stronger than statutes or conventions, she will be conservative of all that the true man loves and honors in woman." Quakerlike the poet added, "I have no fear that man will be less manly or woman less womanly when they meet on terms of equality before the law."

In the turmoil of the fierce conflict over the participation of women in the anti-slavery agitation he had confided to Lucretia that "give woman the right to vote, and you end all these persecutions by reform and church organizations."

LUCRETIA MOTT, SOCIAL PIONEER

The red-blooded editors of the newspapers went particularly out of their way to deride the male supporters of the movement. Many an unknown "he-man" editor of a weekly rural paper wrote slashing editorials about the "Aunt Nancy" men, the hermaphrodites and "ismizers," and fanatical Abolitionist preachers of "damnable doctrines and accursed heresies" who sympathized with the woman's cause. They were pictured either as weak-minded males, or as persons infatuated with a desire for notoriety. Woman's rights men were "men who comb their hair smoothly back, and with fingers locked across their stomachs, speak in a soft voice, and with upturned eyes." Editors reported conventions of "masculine women" and "feminine men," described the bloomer dress very minutely, and said little of the arguments of the speakers.

In the welter of "pros" and "antis" there occasionally appeared in print some self-appointed Solomon who deemed himself so devoid of bias that he sought to analyze in a judicious manner the whole fabric of woman's rights. Like the man who was willing to be convinced (but would like to see the person who could do it), the purpose of such writers was to put an end to the controversy by showing that, whereas women were deprived of certain rights, they were wrong in their battle against "nature and God."

Such an arbiter was L. P. Brockett, M. D., of Hartford, Connecticut, author of many books. In a thick volume he entombed his reflections and dissected the capabilities of women in a sort of female vocational "Gray's Anatomy." School-teaching the author recommended, but the spectacle of a woman standing before a congregation and teaching the lessons of Christ, he conceded, was something "contrary to our ideas of propriety and womanly delicacy," a sufficiently Victorian reason. The doctor admitted that a well educated and deeply religious woman *might* be able to write a sermon as systematic, earnest, pungent, and practical as most clergymen; which would seem to indicate that he had not heard many of the current sermons of his generation.

Medical treatment of women and children the doctor hoped some day to find in the care of highly educated female physicians, but on the whole he recommended the keeping of bees, the rearing of silkworms, and the care of some of the "fanciful varieties" of domestic fowls, and pigeons, guinea hens, ducks, geese, turkeys, and rabbits, as employments better suited for women.

He viewed the stage with mingled emotions. He recognized the artistic merits of Fanny Kemble, Charlotte Cushman, and Mrs. Siddons, and graciously admitted there were ballet dancers whose purity of life strangely contrasted with the performances which formed a part of their daily duties, but on the whole he was convinced no pureminded woman had the right to imperil her hopes of eternal life by entering upon a theatrical career.

Having put woman in her place, specifically about halfway between the cook stove and the cradle, Dr. Brockett sighed for the return of the spinning wheel. It was such good exercise!

The man who did not believe that women had the power of mind sufficiently to qualify them to teach the higher branches of mathematics, then paid his disrespects to J. Stuart Mill, the English philosopher who had come out in compliment of woman's intelligence. The doctor was not surprised that a "deist" should declare that woman was substantially man's equal. Despite his great reputation, Mr. Mill lacked wisdom because he wilfully ignored the Scriptural accounts of the creation of woman. For that reason Mr. Mill failed to discern the "original design and purpose of her Creator" in placing her in a subject relation to man. Dr. Brockett pointed out that "great men were not always wise."

At this point the masculine counterpart of Sarah Josepha Hale enters a sort of trance (if he had not been in that condition from the start), and takes the interested reader into the future, delineating with colored adjectives election day should women be allowed to vote. He declares it would be a gala day for the prostitutes; "modest, refined, Christian women" would refuse to go to the polls in such company.

What a lesson of evil would be taught children on that day, he moaned. Imagine the innocent offspring, clutching its mother as it stands in the presence of "poor wretches, bedizened in gaudy finery, with bold, brazen faces, many of them half or wholly drunk, and uttering, with loud laughter, horrible oaths and ribald and obscene jests." What an impression the child would receive!

And if the mother attempted to tell her daughter that these were bad women, the little child might query: "But mother, they are going to vote. If they were so very bad, would they have the same right to vote that you and other ladies have?" Unable to answer so precocious a question, the "modest, refined, Christian" mother would scurry home, leaving the polls to her male representatives, and the women of the underworld.

To drive home the lesson the book is illustrated with a picture showing the refined woman at the polls completely surrounded by a vicious group of derelicts of both sexes. The picture vividly warns any woman who is on the verge of becoming a follower of Lucretia Mott, the type of men and women with whom she must associate if she votes. It also discloses the unintentional fact that the voting male is the uncouth immigrant, the bowery heeler, and the pimp; the same male hailed by opponents of female rights as woman's natural representative in affairs of government. One glance at the men in the picture convinces the reader that woman's benign influence in the home had gone awry, despite this best chosen argument of anti-suffragettes.

Dr. Brokett's electoral prognostications are a sample of fears that never have come true. Or perhaps the modern concept of the ideal woman has changed; if so, Dr. Brockett would grieve. Listen while he describes the anatomical changes in woman's face produced by equal rights. "The blush of modesty, the timid, half-frightened expression which is, to all right thinking men, a higher charm than the most perfect, self-conscious beauty, will disappear, and in the place of it we shall have hard, self-reliant, bold faces, out of which all the old loveliness will have faded, and naught remain save the look of power and talent, blighted like that of a fallen angel."

Dr. Brockett is now doubtlessly floating in heaven (where women with "timid, half-frightened" faces are taking care of the more "fanciful varieties of the domestic fowls"), secure in the beautiful thought that all the hardened, bedizened faces are sizzling in hell together with John Stuart Mill, who didn't rate very high at Hartford, Connecticut.

CHAPTER XIX
THE HEN CONVENTIONS

Lucretia endeavored to awaken sufficient interest in her home city to hold a woman's convention, but the interest she aroused was mainly antagonistic. Staid Philadelphians lacked the venturesome temperament which characterized the spirit of western New York.

Lucretia did her best to entice Elizabeth Stanton to Philadelphia. "Thou art so wedded to this cause that thou must expect to act as a pioneer," exhorted the busy Quakeress to her friend. Already, a speech by Mrs. Stanton delivered at Waterloo, New York, had aroused favorable comment among the "respectable inhabitants" of that town, and Lucretia encouraged her friend to exercise her talents in lecturing, that her sex might "go forward." And, continued the mild appearing radical, "do write to Rochester and stir up those women to their duties. We must not depend upon any who have been apostles before us."

Lucretia was cognizant of advancing years and the fact that her time was consumed in the anti-slavery movement. She sought younger women for active leadership in the latest reform. This was forthcoming in the persons of Lucy Stone and Susan B. Anthony, who were to carry the torch until they, too, were to become old, and likewise seek fresh hands and strong hearts to succeed them.

Though Pennsylvania was not ready for a woman's convention, there broke in Philadelphia an opportunity to focus public attention upon the sluggish cause. Richard Henry Dana, one of the literary leaders of the day had, in a moment of unfortunate judgment, selected Philadelphia as the place to deliver a lecture on what he considered the proper sphere of woman. Writer and poet, descendant of the Federalistic gentry of New England, he thought himself an hereditary guardian of public morals. He had little sympathy with, or interest in, the affairs of the world. He was unsparing in his ridicule of the new demands of women for a larger stage of action. To add salt to open wounds he made it a point to eulogize Shakespeare's heroines, especially Desdemona, Ophelia, and Juliet, as models of innocence, tenderness, and woman's confiding love in man.

LUCRETIA MOTT, SOCIAL PIONEER

When Mr. Dana gave his lecture in Philadelphia there was a woman in his audience who for beauty of character out-lustered any character in Shakespeare's insipid female cast. That woman was Lucretia Mott. At the close of the great man's lecture, the friend of Emerson sought introduction. This was effected, and after the formalities of polite greeting had been exchanged, Lucretia started to discuss with Mr. Dana his ideals of womanhood as she would have done with any of her intellectual friends. She told the speaker she had been much interested in his lecture and profited by the information it contained, but that she could not respond to his ideas of woman's true character and destiny.

Mr. Dana was a gentleman of the professorial type; a fountain to spout knowledge into empty vessels, not a debater. The co-founder of the "North American Review" was accustomed to worshipful admiration and was unfamiliar with the type of woman who would take issue with him. When, therefore, Lucretia uttered her first words of criticism, he quickly mumbled, "I am sorry," and rushed out of the hall, leaving Lucretia transfixed with astonishment.

Dana's lecture seemed to Lucretia unworthy the serious subject of woman and, coming from an eminent source, pernicious in its influence upon the young generation. She resolved to answer it in order that she might correct its misconceptions. Her resolution resulted in one of her best known public orations, rendered the seventeenth of December, 1849, before an audience as choice as the one that had listened to Mr. Dana. It was one of Lucretia's few speeches to be fully reported. A limited number were printed in pamphlet form, and twenty years after reprinted at the request of an English lady for circulation in England.

Lucretia began her speech with the assertion that there was nothing of greater importance to society at large, men and women, than the true position of the latter. The subject many years had claimed her earnest attention. She had long wished to see women occupying a more elevated position than custom allotted her.

The theme of woman had been one of ridicule, satire, and sarcasm. Not more was to be expected from the vulgar and the ignorant, but a woman had the right to expect that coarse epithets would not be resorted to by intelligent and refined persons. She thought Dana's lecture fraught with sentiments calculated to retard the progress of women to the high elevation of dignity destined by her Creator. Dana in his talk presented a sentiment rather than an argument. Woman too long had been satisfied with homage, and flattering appeals to her mere fancy and imagination. Woman was now claiming stronger and more profitable food.

Woman, urged the speaker, needed all the encouragement she could receive by the removal of obstacles from her path in order that she might become a "true woman." Let her not be satisfied with the narrow sphere assigned her by man, or fear to aspire to a higher level lest she should transcend the bounds of female delicacy. Let woman cultivate all the graces and proper accomplishments of her sex, but let these not degenerate into the kind of "feminacy in which she is satisfied to be the mere toy of society," content with outward adornments and the flattery and fulsome adulation with which she is often addressed.

Nature had made a difference in woman's configuration, her physical strength, her voice—and Lucretia asked no change—she was satisfied with nature. But artificial practices had increased this difference. It was woman's duty to develop her natural powers by suitable exercise so that they might be strengthened by reason of use.

The founder of the woman's movement attacked the old belief of the desirability of opposites in marriage. Dana had held out the idea that the sexes were opposite, if not somewhat antagonistic, and required a union as in chemistry, to form a perfect whole. He thought of men as being bold in the demonstration of the pure affection of love, in accordance with the idea that women should be somewhat ashamed of love.

Dana's simile appeared to Lucretia "far from a correct illustration of the true union. Minds that can assimilate, spirits that are congenial, attract one another. It is the union of similar, not of opposite affections, which are necessary for the perfection of the marriage bond." The contrast drawn of man and woman seemed to her a fallacy, as "has much, very much, that has been presented in the sickly sentimental strains of the poet, from age to age."

The question was often asked, she said: "What does woman want more than she enjoyed? What was she seeking to obtain? Of what rights was she deprived? What privileges were withheld from her?" Lucretia answered: woman wanted nothing as favor but of *right,* she wanted to be acknowledged as a moral, responsible being. She was seeking not to be governed by laws in the making of which she had no voice. She was deprived of almost every right in civil society, and was a political cipher in the Nation except in the right of presenting a petition. In religious societies her disabilities greatly retarded her progress. She was excluded from the ministry, her duties were marked out for her by man, and she was subjected to creeds, rules, and disciplines made for her by him—this was unworthy her true dignity. In marriage there was assumed superiority on the part of the husband with a promise of obedience on the part of the wife.

She quoted Professor Walker in his "Introduction to American Law," wherein he said if the law in regard to woman's political rights was applied to males, it would be an exact definition of political slavery. Yet applied to females, custom did not teach people to so regard it.

In the intelligent ranks of society the wife might not, in point of fact, be so degraded as the law provided, because public sentiment was above the law. Still, while the law stood, she was liable to the disabilities it provided. Among the ignorant classes of society woman was made to bear heavy burdens and was degraded almost to the level of the slave. In Lucretia's intercourse with the poorer classes she had known cases of extreme cruelty resulting from the taking of the wife's earnings by the husband, with no redress at law.

When the husband died, property accumulated by the joint efforts of husband and wife was distributed in such manner that the widow was dispossessed of her rightful share. The husband either "gave" his wife a share of her earnings, or the law apportioned her a share, while her son, who inherited the bulk of the estate, would speak of "having to *keep* his mother."

Said Lucretia: "Reform is loudly called for. There is no foundation in reason or expediency for the absolute and slavish subjection of the wife to the husband, which forms the foundation of the present legal relations. Were women, in point of fact, the abject thing which the law, in theory, considers her to be when married, she would not be worthy the companionship of man."

The cause of woman's rights made gradual headway in Philadelphia after Lucretia's speech. Public interest in the movement was accelerated by the social unrest of the decade between 1850 and the Civil War.

Gold was discovered in California, 80,000 men departed for the western empire. Famine in Ireland and political conditions in Continental Europe increased immigration to America. The industrial revolution drove women workers into factories where they labored at tasks previously performed in the home at looms and spinning wheels. The world was in turmoil, made no less hazardous, in the opinion of the timid, by a rapid succession of "Hen Conventions."

"Hen Convention" is not an elegant phrase, but this was the designation whereby the press identified meetings attended by mothers, wives, and sisters, otherwise known as "Madonnas" when they stayed at home. The press gathered inspiration from the Universalist preacher who announced a woman's meeting from his pulpit with the statement that "tonight, at the Town Hall, a hen will attempt to crow."

Nowhere was discrimination against women more unjust than in the payment of wages. Conventionalities permitted women three primary sources of income: school teaching, which paid her one-fourth to one-half the salary paid men for similar labor; menial housework, and sewing, the latter so illy paid as to constitute a form of white slavery.

There was, of course, prostitution, but this was *ex cathedra*. When one considers the mental sterility and moral repressions of the Victorian wife, her training, attitude, and environment, one is not surprised at the lusty spread of prostitution, which in every great city in England and America was open, rampant, and notorious; a colorful and luscious weed concealing well its germs of disease in a garden of wilted hothouse plants.

Prostitution was not talked of. Its existence was not recognized. A woman's degree of refinement was gauged by the number and quality of things she did not talk about. Small attempt was made to reform or alleviate the sorrow of the prostitute. It was feared that a helping hand to the wicked would encourage other women to enter the profession. This was an argument which smacked of a famous woman's opinion that the generous sympathies of the philanthropist (by urging one system of reform) often introduced another and greater evil. For example, philanthropy had established Foundling Hospitals in Stockholm to save illegitimate infants from exposure, and what had been the pernicious result? One out of every three children thereafter born in the city had been illegitimate: couples did not have to worry about supporting the offspring of illicit intercourse.

Ernestine Rose criticised women for not daring to take their fallen sisters to heart. "I will not mention names," commented she on one occasion, "I must, however, mention our sister, Lucretia Mott, who has stood up and taken her fallen sister by the hand, and warmed her at her own heart. But we cannot expect every woman to possess that degree of courage."

Lucretia was not able, because of the exactions of a multiple life, to attend all sectional gatherings of the woman's movement, but she was a prominent figure, and often presiding officer, at anniversary meetings. She traveled widely. On one occasion newspapers would report her near at home at West Chester, Pennsylvania, and a few months later in the chair at Syracuse, New York. In 1855 she was as far away from Philadelphia as Cincinnati and Indianapolis.

A woman's convention presided over by the Philadelphia Quakeress presented an interesting picture. In the audience one might see members of both sexes, and a variety of colors and costumes. Here an occasional woman in bloomers sat, walked, or conversed with timid-looking Quaker dames in quiet-colored gowns and shawls, and there was always a goodly sprinkling of ladies genteelly dressed in the latest Paris fashions. In one crowded hall, on the steps leading to the platform, sat William Lloyd Garrison and James Mott side by side with men of the darkest hue. This was a reason why woman's rights, non-resistance, and liberal religion made slow headway in the South, where the reforms of the century scarcely penetrated.

Wendell Phillips reported to Elizabeth Pease in far off England:

You would have enjoyed the Woman's Convention. I think I never saw a more intelligent and highly cultivated audience, more ability guided by the best taste on a platform, more deep, practical interest, on any occasion. It took me completely by surprise; and the women were the ablest speakers, too. You would have laughed as we used to do in 1840, to hear dear Lucretia Mott answer me. I had presumed to differ from her, and assert that the cause would meet more immediate and palpable and insulting opposition from *women* than *men*—and scolded them for it. She put, as she so well knows how, the silken snapper on her whiplash, and proceeded to give me the gentlest and yet most cutting rebuke. 'Twas like her old fire when the London Quakers angered her gentleness—and beautifully done, so that the victim himself could enjoy the artistic perfection of his punishment.

Unfortunately Wendell Phillips was right, and Lucretia wrong. From the days of Mary Wollstonecraft to Margaret Sanger, women have been the most vicious opponents to every move to better the conditions of their own sex.

Lucretia found the majority of women of her day seemingly satisfied with their lot, and from their conduct it was natural for male adversaries to assume that the discontent of the minority was the consequence of individual idiosyncrasies. In vain Lucretia explained how the majority of the people of each generation have passively accepted the conditions into which they have been born, while those who demand larger liberties are ever a small dissatisfied minority whose claims are ridiculed and ignored. The Chinese woman bound her feet, the Hindu woman mounted the funeral pyre, and the Turkish woman veiled her face, in seeming contentment.

Lucretia defended this type: "I blame her not so much as I pity her. So circumscribed have been her limits that she does not realize the misery of her condition. Such dupes are men to custom that even servitude, the worse of ills, comes to be thought a good, till down from sire to son it is kept and guarded as a sacred thing."

She presided over a remarkable series of meetings at Syracuse, New York. "Some of the most able women of the country" were in attendance, reported a not unfriendly paper, though a pro-slavery sheet sounded the alarm, thus: "The women are coming! They flock in upon us from every quarter, all to hear and talk about Woman's Rights. The blue stockings are as thick as grasshoppers in hay-time, and mighty will be the force of 'jaw-logic' and 'broom-stick ethics' preached by the females of both sexes."

Present at a woman's meeting for the first time was Susan B. Anthony. Already established locally as a temperance worker, she was welcomed into the greater cause and made a secretary.

She helped to enliven proceedings with what has become an anecdote. Paulina Wright Davis, of Rhode Island, had come to Syracuse with the determination to put in office as president her dear friend Elizabeth Oakes Smith, a fashionable "literary lady" of Boston. Both women went about the convention hall dressed in ultra-fashion, wearing gowns that left neck and arms exposed in a manner not calculated to stimulate deep reformatory thought—among males, at least.

At the meeting of the nominating committee, James Mott put Mrs. Smith's name in motion. Perhaps he experienced a qualm at the sight of pink and white embroiderings, but he was too liberal to let fashionable apparel prejudice his vote. However, blunt, earnest Susan took occasion to express herself boldly that in her opinion no woman, dressed as Mrs. Smith, could represent the earnest, hard-working women of the country. Quaker James Mott mildly expostulated that the committee could not expect all women to dress as plainly as Friends, but Quaker Susan held her ground, and Lucretia was nominated as a compromise candidate.

"It was a singular spectacle," informs the Syracuse "Standard," "to see this gray-haired matron presiding over a Convention with an ease, dignity, and grace that might be envied by the most experienced legislator in the country." The fifty-nine-year-old matron had gone far since the day she had declared her inability to put a "vote" at the first meeting of the Female Anti-Slavery Society, or even in the four years since Seneca Falls when it had been necessary to call James Mott to the chair.

The impression of her "sweet face and placid manners" at Syracuse was strengthened by her opening remarks. The press declared them to have been "better expressed and far more appropriate than those heard on similar occasions in political and legislative assemblies." Reporters accustomed to the blatant cheapness of political conventions were impressed by the woman who devoted her talents to something more elevating than the spread-eagle oratory of the day, and speeches calculated to arouse the prejudices of an ignorant citizenry.

One paper informed its readers that a greater amount of talent was present in the woman's convention than had characterized any public gathering in the State during ten years back, and probably a longer period, if ever. The appearance of the speakers before the audience was modest and unassuming, though prompt, energetic, and confident. For compact logic, eloquence, and correct expression, and the making of plain and frequent points, the editor had never met the equal of two or three. "The officers, and most especially the distinguished woman who occupied the president's chair, evinced a thorough acquaintance with the duties of their station, and performed them in an admirable manner."

Said a co-worker of many years' standing, of Lucretia:

As presiding officer in a woman's convention nothing escaped her notice. She felt responsible that everything should be done in good taste and order. Her opinions on woman's nature, sphere, destiny, were thoroughly digested, and any speaker who did not come up to her exact ideal, was taken delicately to task when her turn came to speak.

When she arose she touched them all round with her gentle raillery, offending no one, just pronounced enough in her speech to be effective, and in no way compromising herself.

Her influence was always for harmony, good will, and the broadest charity. She endured too much persecution herself to join in persecuting others. Asked once to study-up the precepts of the free-lovers in order to publicly refute them, she replied, even of a cause she disapproved, it was a task not to her liking. In every reform the Hicksite preacher stood in the foreground of battle. She never dodged responsibilities, or disagreeable duties, and could be relied on to share in every trying emergency. An observer once said that it was easy enough to antagonize the brilliant *esprit* of Elizabeth Cady Stanton, the aggressiveness of Susan B. Anthony, or the free thought of Ernestine L. Rose, but that even a Morgan Dix of the Episcopal Church or St. Paul would have been mollified (if not persuaded) by Lucretia Mott—"that winning womanly figure, so essentially feminine in its aspect, with the Quaker garb and meekly-folded kerchief" and "dark, appealing eyes and gentle mouth. . . . ."

After her death a gentleman opposed to woman suffrage uttered a singular tribute when he said: "I never felt the slightest antagonism to anything she said, no matter how much I differed from her."

A stranger remarked that she was "apparently a good-natured woman," one whose face did not indicate her character as a "fiery and enthusiastic advocate of reform."

This was the woman who, in the almost unanimous opinion of the American public, should not be allowed to lift her voice in public gatherings for the discussion of social and moral problems, but should grow like the modest violet until plucked by a masculine hand for the fragrance of one man's home.

LUCRETIA MOTT, SOCIAL PIONEER

The movement which had raised a gust of laughter all over the country, in five years made such progress that one hundred per cent. Americans became alarmed. Neither Washington, nor Franklin, nor Jefferson had advocated sex equality, hence any move to give woman her rightful place in society was a menace to American traditions. Old Glory conceived by radicals and colored by the blood of traitors, must be uplifted in the name of conservatism.

Persons who perceive patriotism in symbols of war can not long endure oral argument. Comes the time when they must demonstrate their opinions by the use of force. The year 1853 witnessed the first definite efforts to crush woman's rights by physical violence. Ideal for anything of this sort is a great city with its teeming tenements. Ignorant New York was agog when in the September of that year representatives of all the unpopular reforms convened in the city to hold a series of celebrations. The combination of anti-slavery meetings, a sermon by a woman preacher, and a woman's rights convention, all within a few hours of each other, was too much for the taut nerves of the Bowery, the press, and the patriots.

Just as New York brags it is able to do anything bigger and better than it can be done elsewhere, so its mobs of 1853 held the same exalted position. Abetting the unlawful element stood three great metropolitan newspapers. Backed by this potent influence the mob element of the city held carnival. The slum excreted its foul matter. Boweryites attended the temperance conclaves, the anti-slavery meetings, and without fail every session of the woman's rights convention, interrupting alike gentlemen and ladies who attempted to speak. Ignorant peasants indulged in rude shouts, hisses, and stampings of feet, ironic cheers, and all manner of noisy demonstrations.

The leading patriot of the week was a citizen of mixed German and Irish lineage, a plug-ugly by the name of Isaiah Rynders. This notorious character had passed easily from a life as a boatman on the Hudson into the sporting ranks of the great city. Later he had sought his fortune as a professional gambler in the paradise of the Southwest. In this region he had become refined in whatever forms of violence he hithertofore had failed to master, and after a career more dangerous than polished had returned to New York to embark in the practice of the mysteries of his various crafts and trades.

His wide experience and acquired education qualified him for political leadership in Tammany Hall. A sporting house which he opened became a Democratic rendezvous and the headquarters of the Empire Club, an organization of roughs and desperadoes who acknowledged his captaincy and helped elect a President of the United States.

It was the prophet Isaiah, posing as a savior of society against blasphemers and infidels and persons traitorous to the Union, who took upon himself the burden of engineering the riots that made the meetings at the Tabernacle, presided over by the cultured Lucretia, a bedlam of insanity. The rowdies were citizens and voters. Many of them a few years before had been uncouth peasants roaming the countryside of Ireland, or disfranchised tillers of soil in some continental country, but in America all were the political superiors of Lucretia Mott, who had been raised and educated in circles of gentility, and whose traditions embraced the finest in American life. The audience jeered and hooted when she reminded them that few reforms were ever begun or carried on with any reputation in the day of inception. The learned men of Fulton Street knew the time would never come when women would be allowed to vote. It was preposterous!

The height of excitement came when one of the great intellects of the Nation—William Henry Channing—managed to incite the audience into an uproar, merely by reciting the inconsistencies of society in regard to woman's sphere. Said he: The largest assemblies greeted Jenny Lind when she enchanted the ear with the strains "I Know that my Redeemer Liveth," but let Mrs. Mott attempt in simple voice to preach the word of God, and respectable Christians veiled their faces! Fanny Ellsler danced to raise money for Bunker Hill Monument, but let Mrs. Rose stand up to lecture on woman's rights and she was out of her sphere, and men left her to be the victim of disorder. It was not out of character for Fanny Kemble to read Shakespeare on the stage, but if a living female Shakespeare should appear on the platform, delicacy would be shocked, decency would be outraged, and society would turn away in disgust.

This was too much for Bowery nerves. There were loud bellowings, screams, laughter, stampings of feet, and cries of "Burleigh," "Truth," "Shut up," "Take a drink," and "Greeley!" The latter especially was a synonym for all that was freakish. The tumult assumed such proportions that police assistance was sought by the managers of the convention. Lucretia vacated the chair. It was contrary to her principles to preside over a meeting sustained by force. Considering the feeble efforts made by the authorities to maintain order, Lucretia might conscientiously have retained the chair.

The right of free speech in the Nation had become a Fourth of July boast, but then, as now, most persons thought a radical, by thinking differently than his contemporaries, thereby forfeited the protection of the law. The police have always been loath to defend radicals against even the unlawful anger of "respectable" taxpayers. The editor of the "State Register" expressed public opinion when he wrote:

People are beginning to inquire how far public sentiment should sanction or tolerate these unsexed women, who make a scoff at religion, who repudiate the Bible, and blaspheme God; who would step out from the true sphere of the mother, the wife, and the daughter, and take upon themselves the duties and the business of men; stalk into the public gaze, and by engaging in the politics, the rough controversies, and trafficking of the world, upheave existing institutions, and overturn all the social relations of life.

The woman's movement stirred not only a lavender odor among lovers of ancient customs, but also a Rabelaisian humor that was peculiarly annoying to a woman of Lucretia's dignity. Unfortunately the woman's movement pollenized its own pistil of ridicule. It had a visible peculiarity that even the most slothful dullard could perceive. That was the bloomer costume. Loud and many were the jests showered upon the handful of women who wore it, and their martyred husbands. The latter were identified as hen-pecked males and attenuated vegetarians who were afraid to say "no" to a strong-minded woman for fear of infringing her rights. The wearers were "unsexed women" who met in broad daylight to propound the doctrine "that they should be allowed to step out of their appropriate sphere, to the neglect of those duties which we and our fathers before us have imagined belonged solely to women."

There was talk that the world might become depopulated because of masculine women, while in another quarter of the same camp it was feared the population would be illegitimately increased by "free love." Criticism of the bloomer costume became so offensive that Lucy Stone, visiting the Motts, was labored with by the daughters of the house to abandon the costume. They, in fact, said they would not go upon the street with her, and when the popular writer, Grace Greenwood, called, Lucy was convinced it would have been a real relief to them if she had not been present in her baggy bloomers and long coat. Of course, James and Lucretia defended her bravely. But Lucy concluded that no worth while cause (like woman's rights) could be impeded by long dresses, so she went back to the fashions of the 'fifties. Shortly after, the bloomer became an object of archæological curiosity.[1]

Lucy's retention of her maiden name after marriage was likewise the scandal of good people who saw in it the beginning of the long prophesied reign of sex immorality. It was still a matter of public controversy three years later when in a letter Lucretia commented on Antoinette Brown's marriage, writing she was agreed to Lucy's right to her own name, while glad also that Antoinette was independent enough not to be governed by Lucy's example, if she did not choose to follow it. And, continued Lucretia, "it has amused me to see the wrath of some, because of Lucy's retaining her name, and how it is made an excuse for having no more to do with the cause."

---

1. Lucy Stone: Alice Stone Blackwell.

CHAPTER XX

THE BLACK MAN'S HUNTING GROUNDS

It is doubtful if Lucretia's interest in the woman's cause ever supplanted, if in fact it equaled, her interest in anti-slavery.

A great movement had quickened at Seneca Falls, but the Nation's attention, even more than her own, was focused on capitol hill, where Congress was in daily turbulence. On one point only were its members agreed—and that was that something had to be done. The scratch of pens on the document signed at Guadalupe Hidalgo had been the signal for a fresh outburst of strife. The controversy was whether the millions of acres of fertile land acquired by "fair purchase" of Mexico should be free, or half free and half slave.

Under a democratic form of government, where a wide divergence of opinion exists on any given question, a legislative body can deal only in palliatives without prescribing a course of conduct calculated to cure the disease itself. By 1850 Congress was ready for another political compromise. Tottering John C. Calhoun—champion of the freedom of states and the enslavement of men—was led into the capitol to have his last speech read to the Senate. The gaunt old leader from South Carolina did not sense that the day of agrarian rule by a planter aristocracy was tottering on legs as weak as his own. He was firm in the conviction that the prosperity of the free North was due to a protective tariff and the refused expansion of slavery into the new states.

And so, adding fuel to the fire with the thought that it was dashing water on the blaze, Congress passed the Fugitive Slave Act, and President Fillmore blotted his signature on the warrant of misery of thousands of unfortunate negroes—freed, escaped, and enslaved. The Fugitive Slave Law was written into the compromise of 1850, says a prominent historian, by "cool-headed men, business interests, and conservatives generally," who recognized the necessity of compromise, and party managers alarmed by the way negro slavery had come to interfere with old political alignments.

Lucretia was not concerned with political alignments. The country got along equally well under Whigs or Democrats, and doubtless the rule of party was of small moment to the millions of negroes in slavery. Lucretia read the Fugitive Slave Act. Her indignation boiled. She saw that the new law made the free soil of the North a reservation for the rich and the powerful to run down the poor and the weak.

Into the North from all quarters rushed the minions of slaveholders to seize their prey. With the leash of the bloodhound in one hand and a volume of Federal statutes in the other, these men tracked and hunted the negro like harried rabbits, not infrequently seizing free negroes and making life intolerable for those who had escaped from slavery and long thought themselves free. The happy hunting grounds of the red man had become the unhappy hunting grounds of the black man.

Among "pros" and "antis" the "Bill of Abominations," as the act was stigmatized by opponents, was upheld or denied with equal vehemence. It was a scandal to the patriots of the South (who later seceded) when at Faneuil Hall Wendell Phillips thundered: "We presume to believe the Bible outweighs the statute book. When I look upon these crowded thousands, I see them trample on their conscience and the rights of their fellowmen, at the bidding of a piece of parchment, I say, my CURSE be on the Constitution of these United States!"

A patriot from Andover Seminary stated that all the talk about conscience setting aside the Constitution was an imputation against the men who had formed the government; it held them up to the world as having had neither justice nor humanity. It did not occur to the speaker that, by his own reasoning, every amendment to the Constitution had been an insult to the Fathers, including the Bill of Rights—the very soul of the Constitution—which had been added at the demand of a few of America's earliest radical agitators.

The dogma of the plenary inspiration of the Bible was brought over into the Constitution. Theological training made it easy for churchmen to make saints out of politicians, and Bibles out of statute books. The Fugitive Slave Law brought sharply to the focus of moderate citizens of the free states the realization that slavery was a problem they could no longer ignore. They were confronted with the miserable alternative of either obeying the law and thereby perpetuating slavery, of which they were not fond, or of doing the bidding of the heart to the disobedience of law.

LUCRETIA MOTT, SOCIAL PIONEER

Dr. Sharp, a Baptist minister, well expressed the view of the conservative, yet not pro-slavery, church when he said that it was the "duty" of such persons to submit to the government extending over the region wherein they dwelt, and to obey their magistrates. This was cool reasoning calculated to prevent anarchy, but it never has been the reasoning of the American people who from earliest colonial days to prohibition have nullified acts of Parliament or the Constitution and talked secession whenever the pocketbook or the national conscience has been pricked. The era of the Fugitive Slave Law was a high watermark of this history.

A brother of the cloth less calculating than Dr. Sharp spoke in defense of the law, warning his congregation that to assist a fugitive slave in the face of governmental authority was not merely aiding a negro to freedom but was substituting force for law, a terrible thing, said the orator, who then went on to say if Abolitionists insisted in the spirit of sedition and rebellion (*i. e.,* substituting force for law) the magistracy would eventually be obliged to muster the citizenry to defend the Constitution. "Arm! Arm!" shouted the preacher who detested force in freeing a slave. "If they call you to the field of battle, stand in your ranks as your fathers stood, shoulder to shoulder; if to take human life, take it; and if you fall, your memory shall be hallowed with those whose bones moulder on the slopes of Bunker Hill."

Fighting to defend a flag, a constitution, an established government, is so fortified by precedent that it is considered an ideal thing. To defend human liberty, to free a slave, to think more of mankind than of a piece of bunting, is a ridiculous thing meriting public contempt. Lucretia never gave more than passing disrespect to any argument that made it proper to kill one's fellow-man on the battlefield in the name of the law, but a sin to help a slave escape from servitude without bloodshed. No compact by the Fathers could annul Lucretia's obligations to mankind.

Congress rocked with debate, knives and pistols gleamed in council chambers, synods were torn with dissensions, the air was filled with questions how the Fugitive Slave Law should be accepted by persons who loved the Union, and by persons who respected Southern rights and yet disliked slavery.

Through all the discord Lucretia continued her way quietly, but none the less actively, to advance the morn of the day of universal

225

freedom and the culmination of the spirit of the Constitution, the Bill of Rights, and the Declaration of Independence in their broadest and better senses. She bore no arms, she respected virtue, but she defied law which was passed by man in the spirit of expediency. Like Thoreau she refused to resign her conscience to legislators. The spirit of bloodless rebellion prevailed North and West. The Fugitive Slave Bill was law, but Abolitionists did not trouble themselves about its legality. Abolitionists saw precedent in the fact that so many progressive steps have been taken in violation of authority. Some of the best known citizens of Syracuse, New York, openly declared the Act should not be enforced in that city, and a large number of them made an arrangement to stand by each other in resisting the law.

In the South there were rumors of a strange and mysterious institution known as the Underground Railway, over whose roads escaped slaves were assisted in their flight to the Canadian border. The Underground Railway had no physical properties. Its inventories showed no steel rails, no coaches, no engines. Its conductors collected no fares. Its trains did not even pretend to run on schedule. The railway merely was a network of routes of travel through the free states to Canada over which slaves were hurried from one town or farmhouse to another, by wagon, horse, or afoot, on their way to freedom. Over all the North and West, express trains rumbled over "that memorable but dark and dangerous highway out of democratic despotism to freedom in a land of kings and queens."

The Motts' roomy house at Philadelphia was a "station," and the Motts were "conductors" of the U. G. R. R. Through their station house were billed ladings of human merchandise which did not attain the dignity of humanhood until they had passed the Great Lakes. In some of the free-soil states association with the railway was not a necessarily dangerous avocation; in the border State of Pennsylvania and especially the city of Philadelphia, there were times when it was hazardous and unpopular.

Closely associated with Lucretia and James in the work of evading the Fugitive Slave Act were John and Hannah Cox, of Longwood, Pennsylvania, and large, stout, benevolent, and good humored Thomas Garrett, of Wilmington, Delaware. John and Hannah Cox were members of a little band of liberal Quakers in which Lucretia was much interested, well known for their staunch support of modern reforms. Their house was the first station on the railway across the Maryland border on the Pennsylvania side. It was linked with Garrett's station in Delaware and northward with the Motts'.

At the time of the abolition of slavery Garrett had preserved a record of 2,545 fugitives he had helped to escape from slavery, and had assisted something over two hundred others before he commenced the compilation of his remarkable record. While all the fugitives freighted through the Cox and Garrett homes were not "billed" to the Mott station in Philadelphia, it may be assumed that a large percentage found their way there, as we are told by a contemporary that the Motts' house was the principal station between the Coxes and the home of Isaac T. Hopper in New York.

Whole families of negroes were at times secreted, fed, and clothed in these staunch Quaker homes. Occasionally a zealous officer of the law would swoop down and capture a railway operative "black-handed" with his human cargo. Garrett was several times threatened with bowie knives, and heavily fined in the courts. Once James was the target of a heavy stone thrown by a member of an angry mob while he stood at the doorway of his home, lighted lamp in hand, protecting a frightened negro who had pushed past him, and run through the house and out the back door. The indentation caused by the missile remained many a day in the casing, close where the master's head had been.

Arrests of negroes took place more frequently in Philadelphia than in any northern city. Many fugitives were caught and hurried back without the formality of legal proceedings. Neither side was very scrupulous in observing the letter of the law, except as against the opposing party.

Six years before the opening of the Civil War, Lucretia wrote a friend: "We have had some interesting fugitives here lately. How I wish thousands more would escape, and the remainder resolve that they would no longer work unpaid!" The most remarkable escape recorded was one which, prophesied Lucretia, would "tell well in history some time hence." A citizen of Richmond, Virginia, had called at the office of the Abolition Society in Philadelphia and there unfolded a preposterous tale about a Richmond slave who was meditating escape from bondage by placing himself in a box to be conveyed to Philadelphia as merchandise by Adams' Express.

The visitor was warned of the great danger of suffocation as well as risk of detection. But the slave was obdurate, and after some delays a telegram was received by the Abolitionists that the strange lading of freight was on its way. Fear of detection being great, it was arranged that Edward M. Davis, who had frequent contacts with the local express office, should have a trusted man call for the box. The box was duly claimed at the depot, and being handled carefully as never before, was safely deposited at the anti-slavery office, where four anxious men awaited the resurrection. A trembling query, "All right?" by J. Miller McKim was responded to by a muffled voice within, "All right, sir!" Hasty hands removed the lid as quickly as hoops could be loosened, and a two hundred pound negro greeted his benefactors with a rising welcome, "Good morning, gentlemen!"

McKim's excitement at finding the man alive was so overwhelming that he joined in singing the freedman's hymn of exaltation: "I waited patiently for the Lord, and he heard my prayer." The scene would have astonished the chance intruder; the opened box with scattered fragments on the floor, and the negro crawling out like a chick that had burst its shell, and the participants singing as though their throats would break.

No home in Philadelphia being more discreet than the Motts', the newborn man was sent to the residence of this daring couple. So long had he been doubled up in the box that he felt the need of exercise in the open air. In order to prevent detection he was supplied with one of James Mott's broad-brimmed Quaker hats. Under this capacious refuge the escaped slave promenaded the yard, perhaps the darkest-skinned looking Quaker that ever failed to say "thee" and "thou." Lucretia wrote of the escape:

He [Brown] is a large man . . . . and was incased in a box two feet long, twenty-three inches wide, and three feet high, in a sitting posture! He was provided with a few crackers, and a bladder filled with water, which would make no noise in being turned over, nor yet liable to be broken; he however ate *none*, as it would have made him thirsty, and he needed all the water to bathe his head, after the rough turns over, in which he sometimes rested for miles on his head and shoulders, when it would seem as if the veins would burst. He fanned himself almost constantly with his hat, and bored holes for fresh breathing air, with a gimlet or small auger furnished him. The cracks of the box had canvas over, to prevent any inspection, and to appear like goods. Dr. Noble says, if he had been consulted, he should have said it would be impossible for the man to be shut up and live twenty-four hours, the time it took to reach here; it was fanning so much, which kept the exhausted air in motion and gave place to fresh. . . . .

Because of the mode of his escape, the fugitive was renamed Henry *Box* Brown. He was exhibited shortly after at Faneuil Hall, where Wendell Phillips took occasion to point him out on a platform crowded with fugitives from "church and State of America," exclaiming amidst applause: "We say in behalf of this man, whom God created, and whom law-abiding Webster and Winthrop swore would find no shelter on the soil of Massachusetts—we say that they may make their little motions, and pass their little laws, in Washington, but that FANEUIL HALL REPEALS THEM, in the name of the humanity of Massachusetts."

Not infrequently negroes were arrested in Pennsylvania on false charges of robbery by marshals holding warrants against them as slaves in order to avoid the danger of a desperate self-defense on the part of the prey. At the courthouse the negro would be suddenly introduced into the presence of the man who claimed him as his property. Ignorant of his rights, cowed by the presence of a slaveholder, surrounded by the tools of his natural enemy, with no friend to counsel him, he would be betrayed into admissions which could be used as evidence to consign him into slavery. Zealous for fees, the magistrates of the Federal courts, many of them appointed by the slave power in control of the Senate, construed a dark skin to be *prima facie* evidence of slavehood.

The Abolitionists of Philadelphia did the best they could to prevent the illegal return of negroes, and some member of their several societies was present at any court hearing of which they had notice, to assist in giving the prisoner legal advice and moral support. Reputable attorneys freely gave their services. When all else pointed to failure, effort would be made to buy the captive free of his master.

Lucretia was often in attendance at these trials. One day the information was brought to her that a negro named Daniel Dangerfield, *alias* Webster (by fate of irony), had been seized on a farm near Harrisburg and was being arraigned before the United States Commissioner in Philadelphia on the charge of being a fugitive slave.

The word spread rapidly through the city and it was not long before Lucretia and other members of local anti-slavery societies were in conference. The case had more than usual interest because of the presence on the bench of a new commissioner. Heretofore the Federal judge for the district had been the Honorable John K. Kane, a member of the socially select "Wistaria" group of Philadelphia intellectuals. Under him had served a commissioner friendly to the pro-slavery element. The customary outcome of all fugitive slave cases had been hopeless to the Abolitionists.

Death had removed the old judge, and politics had brought in a new commissioner, a man of Quaker antecedents. Abolitionists regained heart. Leaders who had sat through many discouraging sessions of court under the old régime flocked to court with the hope that the son of a Quaker might better reflect the humanities.

Eminent counsel was hired to defend Dangerfield; Edward Hopper being one. A great crowd collected in the building that lodged the court room. In a small basement, Commissioner J. Cooke Longstreth sat at a table writing, surrounded by a group of officials, anti-slavery men and women, and others interested in the trial of Dangerfield. Knowing the commissioner to be a birthright member of the Society of Friends, Lucretia naïvely approached him, expressing in an undertone her earnest hope that his conscience would not allow him to send the poor man into slavery. The young commissioner listened civilly to the pleader, but replied that he must be bound by his oath of office. The line of the poet sprang into the woman's mind, and she concluded simply:

But remember
The traitor to humanity, is the traitor most accursed.

When Dangerfield was brought out of jail, a rush was made for the courtroom by spectators. A son of the late Judge Kane conducted Lucretia to a seat. The trial lasted all of one day and through the night and into the next day. Ladies of the female society sat through the night. As a number of them walked home in the dawn, they were sad and hopeless.

Through the day the trial continued, Dangerfield sitting by his counsel, clothed as when seized by the authorities, in an old hat and red flannel shirt, a ragged coat and similar apparel.

The question was whether, for no crime but the color of his skin, he should be deprived of his liberty and degraded to the status of a chattel. It was a question dearer to Dangerfield than life, yet it was discussed in the cold logic of law and evidence rather than morality and justice. The prisoner sat mute with terror, puzzled by it all. Close by him on one side stood the minister of the law ready to send him into slavery. On the other side, we are told by an eyewitness in the extravagant language of the day, sat a devoted woman "blind to all outward distinctions and defacements, deaf to the idle babble of the world's tongues, cheering her poor hunted brother with the sisterly sympathy of her silent presence."

Lucretia's presence near the prisoner impressed another person in the courtroom, the claimant's counsel, who was disturbed by the intensity of her unflinching gaze. Her heart seethed with hatred of oppression. Her ordinarily placid features were stern, and the mild expression of her face was transformed into something coldly hot. She was a revelation even to members of her family who knew the depth of her love of justice.

Though she sat quietly, claimant's attorney no longer could bear her presence and caused her chair to be moved. There was no cause for alarm. Lucretia was a known non-resistant. Police officers were in attendance on the prisoner. The claimant and his counsel were close at hand. Yet in the presence of the woman described as "that impersonation of righteousness and sympathy with the victims of wrong," the customarily impervious lawyer quailed. The incident was eagerly seized upon by one of the opposing lawyers who dramatized the situation for the benefit of his client, by returning the chair to its former place.

The evidence was in, and the arguments made. Inside the crowded, dingy courtroom with its low ceiling, sweating humanity ceased to whisper, almost to stop breathing the foul air of the room. The tenseness fell which always precedes a verdict. The throngs in the street, with strange mob perception, passed along the word that the supreme moment had come. The commissioner perceived the anxious crowd in the courtroom facing him. He heard the murmur of the outside mob. He knew the pro-slavery sympathies of Philadelphia. His face paled, but there was determination in the set of his mouth. Slowly he spoke the judgment of the court. The evidence of the escaped slave's height, he found, did not tally with that of the prisoner at bar; he ordered Dangerfield released.

An undulation of excitement rippled around the courtroom. Persons friendly to the prisoner pushed eagerly to his side. The claimant was astounded. The Federal Court had gone mad! The word spread outside; the crowd, surging up and down the street, broke into threats that it would deliver up Dangerfield to his alleged master.

If its members were resolved upon the one thing, an equally strong-willed group of young men were determined that Dangerfield should taste the freedom the law had given him. Ostentatiously they escorted another colored man to a carriage, and while the baffled crowd was trying to decide who was who, drove him off. The real Dangerfield quietly walked out of the building and away in the company of some friends to a retired place where a conveyance awaited him. Thence he was taken to an unsuspected station of the Underground Railway, the country seat of Morris L. Hallowell, eight miles distant from Philadelphia; and a few days later was safe in Canada.

When the claimant's attorney, later Attorney-General of the United States, met Lucretia's son-in-law outside of court, he gave utterance to a friendly sentiment as one lawyer to another: "I have heard a great deal of your mother-in-law, Hopper," said he, "but I never saw her before today. She is an angel."

The impression that the woman made upon him as she sat that day in court and listened to him make an able argument on what she deemed the wrong side, was so indelibly marked on his memory that years later on changing his political affiliations and being asked how he dared to make the switch, the eminent barrister retorted, "Do you think there is anything I dare not do, after facing Lucretia Mott in that courtroom, and knowing that she wished me in Hell!" Lucretia never wished anyone in hell, but perhaps she came nearer that day than ever before, or since.

Another case famous in Abolition annals, but one not directly involving a negro, was the Passmore Williamson case. Williamson was a respected citizen of Philadelphia and secretary of an Abolition society. In performance of his duties he informed a slave mother brought into Philadelphia by her master that she and her two children were free under the laws of the State. The mother, availing herself of this knowledge, took possession of herself and her children. The astonished master—the United States minister to Nicaragua—immediately endeavored to repossess his property. He found many officials in Philadelphia anxious to help him, but was unable to find a lawyer who felt that he could recover the negroes by process of law in the State courts, the master being at fault in bringing his property onto the free soil of Pennsylvania.

The master, finding that he could not recover his property, determined that punishment should be meted the man responsible for his predicament. Williamson was indicted and arrested for participation in freeing the slaves. The trial was necessarily held in the friendly State court, a fact which encouraged the Abolitionists to try a hazardous project. They confronted the prosecution with the sudden and unexpected presence in court of Jane Johnson, the negress mother, who testified that Williamson had not forcibly taken her from her master's custody, but that she had left the latter freely. The prosecution's case collapsed. It had been built on the supposition that the defense would not dare jeopardize the newly-won freedom of Jane Johnson by her production in court as a witness.

The scene was a trying one to the Abolitionists. Although the State of Pennsylvania was pledged to protect Jane Johnson, it was feared United States officers would overpower State officials and make away with the woman. But the energy and skill of the presiding judge and State officers accomplished her safe egress from the courtroom.

Jane Johnson was hastily escorted to a carriage and rapidly driven off under armed guard. The white woman who sat by her side was Lucretia Mott. They went to that sanctuary of refuge, the Mott home on Arch Street, entered the front door and, hastily passing through the house, emerged out the rear where another carriage awaited, and Jane Johnson was whisked away to a place of safety. In that moment of confused excitement in the house when everybody was wholly absorbed in the thought of escaping pursuit, Lucretia hastily seized apples and crackers from her storeroom and potatoes from the kitchen fire, and ran with them to the carriage.

Twenty years after the escape of Jane Johnson, one of Lucretia's grandsons, in the course of business at Washington, met a gentleman by the name of Wheeler who, after talking with him of the changes wrought by the Civil War, asked, "Do you happen to remember the case of Jane Johnson and her children, a fugitive slave case in Philadelphia?" The grandson replied that he did, whereupon Mr. Wheeler explained, "Well, those were my niggers!"

To which the grandson replied, in mutual laughter, "And I helped to run them off!"

CHAPTER XXI

THE FERMENTING 'FORTIES

The history of man indicates that it is not what one says, but that one says it too soon, that brings down upon the reformer's head the wrath of Tory brethren. Were a Christian clergyman to advocate, on Biblical grounds, the reintroduction of African slavery into twentieth century America he would be called insane, where once the charge had been the other way.

The acts on the stage in the great drama of Human Evolution in which Lucretia played an active rôle are largely done. The scenery has been shifted, but characters speak old lines in new situations. Fresh "isms" and phases of old "isms" are attacked in the twentieth century in the same language and with the same hysteria that antislavery, woman's rights, and similar reforms were abused in Lucretia's generation.

The 'forties of the last century was an era of new hopes and a marvelous multiplication of ideas to promote human happiness. A handful of intellectuals, called "infidels" and "traitors," made it their business to break the mental fast day of conservatism. They gave utterance to thoughts long pent up. They stirred the Nation with currents of inquiry and criticism—many reactionaries became seasick.

Their outbreak was against the hard shell of precedent in which Emerson saw the tendency of the priest to become a form, the attorney a statute book, and the mechanic a machine. They promoted the idea of the possibility of the evolution of man to a degree of perfection, contrary to the dogmas of moral depravity and human helplessness. The keynote of the message of the ripest minds of the day was liberty and freedom for all mankind, irrespective of race, color, or sex.

The Reformation had been a struggle to democratize religion, the American and French revolutions to democratize government; the movement to democratize industry was many years yet to come.

The ferment of the 'forties was a phase of the first two agitations. Out of the welter of nineteenth century discord in time came freedom for the negro slave, partially equal rights for women, the abolition of property and religious tests as prerequisites for the ballot, and the breakdown of harsh religion. Humanitarian movements for world peace, prison reform, the education of the deaf and the blind, and the intelligent and humane treatment of the insane and criminal, made enormous gains.

The advocate of one reform is nearly always the espouser of others, and Lucretia was no exception. While her enthusiasm went for a number of primary reforms she had minor interests in which she played no small part. The words of Whittier might have been written of her that the purpose of her life was "to render less the sum of human wretchedness." She followed none of the now considered follies of her generation excepting only an interest in phrenology, the nineteenth century equivalent of the twentieth century flurry for applied psychology.

Even as Americans once thought they could become healthy, wealthy, and wise by reciting, "Every day in every way I am growing better and better," in Lucretia's day professors of phrenology traipsed the Nation measuring cranial protuberances in order to determine predilections for banking, medicine, or matrimony. The science became so exact that it could be determined by measurements of the head whether a man or woman was fond of water for drinking purposes, or shrank from a sea voyage. Phrenology was eminently respectable, much more so than anti-slavery or woman's rights, yet it was the only reform in which Lucretia appears to have been wrong by the test of time.

Her interest in the pseudo-science, or fad, was stimulated by her admiration for the social teachings of George Combe, who was one of the foremost exponents of phrenology.

Of Lucretia's so-called minor interests, the temperance reform was probably the one most prominent before the public. Lucretia gave the cause, besides personal example of abstinence, some aid and encouragement, but she was not one of the outstanding temperance workers of the age nor was she extremely active in the movement. She left the field to earnest workers in order to devote herself to less popular reforms.

The temperance movement (more properly a total abstinence movement) had been one of the strange heresies carried to England by the American anti-slavery delegates in 1840. Lucretia's diary contains several references to the subject. At Samuel Gurney's party the host had genially invited the young people present to help themselves to the wine, and had been "gently reproved for it" by Lucretia. "He bore it well," commented the rebuker. This conduct of a guest shocks the modern sense of social propriety, but the incident loses importance when it is remembered that Quakers were plain people who spoke frankly to one another on matters of morality. Words were never minced and problems were openly discussed. This practice did not always promote harmony, but it did tend to good morals.

When sixty-seven years of age Lucretia reflected how the temperance reformation had accomplished "almost a revolution in our age," but expressed the opinion that the movement was being retarded by running "too much into political . . . . channels." She reposed faith in moral education, and not law.

Another evil which aroused the heed of the Philadelphia Quakeress was the deplorable condition of laborers. The oppression of the working classes by existing monopolies and meagre wages often engaged her attention. She held many meetings with manual toilers and heard their appeals with compassion and a great desire for a radical change in the prevailing system of exploitation.

In a sermon delivered at Yardleyville, Pennsylvania, she pleaded: "There is need of preachers against the existing monopolies and banking institutions, by which the rich are made richer, and the poor poorer. . . . . It is contrary to the spirit of this Republic that any should be so rich." This statement contradicted the principle enjoyed by many Christian persons that God thoughtfully had provided the rich with the raw materials of philanthropy (the poor) whereby the rich might save their souls in the performance of deeds of mercy.

"It is not enough," Lucretia continued in words which are still in the van of enlightened social thought, "to be generous, and give alms; the enlarged soul, the true philanthropist, is compelled by Christian principle to look beyond the bestowing the scanty pittance to the mere beggar of the day, to the duty of considering the causes and sources of poverty. We must consider how much we have done towards causing it."

She had some hope that coöperative trade unions would effect something toward a better state of society. At this time the labor movement, like every change in society's structure, was being met by the armed forces of the law and the enmity of the courts. In Scotland, Chartists had posted themselves outside the meeting of the Emancipation Society and distributed handbills that pleaded for something to be done at home to ameliorate the conditions of the poor "white slave" laborer as well as the American negro. The justness of the plea had impressed Lucretia and when a Socialist and a Chartist stole the floor "and made good speeches" she was "not sorry that they could be heard to plead the cause of their own poor."

Lucretia was distressed by bloody wars in India and penned Elizabeth Pease the only gloomy paragraph found in her correspondence: "A monstrous sacrifice of human life, by a professedly Christian nation! And your poor starved people at home too, overworked and underpaid until driven to desperation; what is to be done, in view of all these evils? The remedy looks at times so hopeless, that I am ready to choose death rather than life, if I must feel as I have done for these classes. There was an extensive strike of the hand-loom weavers in this city, last winter. They were reduced almost to starvation; but they did not gain the added wages claimed, for 'with the oppressor there is power.' I could but sympathize with them in their demand for a better recompense to their early and late toil. . . . . "

A prominent feature of the labor movement was an almost fanatical insistence by leaders upon the importance of an adequate system of universal education. An especial defect in education was its failure to afford equal advantages to the sexes, and on this point Lucretia centered her attention.

When in the 'forties women claimed intellectual capacity, it was commonly charged that they had stepped out of their sphere. A woman's quest for knowledge was believed to be a moral calamity. A mother required no knowledge of trigonometry to count twelve or fourteen children. Gentlemen respected the opinion of the writer in the time of Charles I who wrote that a woman who knew how to compound a pudding was more desirable than one who skilfully composed a poem. Lord Byron (an authority on women, though scarcely an idealist) had thought a woman's library should be limited to the Bible and a cookery book. It was commonly asserted that "chemistry enough to keep the pot boiling and geography enough to know the location of the the different rooms in her house, is learning sufficient for a woman."

What the nineteenth century woman thought of education was a matter of small importance, and most women gave the subject their attention not at all. In an age when the average run of lawyers and doctors and school teachers was homespun, it was ridiculous to talk of education for girls beyond reading and writing and sewing. Even so famed an authoress as the Danish Miss Bremer had thought mathematics and physics not proper subjects for a girl's investigation. She found that "the young girl in her zeal to prepare her lessons, snubs her mother and looks cross at her father, if either ventures to interrupt her. It arouses ambition at the expense of her heart. It lays too much stress upon school learning." This recapitulated the idea that womanly delicacy and morality were fattened on the food of ignorance.

Under the influence of this philosophy the sensitive were shocked, the indolent vexed, and the wildest apprehensions excited by the demand for intellectual equality. Lucretia was interested not only in education that enriched the mind, but that which would give women economic independence, if necessary. This was popularly disapproved because it was thought that women capable of earning a living would be prone to leave husbands freely, thus disrupting the charmed home of drunkenness and brutality.

Lucretia had taken opportunity when abroad to visit a number of schools in England, Ireland and Scotland, where various methods of education were in operation. Her criticism had been that boys were well instructed in mathematics and similar studies, but the girls too much confined to sewing. The lively Lucretia had great respect for the needle, but her sunny spirit rebelled at a superabundance of confining work while all outdoors was filled with joy.

Much of her attention in her famous "Discourse on Woman," delivered in 1849, had been devoted to the problem of education which she thought would not cease until girls and boys had equal instruction in all elements of useful knowledge. She had complained that none of the great colleges of the country admitted women, while women's property was taxed to sustain State endowed universities.

Because of the prominence of her name, Lucretia was appealed to by Dr. Marie Zakrzewska to assist in the latter's campaign to establish female medical colleges and training hospitals for women physicians. Though the discussion of woman's rights had at first shocked the Polish physician, she was glad to have the asset of the name of America's most liberal woman to promulgate her theories in Philadelphia.

Graciously Lucretia gathered another group of friends in her parlors, this time to be addressed on the subject of medical schools. Good people were appalled at Dr. Zakrzewska's grotesque proposition, for in popular imagination women physicians were abortionists in thin disguise, and any plan to disseminate knowledge among laywomen of anatomy and physiology was highly discountenanced.

Like a sawdust doll, woman had no anatomy. She was stuffed with delicacy and virtue. Although the chrysalis of posterity, she was refused enlightenment on the subject that was to her of the utmost importance. It was woman's business to bring children into the world, not to know the mechanics of her trade.

A charming state of ignorance on all vital matters of a female significance existed among married women, and few had progressed beyond the classic myth of the stork which winged its arduous journey of nine months out of Heaven to the doctor's office where, after reporting for duty, it was escorted to its destination by a physician duly qualified and licensed for the practice of obstetrics. From time immemorial females had been herbalists, witch doctors, and midwives. But their knowledge on these subjects had been so empirical that the delicate bloom of innocence, which was woman's prerogative, had been little tarnished by any accurate knowledge of gynecology.

Among women of the upper classes it was a day of enforced idleness and white skins and the pallid look which was thought highly attractive. No well-bred lady who could afford to be ill was willing to admit that she possessed a sound nervous system. This was something for servant girls who could not afford the luxury of enthronement in the best chair, with no other obligation in life than to exert a noble and uplifting influence over the male members of the family both by word of mouth and the distribution of religious tracts.

The idea of feminine softness, physical as well as mental, was associated with delicacy, and men recoiled at any demonstration of extraordinary appetite or ability to endure fatigue. At sports the fair sex was a total liability. Girls had to be lifted over fences and guided around rocks and carried over streams an inch deep. Like falling leaves they swooned left and right.

It is not to be wondered that the dog has become the outdoor man's symbol of companionship.

Lucretia pressed the matter of medical education for women and went so far as to give a special public address on that topic. She made the point how people twenty years before had wondered how a modest girl could attend lectures on botany. But modest girls did attend them and other places formerly frequented only by men, and the result was not a loss of delicacy, but a higher and nobler development —a true modesty. This was radical talk, for the study of botany included the study of plant reproduction!

Emersonian transcendentalists were believers in the philosophy of living in harmony with the known forces of nature. Thus it was that Lucretia was impressed with "the necessity of the observance of the laws of health." She warned a friend to be careful to heed these laws for, added she, "I can't learn resignation to the good and the useful not living out half their days."

Lucretia's last overt interest in education was participation in the founding of Swarthmore College, an institution organized by members of the Hicksite Society for the education of members of both sexes. At the dedicatory exercises, in her seventy-seventh year, she was elected to honorary membership and invited onto the platform. With her own hands she planted the first tree which now adorns the spacious campus. Her husband was an active member of the board of managers, and later a daughter, Anna Mott Hopper, carried on the family tradition as a member of the college's executive committee.

One of Lucretia's most radical reforms, if choice must be made among many, was that to broaden the grounds of divorce. This was a project too far "beyond the beyonds" for the majority even of radical women. The subject of divorce became prominent as women set up higher standards of happiness for their sex, and refused longer to tolerate inequitable domestic situations once thought insolvable, albeit highly regrettable. Lucretia found that the subject of the marriage status was closely allied to divinity, a feat made easy by the aura of mystery and superstition that ever has clung to sex. Once shackled with immutable laws of allegedly divine origin, the problem ceased to be one of common sense. Even to ascertain the facts was to damage one's reputation.

Society enmeshes itself in customs of its own formulation until, like a statue of Laocoon, it becomes a thing immovable.

LUCRETIA MOTT, SOCIAL PIONEER

It was the consensus of current opinion that divorce should be limited to the ground of adultery. The mental cruelty inflicted on wives by drunken or diseased husbands, the tragedy of imbecile children, were factors not consulted in a civilization based on Hebraic law.

When Susan B. Anthony counseled wives and mothers present at a lecture "to separate from their husbands whenever they become intemperate, and particularly not to allow the said husbands to add another child to the family," a newspaper reported the address as a "startling and disgusting" speech. "Think of such advice," squirmed the editor, "given in public by one who claims to be a *maiden* lady."

Better that women and posterity suffer the tortures of ignorance than make sane remarks on the platform couched in language more dignified than that used by the editor who closed his tirade against bloomered Miss Anthony, saying: "After which she gathered her short skirts about her tight pants, sat down and wiped her spectacles."

When the divorce question ran high there was resurrected the waning hue and cry about free love.

Needless to say the nineteenth century outcropping of the Free Love cult was in no way even distantly related to Lucretia's equal rights party.

The Free Love movement had its votaries, its preachers, its poets, and its colonies. Some were Spiritualists who believed that Heaven could be entered only with one's natural mate, and made conscientious effort to ascertain the identity of their heavenly traveling companion. Others were intellectuals who assumed the position that the State had no jurisdiction over the individual's affections. But whoever they were they were not on bowing terms with Lucretia Mott, Ernestine Rose, or Elizabeth Cady Stanton.

The subject of divorce particularly interested Mrs. Stanton, who made it an issue in New York State where she was well connected with politically influential members of the old aristocracy. She brought pressure to bear on the Legislature of 1861 to put through a bill enlarging the grounds of divorce so as to include desertion and certain types of inhuman treatment.

There was at the time considerable dissipation among male scions of the old Dutch stock. The estates of large farmers accumulated by the dint of many years of laborious thrift were often quickly wasted by dissipated sons-in-law who, under the laws of the State, had complete control of property inherited by their wives. This situation excited a number of anguished capitalists to the point where they were willing to reread their Bibles in the light of modern circumstances. The opinion that God never intended worthless sons-in-law to run through the property of virtuous Dutchmen in New York State, gained converts. It was thought that it might be well to listen to the radicals, for once.

Invited to speak before the Legislature in support of the bill, Elizabeth describes what took place in her own inimitable language:

We chose the time at the close of one of our Conventions, that Mrs. Mott might be present, which she readily consented to do, and promised to speak if she felt moved. She charged Ernestine Rose and myself not to take too radical ground, in view of the hostility to the bill, but to keep closely to the merits of the main question. I told her she might feel sure of me, as I had my speech written, and I would read it to her, which I did, and received her approval.

The time arrived for the hearing, and a magnificent audience greeted us at the Capitol. The bill was read, I made the opening speech, Mrs. Rose followed. We had asked for the modification of certain statutes and the passage of others making the laws more equal for man and woman. Mrs. Mott having listened attentively to all that was said, and coming to the conclusion that with eighteen different causes for divorce in the different States, there might well be no laws at all on the question, she arose and said, that "she had not thought profoundly on this subject, but it seemed to her that no laws whatever on this relation would be better than such as bound pure, innocent women in bondage to dissipated, unprincipled men. With such various laws in the different States, and fugitives from the marriage bond fleeing from one to another, would it not be better to place all the States on the same basis, and thus make our national laws homogeneous?" She was surprised on returning to the residence of Lydia Mott to hear that her speech was altogether the most radical of the three. The bold statement of "no laws" however, was so sugar-coated with eulogies on good men and the sacredness of the marriage relation, that the press complimented the moderation of Mrs. Mott at our expense. We have had many a laugh over that occasion.

The joke being too good to let die, Elizabeth wrote Lucretia's sister: "Do you fully appreciate our triumph at our recent convention in taking your dear sister Lucretia before the Judiciary Committee of the Empire State on Divorce? And do you grasp the full force of the radical sentiments which she expressed on that occasion? 'All your legislation on that whole subject should be swept away.'"

Lucretia soon after sent a letter to a friend in which she quoted an extract from a speech made by Lord Brougham which she likened as being as radical as her own.

"So," defied Lucretia, "Elizabeth Stanton will see that I have authority for going to the root of the evil."

Another radical cause which brought down almost equal infamy upon Lucretia was her sponsorship in 1848 of a convention instigated by William Lloyd Garrison to examine into the authority of Sabbath enforcement as a day of rest.

A striking feature of the 'forties was the rigid observance of Sunday; a period of twenty-four hours of uncomfortable clothes and postures, when every red-blooded idea, every natural exuberance of feeling, every desire for normal action, was repressed by law. John Quincy Adams made the doubtful boast that this form of austere and gloomy worship was peculiarly American.

In her twenties Lucretia had corresponded with her husband's grandfather on the subject of Sunday idleness, and he had replied that he wished all were as liberally minded as she. "But some are so tenacious of the observance of the Sabbath, that they seem disposed at least to set a black mark against those who do not deem it so obligatory; while on the other hand, some of these latter brand the former with bigotry."

Lucretia was early satisfied that the Sabbath day had no particular sacredness. In order to accomplish her many philanthropic duties she had adopted the custom of sewing on that day, whenever necessary. Respectful of the opinions of others, and with no desire to cause them pain, she had made it a practice for a time to lay aside her work or conceal it when a servant entered the room. On being asked why she did not also, for the same reason, go to the communion table or submit to baptism, she could not answer satisfactorily, and at length had been convinced that more harm was done in the practice of the little deception than in working openly, as she thenceforth did.

So fanatically was the Sabbath observed during the first half of the century that on the day that ministers preached human slavery as a divine ordinance, Abolition workers would be arrested for distributing literature or for traveling from town to town. As early as 1840 a gathering, largely of Abolitionists, had been held at Chardon Street Chapel in Boston for the purpose of considering the validity of the opinions which prevailed in general as to the divine appointment of the Christian Sabbath, and the institutions of the ministry and the church.

Lucretia had been in sympathy with the convocation, but had expressed little faith of its success, commenting, "I fear the Sabbath, Church, and Ministry Convention will not effect much, the time is so occupied by St. Clair, Phelps, Colver, and other bigots. It may set the people of priest-ridden New England to thinking for themselves, and ultimately do good."

The eight years that passed had seen little growth of liberal sentiment. A society styled "The American and Foreign Sabbath Union" had been organized with the specific object of imposing the Sabbatical yoke yet more heavily around the necks of the American people. All secular travel, business and amusement, were to be confined to six days of the week, and on the seventh the people, whether gentiles, Jews, or atheists, were to assemble, under threat of the law, for the worship of God.

Because Sabbath worship was a fetish in which nearly all Christian sects were united, the power of unorganized persons for a sane Sunday was nil. Lovers of freedom thought it proper that the activities of the Sabbath Union should be met by a corresponding energy on the part of the friends of civil and religious liberty. The Sabbath, in their opinion, was mute evidence of ecclesiastical tyranny and disregard for the views of dissenters and non-Christians.

The projectors of the convention of 1848 were persons of high moral conduct and deep religious convictions, and it seems hardly possible to the modern ear attuned to a Sunday of either play or rest that the Pharisees of that day should have accused them so violently of being anti-religious. One can scarcely find a woman of her day more religious than Lucretia Mott.

As she had been a factor in bolstering the courage of the men who had founded the American Anti-Slavery Society fifteen years earlier, and as she had charged the members of the Unitarian convention to assume a more radical position in religion, so she took the floor at the anti-Sabbath convention, and spurred the delegates to greener pastures.

She thought there had been too much yielding by previous speakers to prevailing ideas of Sunday worship. Many feared to go the whole way. "The time is come," encouraged the fifty-five year old Quaker woman, "and especially in New England is it come, that man should judge of his own self what is right. . . . . "

. . . . Those who differ from us would care little for an Anti-Sabbath Convention which should come to the conclusion that, after all, it would be best to have one day in seven set apart for religious purposes. Few intelligent clergymen will now admit that they consecrate the day in any other sense, or that there is any inherent holiness in it. If you should agree that this day should be for more holy purposes than other days, you have granted much that they ask. Is not this Convention prepared to go farther than this? to dissent from this idea, and declare openly that it is lawful to do good on the Sabbath day? That it is the consecration of *all* our time to God and to goodness, that is required of us? Not by demure piety; not by avoiding innocent recreation on any day of the week, but by such a distribution of time as shall give sufficient opportunity for such intellectual culture and spiritual improvement, as our mental and religious nature requires.

She pleaded:

Let us not be ashamed of the gospel we profess, so far as to qualify it with any orthodox ceremonies and expressions. We must be willing to stand out in our heresy; especially, as already mentioned, when the duty of Sabbath observance is carried to such an extent, that it is regarded, too generally, a greater crime to do an innocent thing on the first day of the week—to use the needle, for instance—than to put a human being on the auction block on the second day—a greater crime to engage in harmless employment on the first day, than to go into the field of battle, and slay our fellow-beings, either on that day or other days of the week. While there is this palpable inconsistency, it is demanded of us, not only to speak plainly, but to act out our convictions, and not seem to harmonize with theirs.

The Quaker orator was one of the oldest members present. She drew attention to this fact, saying how these views had been familiar to her from early days, having heard them from the lips of Elias Hicks, who had taught that there should be such regulation of time as to overtax none with labor on any day of the week, and that man should have the advantage of innocent relaxation on Sunday after such devotional exercises as he might choose for himself. She knew while she spoke that the aftermath of the anti-Sabbath convention would be the customary public explosion of wrath.

She was not disappointed. Persons who had thought Garrison an American Wilberforce, and supposed him a pious, though deluded, person about slavery, felt they had discovered him out. "Would Wilberforce have spoken thus of the day on which the Son of God rose from the dead?" Clearly not, so the cause of the Abolitionists received another stripe on its welted back.

CHAPTER XXII
CONVERTS

The scope of influence of a public character never fully can be determined. A single sentence of an address may influence some auditor and set in motion the currents of an epoch. Miss Sarah Holley has preserved in her reminiscences an event in Lucretia's life. It was told Miss Holley one evening by a gentleman while she was resting at a friend's house.

When Lucretia was in England—ran the story which may be true only in part—Florence Nightingale was a young girl, and heard Lucretia talk about the importance of young ladies having some other ambition than solely that of being married, and how much happier they would be in some career of useful benevolence; and Florence said she would like to live to do good. Shortly after, she was visiting a hospital with an aunt, and as they went through the wards, Florence would say, such-and-such an improvement ought to be made, when her aunt said, "Florence, you are the very one to make it; this is the work for you to do; you have been wanting something to engage your higher and better energies and here it is."

Lucretia was a liberalizing influence in the lives of several great men. She was the prominent factor in humanizing William Lloyd Garrison from the rigors of Calvinism, which ended in his becoming the father of non-resistance in America, and the inspirer of conventions to examine Sabbath worship and church authority.

At a time when she was being bitterly reviled for her sentiments, Garrison came to her defense in an editorial in the "Liberator," explaining that if his mind had become liberalized in any degree (and he thought it had burst every sectarian trammel)—if the theological dogmas which once he had regarded as essential to Christianity, he now repudiated as absurd and pernicious—he was largely indebted to James and Lucretia Mott for the change.

Especially did Lucretia like to counsel young clergymen in whom she detected evidences of liberalism. A convert of pregnant significance was Robert Collyer, many years a preacher in Chicago, where his church gained the reputation of being "the glory of Christian liberalism."

As a lay Methodist teacher the immigrant Collyer had spent his Sundays preaching to a little group of neighboring farmers and artisans about Shoemakertown, about a mile from the Mott home. "We had started," writes Collyer, "a lyceum the previous winter in the school-house, and were hammering away at a great rate as to which is the most beautiful, the works of art or the works of nature, and whether the Negro or the Indian had received the worst usage at the hands of the white man—a matter we could not settle for the life of us—when Edward Davis, a son-in-law of James and Lucretia, came in and before we knew what was coming, plunged us headlong into the surging and angry tides of Abolitionism."

Mr. Davis had a fondness for quoting scripture that was matched only by genius for misquotation. He quoted the prophets, but got them all wrong, and was given some swift retorts by the laborer whose extensive reading was the talk of the countryside. Apt or inapt, Davis was the first genuine Abolitionist Collyer had ever met, and he had supported the affirmative of his proposition with zeal and power, albeit with lamentable marshalling of scriptural authority.

At the next lyceum meeting Davis came fortified with Lucretia. Collyer denounced the Abolitionists as "busy bodies." He was then, as he had always been, in favor of emancipation by practically letting the thing alone, or putting it away into the future. But Lucretia poured out her soul upon him and Collyer threw up his hands, and admitted, "You are right. I fight henceforth under this banner." From that night in a rural schoolhouse, to the time of his departure for Chicago, Lucretia was one of Collyer's closest friends and, without exception, his most intimate counselor.

Several weeks after the lyceum incident James came to Collyer and said, "We want thee to come to our house." And Collyer had gone as he had gone to the house of Mr. Davis in Philadelphia. He went with the sensitive pride of a self-respecting workingman. He would stand no patronage, no condescension. If ever he felt this in the atmosphere, the Motts should go their way, and he would go his. But he found it was simply falling into another and ampler home of his own. And this was not something the Motts did carefully and by concert. It was as natural to them as life. They had no room in their fine natures for any other thought. "This," Collyer explains, "was how I came to know these friends, and to be at last almost as one of their own kinsmen."

Collyer came to love Lucretia, whom he called that "grand-hearted Quaker preacher." Under her influence he joined a local Abolition society and spoke at public gatherings, sometimes with bursting pride on the same platform as his mentor. Yet his new friend tried never to make him a convert to her sect. She advised him constantly that to be a good Methodist, so long as it was possible, was the best course he could pursue.

Eventually Collyer was cornered by the officials of his church. Certain questions were put to him. Whereupon the young man resigned his office as a circuit preacher and went out of the Methodist Church, alone and lonesome, abandoned by men and women who had loved him once, not one of whom came to him, or held out a hand, or said a word of farewell. In the hour of great loneliness he found comfort in the friendships of Lucretia Mott and William H. Furness. These were the associates of Collyer at the fork in the highway of life. "I love to remember," said Collyer in reminiscence, "with what tender pathos (Lucretia Mott) opened her heart to me, when it seemed almost like death to leave my old mother church, of the trouble it was to her when she had to do this in the days of Elias Hicks— to find she must part with old friends for the truth, and to have the meeting-houses closed to her in which she had loved to meet them, and to suffer reproach that she might be true to her own soul."

Such words were balm in Gilead. What she had done, he could do, and God helping him *would* do!

Another convert was J. Miller McKim. Lucretia first met him at the convention which organized the American Anti-Slavery Society. Between the student of twenty-three, preparing for the Presbyterian ministry, and the Quaker matron of forty, ripened a lifelong friendship. The woman had been greatly pleased with McKim's eager adoption of the despised cause. She took interest in the conflict she knew was being waged in his mind between liberal Christianity and inherited Presbyterianism.

McKim sent her parts of his diary that she might analyse his thoughts. He asked her for books and she regretted she could not procure for him all that had been written opposed to Channing for, much as she loved Channing, justice required, she cautioned the young thinker, "that we should acquaint ourselves with both sides, before we judge." She warned him that the step of quitting his faith was a serious one, and she prayed that he might be rightly directed. "We frequently conversed together, touching the doctrines or dogmas" of the Presbyterian society, "and on his return home, he read some of Dr. Channing's works, and some goodly Friends' books we furnished him, and the result was an entire change of views," reports Lucretia.

Late in the 'forties, George W. Julian, of Centerville, Indiana, and James L. Pierce were among prominent persons who consulted her on religious problems. She did for them as she had done for McKim. She recommended Parker's writings and, in particular, the sermon on The Transient and the Permanent in Christianity. In addition she sent Julian a few tracts and small works, "some of which may prove altogether too radical for thy enquiring mind," she apologized.

At this time of life she made it a practice to refer her friends to the writings of Joseph Blanco White. White had been a Spanish priest whose ancestors had left Ireland to escape the penal law. The Roman church not suiting his mind, he had gone to England, where on a reëxamination of Christian doctrine he had accepted the faith of the Church of England and studied for the ministry at Oxford. But he preached not more than once in an English pulpit, for his mind rested no more satisfied with the Protestant liturgy than the Roman breviary. His life was nearly spent when he entered for the first time a dissenting place of worship and heard James Martineau, of Liverpool, preach an Unitarian sermon. Thereafter he frequently heard the preaching of J. H. Thom, son-in-law of Lucretia's European acquaintance, William Rathbone. Commencing life as a Roman Catholic priest, White ultimately went further to the left than most Unitarians.

The life and writings of Blanco White, sent her by a friend abroad, comprised a two-volume set of books that were in immense favor with Lucretia, depicting as they did the evolutionary progress of an enquiring mind. She carried them with her, quoted them, and circulated them among her friends until they were worn out in the lending. Her notes on them formed three little volumes written on the backs of old letters.

In her correspondence Lucretia apologized to Pierce for her delay in answering his questions, pleading "a kind of instinctive dread of entering the theological field" and discussing points of creed. So many entanglements were found there for the person untrained in the study of astute polemics that one was apt to find oneself bewildered in a maze of contradictions and fine distinctions. She preferred, she admitted, "to walk in the way called heresy," being thereby not troubled with "the difficulties that beset many an honest traveler in his attempt, with the only admitted implement or weapon, the Bible, to smooth this field and 'make straight in the desert a highway for our God.' "

She told Pierce that she did not join in the claim that everything in the Bible was unusual. She admitted the crucifixion of Jesus was a fearful tragedy, but that the ferocity and malignity of the sectarians of that day, who committed the barbarous act, were "unparalleled," she was not sure. Later martyrs who were stoned and sawn asunder were doubtless victims of precisely the same spirit. Ecclesiastical history records the deaths of thousands upon thousands of persons who were the objects of the same priestly hate and bigotry as Jesus Christ.

She added:

I never like to see the Jews pictured with so dark and malignant a countenance, as sinners above all men. Let Catholic and Protestant persecutors be placed in the same category—aye, and dissenters, too, who, in their zeal, are calling down fire from Heaven, be they of the old Puritan order, or belonging to the more modern Hicksite profession. Even though the custom of the times will not sanction the erection of the cross, or the gallows, nor yet other instruments of torture—blessed be the age in which we live!—yet the disposition to cast out the name as evil, to persecute with the pen and the tongue, and by church excommunication, is still as apparent, as when brother delivered up brother unto death.

CHAPTER XXIII
JOHN BROWN'S BODY

"I am worth inconceivably more to hang than for any other purpose."—JOHN BROWN.

In the autumn of 1859 occurred the raid at Harper's Ferry. The butchery of "Ossawatomie" Brown horrified the Nation as the news of his exploit spread from the cities into every nook and hamlet. So much hysteria had been heard on the subject of slavery that the words of taciturn John Brown that Abolitionists did nothing but talk, that "what is needed is action—action!" had fallen on unsusceptible ears.

Brown had little respect for principles of moral reform, adjectives, and non-resistance. Let Garrison and his crew of pacifists baptize the anti-slavery cause with the water of the New Testament; John Brown was of sterner stuff; he stood for the Old Testament purge of blood. He believed in an implacable God, and kept his powder dry. There was a definite place in Christianity for bloodshed, and he was impatient of what had gone on before—which mainly had been nothing but talk.

Supporters of Brown scattered like leaves before an autumnal gust. Gerrit Smith took refuge in an insane asylum, others fled to Canada; all but a few denied they had known Brown's plans to put down slavery by force of arms. The impetuous Higginson journeyed into the mountains to break the news of Brown's capture to the wife and surviving members of the family. Mrs. Brown started to the bedside of her stricken husband, but on the way was halted by friends who advised against such a move. Cool heads thought best that she remain away from excited Virginia. Accordingly, she took refuge in the home of the Motts, outside Philadelphia, while fever raged the country and militia paced the streets of Charlestown.

Lucretia was no believer in bloodshed. She was stout that nothing could be accomplished by force of arms that could not equally, or better, be accomplished through peaceful means. In her opinion the negro was a human being possessed of as many rights as any farmer of Harper's Ferry, though not always the white man's social or intellectual equal; and many a negro had been killed in the name of slavery!

John Brown learned of his wife's whereabout and wrote her from a cot in the jail at Charlestown: "I once set myself to oppose a mob at Boston where she [Lucretia Mott] was. After I interfered, the police immediately took up the matter, and soon put a stop to mob proceedings. The meeting was, I think, in Marlboro' Street Church, or Hotel, perhaps." Thus the man felt he had paid his debt by a pre-existent consideration. The incident he referred to was perhaps the dedication of Marlboro Chapel, the Boston analogue of Pennsylvania Hall.

Whether John Brown actually expected to foment a slave insurrection, buttressed by the thought that the loss of a few lives among the whites could not balance the ledger of negro suffering, or whether he looked on his deed as the dramatic spark that would fire the Nation, can only be surmised and discussed with the question of his sanity. Whatever was John Brown, posterity has elevated him like some mythical hero on a par with Arthur, Wallace, or William Tell. He is one of the characters of history who by a single deed has won to himself the fame that has not come to many a laborious, and truly greater, worker. In a night the reputation of John Brown, of Kansas, had become a national monument. School boys were to die on battlefields with the spirit of a John Brown song on their lips— marching on. Brown was, and always will be, an enigma, but not more so than the people of the Nation who took up his name and called him great after decades of anathematizing the non-resistant Abolitionists as "bloody fomenters of disorder."

Came a strange paradox. Many Abolitionists repudiated Brown's deed while thousands of citizens who never before had been favorable to anti-slavery rallied behind the man who had tried to conquer windmills with Sharp's rifles. Thousands of men who ten years before Harper's Ferry could not endure the lightest word of Abolitionism from Lucretia's lips, now easily swallowed John Brown whole, "and his rifle in the bargain."

On the day that Brown was hanged, some of the church bells of the land rang a muffled requiem. Garrison, listening to the tribute that clanged from white painted towers where his own name had been cast out as evil, cynically observed how the church that had rejected his bloodless principles, held to her bosom the dripping hands of John Brown.

Lucretia's letters of these stirring days are not extant. Being of unusual interest, they were sent the family chain to farthermost relatives, and lost in numerous transfers.

Although John Brown had become a hero to thousands of persons North and West, his deed wreaked upon Abolitionists the multiplied animosity of other thousands of persons who feared disunion. The non-resistants were accused of loading the guns of hatred and dissension, if they did not discharge them.

Daily the South neared the end of its patience. It had tried every means within its power to silence anti-slavery propaganda, by force, by threats, by law, by pleas. Now it girded its loins for the final struggle before disruption. That struggle was the presidential campaign of 1860. The candidate thought most likely to win the Republican nomination was William H. Seward. The South-side view of Seward was pictured by Representative Lamar, of Mississippi, who described how he had actually heard with his own ears Seward say that "he hoped to see the day when there would not be the footprint of a single slave upon this continent. And when he uttered this atrocious sentiment," continued the orator, "his form seemed to dilate, his pale, thin face, furrowed by the lines of thought and evil passion, kindled with malignant triumph, and his eyes glowed and glared upon Southern senators as though the fires of hell were burning in his heart!"

It was a day of taut nerves. Not the least composed was Henry Ward Beecher, the pulpit Barnum, auctioneering negro maidens on the stage of Plymouth Church in Brooklyn amidst orgies of tears. His purpose was to show congregations what reality was like in the nigger-pens of the South. There were no mock auctions at Philadelphia.

When the time came for Lucretia and her associates to hold the annual local fair a leading Philadelphia newspaper asked its readers if they meant to permit the Abolitionists to maintain the event so shortly after Brown's raid. The fair was no more under way than the mayor of the city deemed it necessary, in order to prevent riot, to ask the women to take down the flag which they had hung at their building as an attraction. The distasteful emblem consisted of a copy of the old Liberty Bell, with the well-known inscription "Proclaim liberty throughout the land, to all the inhabitants thereof."

LUCRETIA MOTT, SOCIAL PIONEER

The mayor appeared at the hall in person, accompanied by the sheriff and the latter's lawyer, to serve an order from the lessor to remove all property from the hall within three hours, on the plea that the premises were being used for a purpose which tended to excite popular commotion and the destruction of property.

The managers of the fair assembled in a corner of the hall. Lucretia acted as spokeswoman. Her reply to the guardians of law was typical of her. She told the gentlemen she was glad that her friend, Mr. Gilpin (one of the officers), had expressed regret for the occurrence; she well remembered some service of his rendered to the anti-slavery cause in earlier days; that the managers did not reproach the officers for their part in the affair, but were sorry for them that they held offices which obliged them to perform such deeds. After this quaint speech, the ladies removed their goods to other quarters in the city, where the fair was continued with great success the remainder of the week.

A mob, invoked by the local newspaper, directed its attention to a lecture given by George William Curtis on the "Present Aspect of the Country," a title which affords fuel for controversy during any national crisis. As fearless as in their younger days Lucretia and James occupied seats on the platform; Lucretia sixty-six years of age, and her husband seventy-one.

In due time Seward returned from a tour of the Holy Land and, bidding for the Republican nomination for President, delivered a mild speech wherein he endeavored to lessen the fears of the South and the moderate North about his radicalism. He let it be known that he had not meant all he had said ten years before when he had declared that a higher law than the Constitution demanded the extinction of slavery, or in a later speech when he had uttered the stirring words that the North was engaged in an "irrepressible conflict" which must make the Nation either all slave or all free.

The visit to Palestine had softened his nature!

Seward's speech was received in the North with varying degrees of enthusiasm. Republicans who wished only to suppress the expansion of slavery into the new states, but had no intention of doing away with the institution in the South, were elated by the speaker's preëlection sanity, and refreshed by the thought that the choice of appointive offices might soon be theirs.

J. Miller McKim and other good Abolitionists dropped in at the Motts, where the speech was discussed. Many commentators were profuse in praise, but Lucretia said she was not satisfied. She took notes of the objectionable parts of the oration and commented on them further at the next meeting of the Female Anti-Slavery Society. While uniting with the applause bestowed upon other parts of the speech, she warned her fellow-members against unqualified praise. She perceived that the negro, for the purposes of politics, had been disparaged. Her remarks, she admitted, "seemed unexpected" by the members, but "little reply was made."

Abolitionists so long had esteemed Seward a friend that they were inclined to ignore the unfavorable parts of his discourse. The "Anti-Slavery Standard" concluded to pass over all comment because of a "want of space," but Garrison's "Liberator" boldly faced the facts with a severe criticism.

"How glad was I that Garrison reviewed it as my instincts had led me to do—and with all the faithful rebuke that ever flows from his pen," praised Lucretia.

Politicians played marbles while drums of social revolution rumbled in the distance. Webster had thundered sonorously his Union, one and undivided; Calhoun had shrieked secession, and Clay had proposed his temporizing compromises. One and all, they would not hear, they could not see, the moral issue involved. To them the all important thing was the preservation of current political institutions. The election of a Whig or Democratic President, or considerations of tariff or banking policies were to them of more importance than the freedom of millions of men.

Several of the greatest statesmen in American history passed to rest without solving the real problem of their generation. By 1860 the giants were entombed. A new school of politicians, boned and sinewed by voting Abolitionists, had succeeded them as victims of temporizing politics, and shown themselves not much better.

The several candidates for party nominations aligned and disaligned throughout the year. Blatant conventions were held in the otherwise pleasant months of April, May and June. An ungainly and, what is sometimes an advantage, almost unknown lawyer from primitive Illinois won the Republican nomination for President; and in the same month Lucretia mourned the news of Theodore Parker's death.

LUCRETIA MOTT, SOCIAL PIONEER

Unlike the pro-slavery editor who announced that Parker "was gone, and let no one imitate his bad qualities," Lucretia thought it was "truly mournful that such a gifted spirit should be so early removed from earth, where he was so much needed. . . . . The last time we had his company at our house in Arch Street, he was telling us of the works he had on hand, and the research necessary to complete them. I cautioned him not to overtax his powers of endurance, little dreaming we should so soon hear of a fatal result of his great labors. It is too sad to dwell upon, when we have so many around us who are cumberers of the earth. We have had a succession of melancholy deaths, thinning our anti-slavery ranks. . . . . Who will fill such blanks?"

In November Abraham Lincoln was elected President. At last the followers of Birney and Stanton had indirectly elected a President of the United States—an Abolitionist with strong reservations. Lincoln's "Black Republican" party was little more than the Free Soil Party. It maintained that slavery in the slave states was to be patiently endured while extension of slavery in new territories was to be strenuously opposed.

Despite this timid platform, the Hotspurs of the South were infuriated by the results of the election. The Republican administration was predicted as one which would soon be "coiling its slimy folds around our dearest rights and patriarchal interests." While the Nation awaited the inauguration of Lincoln, especial effort was made to silence Abolition propaganda. It was alleged that the national situation was so delicate that nothing should be said about slavery, else the South might fulfill its threat of secession.

The statesmen of the Nation were talking slavery. James Buchanan was fasting and crying over it, the rowdies of the northern cities were ready to bluster by it, the South declared it would die for it, yet Abolitionists were forbidden to open their lips, in the name of patriotism. So determined were some citizens that the bonds of the Union should be preserved in peace, that riot followed riot whenever Abolitionists met. Ralph Waldo Emerson, at Tremont Temple, for the first time in his life, faced a mob in an address in behalf of free speech. Union meetings threatened Wendell Phillips, who was followed in the streets of Boston by enraged citizens awaiting their chance to do him bodily harm. Constables and justices of the peace invaded halls and broke up meetings at the head of drunken mobs.

In the South extremists described Abolitionists as vulgar men who were getting above themselves . . . . they had grown saucy and dared to be impudent to gentlemen . . . . they had been suffered too long to run without collars . . . . they must be lashed into submission . . . . then they would learn to behave themselves like decent dogs. "Free society" was summed up as a "conglomeration of greasy mechanics, filthy operatives, small-fisted farmers, and moon-struck theorists" not "fitted for well-bred gentlemen," *viz.*, Southerners. There was much ranting about "the chivalrous sons of the old Palmetto" and "their unstained escutcheons."

Beneath the din of the hurdy-gurdy, Northern capitalists shrewdly endeavored to chart a political course that would hold together cotton fields and cotton mills. Cotton was king! It seemed to disgorge wealth with a lavish hand out of a bottomless cornucopia of plenty, but beneath the fibrous padding of cotton was enwrapped a civilization as brittle as glass, retarding the progress of the South as a whole and distributing its wealth unequally upon a favored few. Only about one-third of the white men of the South owned even one slave. While much of the civilized world had undergone the pangs of the industrial revolution, the South was basking in the glamor of a fast dying agrarian prosperity with a frosting of feudalism.

Efforts to conciliate the South, and the cautions of Union men to preserve peace, Lucretia admitted were all very good, yet she doubted statements that the South was the bone and sinew of the country, and the firmest supporter of democracy. "They have ever looked *down* on labor of any kind, calling the free Northern industrial workmen 'the mud-sills of society.'" She asked what encouragement had they ever given to universal education? Even leaving out of view the millions of their bondmen "whom no *true* democrat could trample under foot, denying their every right, as they do. No, they send their own *white* sons to West Point at the government expense, for a military and aristocratic education, and leave the people and children at large in the grossest ignorance. . . . . "

Slowly the Union toppled. Almost daily a column crashed to earth. Northern statesmen staggered about stunned, shrinking from fratricidal war, in no sympathy with the cause that had watered dissension, and half-believing the South was right in everything but the legal power to withdraw from the Union.

LUCRETIA MOTT, SOCIAL PIONEER

Buchanan drained the scattered sands in the hourglass of a four years' administration which was without precedent, shook vacantly his addled head, perceived his debilitated administration was closed, and handed over what was left of the Nation to Lincoln.

Two hundred and forty-two years had elapsed since a very tiny ship had unloaded a cargo of slaves in the James River of Virginia a year before the coming of the "Mayflower." The name of the ship, the name of the captain, and the number of slaves are no longer of importance. Sufficient that the planters of the neighborhood were pleased at the prospect of cheap labor in a land where manpower was scarce, and the captain and the owners of the ship were pleased with their profits, and everybody was pleased except the benighted heathen who were sold into slavery.

It was a happy day, and we can imagine it was a very bright and sunny day. It was also the beginning of a long civil war of hatred and sorrow and bloodshed in America.

CHAPTER XXIV

Civil War

"Were you looking to be held together by lawyers?
Or by an agreement on a paper? Or by arms?
Nay, nor the world nor any living thing will so cohere."
—Walt Whitman in "Drum-Taps."

On the 10th of April, 1861, Lucretia and James celebrated their golden wedding anniversary, and the next day General Beauregard demanded of Major Robert Anderson the surrender of Fort Sumter in Charlestown Harbor. While Northern and Southern soldiers glared at each other over bristling parapets, the 10th of April at Roadside dawned a bright and sunny day. It was the spring of year, the winter of age. Friends of the Motts, and relatives far and near, assembled at the old house to do homage to the venerable bride and groom. Three of the twenty still living of the one hundred and twenty-five witnesses, who fifty years before had signed the wedding certificate in the Pine Street Meeting, were present.

The old document, yellow with age, was brought out and read aloud. All who were present appended their names on the obverse side as a testimonial of reverence for "the beauty and glory of true marriage." Observers expressed curiosity about a blank part of the document towards one edge which had been cut out. Various explanations were guessed until Lucretia confessed the personal commission of the sacrilege forty years before in order to mend a broken battledore for one of her children. No other piece of parchment at hand, she had taken that. Nothing could better epitomize the character of the woman than this act of tearing the paper symbol of the union of marriage for the practical purpose of making someone happy.

Old Roadside, surrounded by trees and warmed by sun, resounded to the cheerful sounds of human voices, including children, grandchildren, and one tiny great-grandchild of the celebrating couple. Little visitors romped through oddly shaped rooms and queer passages, amazed and delighted at unexpected turnings and steps up in one place and down in another. At Roadside there was no Victorian parlor. Where in other houses children were admitted into this hall of state only in event of a funeral or the visit of the pastor, and had otherwise to content themselves with lost-soul glimpses of heaven through the pearly gates of partially opened doors, the Mott parlor had the distinction of being lived in every day.

The windows of the house commanded pleasant views of adjacent countryside. In the comfort of evening, elderly members of the family and guests congregated on the porch and glimpsed tree-framed pictures of the Old York Road, over which once trappers had passed on foot to the Indian country and stagecoaches had lumbered between Philadelphia and New York. When the growth of bushes cut off the view, the plants one by one would be sacrificed because of Lucretia's dislike to be shut in; and trees that spread too much shade came within the same decree.

A glass door opening from the piazza led to the library, the quiet retreat of James and Lucretia in the evening from lively groups in the parlor. Here a bookcase contained not many, but carefully chosen and well worn volumes few, if any, of which were fiction. From surrounding walls gazed the faces of well beloved friends; William Lloyd Garrison, William Ashurst, George Thompson, Elias Hicks, Miller McKim, Robert Purvis; and mixed with these English and American liberals was the occasional portrait of a member of the family.

On one side of the fireplace was tacked a small map of Nantucket Island, and another of the town after the great fire of 1846. Close by hung a genealogical chart of the Coffin family, with patriarchal Tristram's name in the center. The master's chair was high and straight backed as befitted a Quaker elder and stood by a side of the fireplace near the light of a western window. In a corner behind was a table called by the younger members of the family "the colt" because of its ungainly long legs. In the middle of the room, opposite the Franklin stove, was located Lucretia's rocking chair and a table covered with books and paper and writing materials, systematically arranged, and never disturbed save by its mistress' hands. A Nantucket basket stuffed with carpet rags for the work of idle minutes, and another dedicated to mending, occupied a nearby shelf.

Different indeed was the graceful and happy scene at Roadside, the ancient couple surrounded by kin and friends, from the situation at Charleston Harbor a few hours later with Fort Sumter blazing like a furnace, its brick and mortared walls crumbling beneath the poundings of Confederate guns, its defenders returning a steady fire despite the inevitable surrender.

The Nation responded to the call of war. Boston bankers who had sung so lustily the virtues of King Cotton offered to lend the State millions of dollars in advance of legislative action.

Humpty Dumpty Cotton was off his throne, and all the South's courage and all the South's men could never put Humpty Dumpty Cotton back again. The tread of marching feet echoed in the streets. The political Abolitionists (the old Birney-Stanton faction) threw themselves with enthusiasm into war. The Stars and Stripes were pictured on the cover of the "Anti-Slavery Standard." The romantic Higginson—equally at ease in the pulpit or the student's cloister—in time became colonel of the first regiment of freed slaves mustered into the national service. Even the icy Emerson was caught up in the swirl of enthusiasm and repudiated for the time his anti-social inclinations.

War and patriotism are a congenial pair of twin brothers. Phillips, who had shocked Boston for two decades, was cheered to the roof-trees of Boston Music Hall when he cried, "I rejoice for the first time in my anti-slavery life; I stand under the stars and stripes and welcome the tread of Massachusetts men."

Garrison, too, was for war, if war there must be. He could not remain neutral where the freedom of slaves was involved. He was greeted in New York by cheers and repeated bursts of applause. It was good to be popular, to see smiles and hear shouts and claps of approbation where once had been only growling crowds and sullen mobs.

But no cheers saluted the Quakeress of Cherry Street Meeting. Lucretia was one, among all those who had professed peace, who remained true to the principles of pacificism. No cause was enshrined more dearly in her heart than negro freedom. But what avail to humanity to set men free, if men must be slain in the doing? The Nation was rent asunder, hatred filled the air, fathers cursed sons, brothers slew brothers, all for the cause she loved, in a manner she abhorred.

Heredity, environment, religion had budded in her soul a passionate love for freedom. But the same factors had taught her that passive resistance was the stalk of justice. Lucretia was troubled by a large practical sense in her make-up which recognized the probable end of slavery on the battlefield. Yet she could not support the war. "We know full well, that the battle-field is a precarious resort to obtain the Right—that sorrows multiply there; and as to the moral sense of corrupt statesmen, it is 'seared as with a hot iron.'"

She heard hymns of battle exultantly chanted as the war spirit swept North and South. On Sunday the consciousness of Mars was stronger than on any other day of the week, for on this day the people of the Nation went to the fonts of Christ for spiritual food to encourage them to sustain the horrors of another week of bloody slaughter. The cry was that the Union must be saved! Surely God would bring victory to a cause so important as the preservation of a political structure made holy by the blood of a Warren at Bunker Hill and a Nathan Hale on the scaffold. They shall not have died in vain!

Already the negro had been forgotten. At Washington the President was proclaiming that the cause of the negro had nothing to do with the war. The day after Bull Run, Congress passed, under Lincoln's influence, a resolution declaring that the North did not mean to interfere with slavery, but only sought to perpetuate the Union.

The administration's policy was that, after all the bloodshed and all the hatreds of armed conflict, slavery should remain at the close of the war a problem to be disposed of in some way that statesmen and politicians had been unable to solve in decades of peace before the added passions of spilled blood had seared the brain.

Lucretia complained that there had seemed "to be rather a stolid determination of late, among a class of politicians, that this war shall have nothing to do with Slavery, 'The Union, and nothing but the Union,' is their cry—as if that were ever again possible, with the deplorable weight of that incubus [slavery] upon it. Time alone will reveal to us." The woman at Roadside saw that to which the statesmen at Washington blinded their eyes. The Union was tottering on its mudsills—the institution of slavery.

There was a lack of complete frankness in the attitude of the President who sensed the national lack of enthusiasm for a war which would emancipate the negro race. He knew there were hundreds of thousands of persons in the North to whom the cause of the African was not of sufficient moment to sacrifice life or money. He had come to the presidency pledged to preserve slavery in the Southern States, so he cried out that the war had nothing to do with slavery—that the lesser was greater than the whole.

"Preserve the Union!" implored the voice from the White House, and thousands on thousands of boys, not out of their teens, rallied to the flag. Some who recently had crowded the doors of the last anti-slavery convention in Boston, shouting down the speakers by uproarious songs and catcalls, were marching southward. Their blood was to enrich the soil of the states from south Pennsylvania to New Orleans, that there might be one Nation, with or without slavery, but not two.

What was this Union for which so many lives were to be given, and in whose name so much sentiment was written? In the last analysis it was the forcible binding together of mutual haters in order to preserve a partnership distasteful to millions of citizens. It was a desire for latitude and longitude, and Manifest Destiny.

Lincoln's stand did not pacify the South in the quicksands of secession, and it antagonized England. Lucretia advised her friends that petitions should be poured into Washington from all quarters, "that those in power may see how unavailing is their pro-slavery conservatism. It only lays the foundation for future trouble and fighting, when for reputation 'to please men,' they seek to 'build again the things they are called to destroy.'"

As the war progressed (chronologically, but not in military victories), Lincoln was confronted with the tumult of contending counsel, and was torn by a mind trying to cope with a question both legal and moral as though it were only legal. As President of the United States his duty was to follow out the will of the people, and as is always the case in a vital issue, the people were wallowing in troughs of conflicting ideas, and no ideas at all.

The President hesitated, tracked and double-backed. He stressed the unification of the Nation, but the question of slavery haunted long nights of sleepless vigilance as it had done Webster, Clay, Calhoun, and Buchanan, too. Wendell Phillips bitterly attacked Lincoln for hiding behind the Constitution in rejecting recommendations for negro emancipation, and yet suspending the *habeas corpus* after centuries of struggle by ancestors against the tyranny of rulers and nobles. Radicals like Greeley and Robert Dale Owen pleaded with Lincoln to make the war a struggle for human freedom, to make it as holy as possible

NO COMMUNION WITH SLAVEHOLDERS.

"Stand aside, you Old Sinner! WE are Holier than thou."

CARTOON FROM "HARPER'S WEEKLY," SHOWING ABOLITION MINISTER REFUSING COMMUNION TO SLAVEHOLDER

and not a mere trial by combat of fine points of constitutional law in regard to the right of secession. The pressed Lincoln tartly denied the right of presidential emancipation, even while he was toying with the draft of a document in case the minute hand should strike the hour.

Came dark days when all seemed lost. McClellan was no more than a James Buchanan in uniform, puffed with a great conceit. The Peninsular campaign collapsed. Bull Run was a lingering nightmare by day or by night. England threatened war. When there was nothing else to be done, the Chief Magistrate who had persistently denied the power of the President to abolish slavery, was pushed— aye shoved—into his most vital piece of statesmanship, the perhaps unconstitutional Emancipation Act, the document that has made his name enduring.

For reasons not based on any principle of humanity, Lincoln temporarily joined the radicals, and was by the side of Lucretia Mott, who had not shifted her position since the outbreak of war. The mighty document, born in the travail of a painful reluctance, won the popular imagination and its author the title of "The Great Emancipator," which might better have gone to William Lloyd Garrison. The emancipation document was oxygen to the disheartened North. The Nation had been dreary of the thought of a war won at the cost of thousands of its best manhood that a people might live in a United States composed of this, instead of that, number of states and territories.

The years of the Civil War were quiet ones at Roadside. Lucretia's health being not good, they were spent in comparative retirement. Woman's rights conventions no longer being held, and reform movements beating time in general, the woman devoted herself to many personal acts of philanthropy among the poor and unfortunate members of the black and white races in the neighborhood. At home she picked blackberries and peaches from the garden, "a beautiful succession of fruits," she described it, but "constant attention is the price one pays" for crops, "and weeds and briers the penalty."

Thoughts of civil war she could not entirely submerge. Towards the close of the first year she wrote her sister "how trifling are family items when our thoughts and hearts are full of the great events of the day."

She almost despaired of any good result from the outbreak. The resort to bloodshed was barbarous, "besides making the innocent suffer for the guilty."

James Freeman Clarke consoled her with the statement that "the Lord reigned" and would bring forth fruit in fields pock-marked with shell holes. Lucretia answered that the sentiment that everything was in the hands of the Almighty was a superstitious idea which bred indolence. The *"effective instrument,"* said she, was the moral laborer. The advocates of moral education must not rely too greatly on the tented field and the armed camp for the abolition of slavery. They must ever be alert.

When Lucretia's nephew enlisted, she penned the mother what a strange thing it was that the glories of war could, in any wise, reconcile one to the perils. "It is vain to say much on the subject now, but my convictions are as strong as ever, that a better and more effectual way will be found as civilization advances."

The removal from home of the youngest daughter was a trial to Lucretia, who was lonely and a little out of place in the war-torn world. She was glad of the bright prospects that impelled her son-in-law and his family to leave Roadside, yet she was selfish enough to want all her children and grandchildren with her.

Her attention was attracted early in '63. The War Department organized a camp for the mobilization of negro soldiers a short distance from Roadside. With characteristic lack of humor the military authorities conferred upon the camp the peaceful Quaker name of William Penn.

George L. Stearns, the Boston merchant who had strongly agitated the enrollment of colored troops, dropped in at Roadside while on a visit to the camp. He found the mistress still loyal to principles of non-resistance, but accepting "very gracefully," thought Stearns, the present state of affairs, although looking forward to a society when war would be unnecessary as a means of settlement of human difficulties. "So do I," acclaimed Stearns, "but I told her that this war was a *civilizer,* not a barbarism. The use of the musket was the first step in the education of the black man. This she accepted. She is a great woman. . . . . "

While Lucretia disapproved the trappings of war, she could not resist an interest in the public acknowledgment of the negro as a soldier and a human being. "The neighboring camp," she explained to her sister, "seems the absorbing interest just now. Is not this change in feeling and conduct towards this oppressed class beyond all that we could have anticipated, and marvelous to our eyes?" She seldom visited the camp and seemed indifferent to its affairs as a military institution. But she loved to listen to the music of the band as it came softened across the fields. One imagines the melancholy strains of "taps" wafted through the stillness of nights must have struck deep into the gentle heart of the woman as she thought of those young boys to whom taps would one day be requiem.

The fact that the mistress of Roadside displayed little interest in the military affairs of the adjoining camp does not mean that she failed to befriend its inhabitants as individuals. The colored soldiers were interested in the famed Abolitionist whose home adjoined their tented city. One or two regiments, as they left for the seat of war, commanded by white men—some of them sons of old Abolitionists—made it a point of courtesy to march in at the back gate of Roadside and out the front, in order to salute the sweet-faced lady who had proved herself a friend to the black race.

On one of these occasions, as the troops were heard approaching, Lucretia hastened to the cake-box and emptying its contents into her apron ran out to the end of the piazza where, as the men filed by, the woman of threescore and ten years handed each a gingerbread until the supply was exhausted.

The troops faded out, the dust settled; beyond the quiet horizon men were dying while cannon belched destruction. The mistress of Roadside, so tiny and so frail, returned to the silent house, torn between the appeals of a moral nature which told her that war was death, and a heart that beat warm for the childlike grinning men who had just done her reverence.

A meeting of the anti-slavery cohorts in 1863 was called in New York in the same month that witnessed the last great Confederate victory at Chancellorsville. The convention was adjourned to Philadelphia, there to commemorate the thirtieth anniversary of the founding of the society in that city, and to rejoice over the partial emancipation of the negro.

In the interim of seven months the fortunes of the Confederacy surged and ebbed. In the summer Lee made his great thrust into the side of Pennsylvania. The fate of the Union and negro freedom depended on whether he was stopped. The North was tiring of the war, the terms of enlistment of her soldiers were expiring, the crucial moment had come. Ewell cleared the Shenandoah Valley of Union troops, crossed the Potomac and moved to Hagerstown, Maryland. "Jeb" Stuart swung between Washington and the Union Army in another daring raid. If success continued, Southern independence was conceded, and the anti-slavery cause retarded indefinitely.

The lady of Roadside awaited each night the news of the city brought home by male members of the family. Anxious days of the War of 1812 were repeated. Citizens of Philadelphia were enlisted in a corps for the protection of the city. Shops were closed. Silent crowds thronged Chestnut Street and pressed about the State House eager for tidings, fearful lest the word should be that Lee was advancing into the heart of Philadelphia, and knocking at the city's gates.

Quiet Roadside lay in the shadow of butternut gray. At Gettysburg Lee was met by Meade. Muskets crackled. Sick and wounded poured into Philadelphia. On the second day Sickles and Ewell battled on the slopes of Cemetery Ridge, and on the third of July, Lee's charging columns were repulsed. On the field at Gettysburg the dead lay uncounted in trenches, and in Philadelphia 4,000 wounded soldiers crowded the hospitals.

When the Abolitionists came together in December, Philadelphia was a city where relief was everywhere visible in the countenances of citizens. Not only the tide of war had turned, but with it also the sentiment against Abolitionism. As an organized movement of a few men and women, Abolitionism was now nearly swallowed up in the great revolution of Northern sentiment about slavery which had been going on since the bombardment of Fort Sumter. Negro companies, singing the John Brown song, marched down State Street in Boston, where Garrison twenty-eight years earlier had been dragged by a mob. The soldiers were cheered by patriots who with equal enthusiasm had cursed Garrison's name.

A happier spirit pervaded the meeting of 1863 than that of 1833. The clash of arms still was heard on several fields, but already three million three hundred thousand former slaves had been freed.

Lucretia saw no ominous crowd gathered in sullen resentment and heard no mutterings as she entered the hall. Citizens did not throw rocks, burn buildings, or shout threats. They respectfully stood aside for the woman who had given the strength of her body and mind for the cause now so closely allied to the pendulum of war. A squad of colored soldiers from Camp William Penn occupied seats on the platform at the opening session. A slave auction block served as the speaker's stand, and the national colors festooned the walls. Many of the delegates in attendance at the first convention in Adelphi Hall were yet alive. Eleven of the forty-five survivors were present who had lived to rejoice over the almost complete realization of their hopes. Only a few had faltered in the battle of freedom and turned back.

Samuel J. May, Miller McKim, and Lucretia regaled the audience with reminiscences of the first convention. In the triumph of success, and in memory of persecutions mutually borne, estrangements between John Greenleaf Whittier, Arthur Tappan, and William Lloyd Garrison were healed, after nearly a quarter of a century. The popular Henry Ward Beecher was present—he who had not been wont to speak on Garrisonian platforms in the unpopular days of the struggle—and gave belated thanks to God that the Garrisonians had been called into being. He lauded them as a *church*—a church without ordination, but a church of the best and most apostolic kind. Victories of soldiers on the battlefield had made Christians of a host of heretics and infidels!

The convention adopted a memorial to Congress asking for a constitutional amendment to prohibit slavery forever within the limits of the United States and adjourned.

In the first quarter of the next year the news came to Roadside that Grant had assumed command of all the Union armies. The states were to be reunited by the stubborn brutality of this general who was to trudge into the White House in boots that oozed blood at every step. A man who never demonstrated publicly the flickering of a truly great or humanitarian idea, a middle-class unsuccessful storekeeper elevated to the highest military office in the land by the values of war, continued the three-year-old story of slaughter and blunder and colossal expense at Cold Harbor. By midsummer Grant's genius had cost the Nation 75,000 men since crossing the Rapidan.

And because it was thought best not to swap horses while crossing a stream, Lincoln was renominated for the presidency of the

United States by the Republican party. The Democrats nominated General McClellan, famous do-little, believing for no apparent reason that he would make a more active President than soldier. The radicals nominated the erratic Frémont. Gloom descended upon the Nation.

Then out of a prostrate South flashed the word that Sherman had entered Atlanta, and on the basis of this argument Lincoln was reëlected President by a large electoral vote. Lee evacuated Petersburg and the crumbling of the South became painful. The surrender at Appomattox village brought to a practical close the saddest civil war fought in history. The death of thousands of boys proved the legal point that the Constitution was indissoluble. Beyond this the war had accomplished nothing definite. Slavery was actually existent and still legally possible.

The close of the war did, however, make the Abolitionists heroes, because they had been on the winning side. The realization dawned on conservatives that a campaign for the freedom of another race, involving no personal gain and whose rewards had been abuse and ostracism, was something worthy of praise.

In Quaker ranks reigned benign contentment. Doves of peace (shopworn from years of fluttering abandonment) cooed in every meetinghouse. Quakers who violently had been opposed to the Abolition movement, or strenuously in favor of "quiet," talked as though at heart they always had been in favor of emancipation. The fact that they had exercised a cautious restraint in expressing their opinions and at times had been so sane as to entirely conceal their enthusiasm for the negro, while it brought them no reward of public adoration, did not embitter the sweets of self-satisfaction. It is the misfortune of judicious persons that while they sometimes earn the tepid respect of both sides, they neither experience the extremity of martyrdom nor the heights of clamorous approbation.

Never had forbearance, courage, patience, and faith more severely been tried, and never more conspicuously rewarded than in the anti-slavery cause. Few reformers have so long worn a crown of thorns to have it transmuted into a wreath of honor. Lucretia and James were no longer obliged to seek shelter at country inns. A new heaven and a new earth was come, wherein dwelt righteousness. The faithful couple was everywhere received as honored and beloved members of the Hicksite Society. Their charity overlooked the inconsistency of congratulations showered upon them by former opponents.

Persons who previously had disclaimed them were busy to tell their friends how intimate they were with the Motts—splendid people! The mail at Roadside was flooded with demands for autographs and "original anti-slavery sentiments" in Lucretia's handwriting. "Skeletons in my house," she called them, nevertheless she was pleased. She found it agreeable, though novel, to be approved. The long, gaunt, sweet Emerson chanted: "What forests of laurel we bring, and the tears of mankind, to those who stood firm against the opinion of their contemporaries."

It is as much an honor today to have an ancestor who spoke on the same platform with Lucretia Mott as to possess a handkerchief owned by one's great-great-grandmother when she danced with Lafayette. It is proudly emblazoned in genealogical dictionaries that one's ancestor kept a station on the Underground Railway.

There is as yet no Society of the Sons of Those Who Burnt Pennsylvania Hall.

CHAPTER XXV

The Negro's Hour

The shot fired at Fort Sumter signalized the close of an era in American history. After four years of bloodshed and sacrifice the rebellion was suppressed, and the people of the Nation turned again to peaceful pursuits. Gopher-like they groped for the scattered channels of existence, expecting to find them where left. But landmarks of social existence had been shot away in the thunder of guns, and monuments of human conduct were scattered by the ravages of passion.

The close of the Civil War marked the line of demarcation between an old and a new era. It began the day of the triumph of business enterprise. The pioneer was no longer the frontiersman trekking with family and Bible over mountain fastnesses, opening new lands and defending new possessions from Indian depredations. The Builders of Empire were men who fought bulls and bears with margins, stocks, and bonds. They trekked on steel rails laid by the sweat of Irish immigrants and Chinese coolies.

The new world was one of industrialism and mass production and business expansion on a scale before unheard of. The clang of the hammer supplanted the low of cattle and the bleat of the shepherd's flocks. Across green pastures were laid the steel rails of the locomotive, soft wooded slopes of hillsides were cut with ugly gashes, and canyons were filled with quarried rock. The shrill whistle of the engine was heard on the prairies, and its fading smoke was the pyre of the Indian and the buffalo. Squat, ugly factories lay snake-like heads by banks of streams; their bowels rumbled and roared with machinery as they drank waters that had long swept unchallenged to the sea.

Man was no longer a peasant, dumb-spoken and down-trodden, but a brightly burnished cog in the machine of life, an important unit in the smooth running mechanism of economic civilization; a part easily replaced from the storehouse of humanity.

The era of the new democracy was ushered in with a new corruption and a new public immorality. The institution of slavery gave way to unbridled exploitation by Big Business. The war for the free-dom of a race and the preservation of the Union had resulted in the substitution of a Wall Street plutocracy for the slave-owning aris-tocracy. The privileges, emoluments, honors, and powers of old rul-ing families, conditioned on landed wealth and slaves, descended to the capitalistic class whose ultimate power of control arose not out of ownership of land and men, but the control of factories and rolling stock.

As a balance wheel to the gross immoralities of public and busi-ness life, the stuffy conventionalities of the mid-Victorian era were fastened onto the home. It was an age of piety in the home and piracy at the office. In the blatant atmosphere of a middle class elevated to sudden wealth and power, the era of moral reform and philosophic thinking suffered decline. The "isms" of the 'forties and 'fifties depreciated in value. They were not investments. They bore no interest. They were speculations without profits. They had no place in the lives of men like Jim Fiske and Jay Gould. New England turned from philosophy to business, and produced the elder J. Pier-pont Morgan in substitution for his grandfather, the Rev. John Pier-pont, poet and Abolitionist.

Conventions to evaluate the humanities were held no longer with such fertility of imagery and staunch vigor. Gradually were substi-tuted conventions of a different character—those of master plumbers and retail pharmacists and associations for the promulgation of a buying consciousness, or the untrammeled transaction of business with-out governmental interference (except to make large grants of land to railroad magnates or to tinker the tariff). The Nation wore fine clothes and developed an intellectual paunch.

The fiery leaders of the old régime met over the bones of Yorick. Garrison, wearied after thirty-two years of heartbreaking labor, was ready to disband the American Anti-Slavery Society, willing and glad to accept the posies of praise everywhere extended him by associates and former enemies, alike. Said he, the cause of the society was "ANTI-Slavery," and this accomplished, the purposes of the society have come to an end. Its puny membership was engulfed in the new "great ocean of popular opinion against slavery." But Wendell Phillips said "No." We have carried the negro, he contended in sub-stance, to the threshold of freedom, and now propose to drop him through the doorway, leaving him with nothing but the contemplation of an abstract status.

During the Presidential campaign Phillips had opposed, and Garrison favored, the reëlection of Lincoln. This had brought about an estrangement between the pair, a fact which Lucretia had thought Garrison had taken "too much to heart."

In the end, Phillips prevailed, and took over the leadership of the American Anti-Slavery Society. He cherished the sentiment, strong in parts of the North, that the degraded intellect of the negro was due to the repressions of slavery; that given equal opportunities the black man would prove self-supporting and respecting, and become a desirable citizen. Northern clamor, which once had jeered Lucretia, now demanded the ballot for the negro. The South, more consistent, reiterated its monotonous boast that it, alone, understood the negro.

In the midst of the controversy, an earthquake shook the Nation more severely than had the news of Brown's raid at Harper's Ferry. In a box at Ford's Theatre in Washington, Abraham Lincoln, sixteenth President of the United States, was shot and fell into a coma that ended with death.

"A beautiful day!" ejaculated Lucretia. "When a great calamity has befallen the nation, we want the sun to be darkened, and the moon not to give her light; but 'how everything goes on,' as Maria said after her dear little Charley died, 'just as though such an awful event had not occurred.' Was there ever such universal sorrow? The 'mirth' of the day before so suddenly 'turned into heaviness.' Men crying in the streets! As we opened our paper, the overwhelming news stunned us, and we could hardly attend to our household duties. . . . . "

Lincoln's death accelerated the growing conflict between Congress and the presidency over Reconstruction. By a resolution passed February 1, 1865, Congress submitted to the legislatures of the several states the constitutional amendment which forever banished slavery from American soil.

How changed the land! Slavery was dead. The thing which the timid had thought impossible or dreadful in the middle of the century was accomplished and, being done, the timid rejoiced with the brave. Whittier, who once had feared tar and feathers, dashed off a poem:

> "It is done!
> Clang of bells and roar of gun,
> Send the tidings up and down.
> How the belfries rock and reel!
> How the great guns peal on peal,
> Fling the joy from town to town."

Shooting guns and ringing bells were easy enough, but there were problems spawned by the war besides political reconstruction. Not the least important were those of feeding and educating the new-freed negroes—men, women and children—a situation which had presented itself early in the war when the advance of Union armies had swept hordes of slaves within military lines.

As women had no participation in politics, Lucretia's energies were attracted to the organization and maintenance of Freedmen's associations for the purposes, first, of relieving the acute demand for bread and, next, of promoting industry and the power of self-support among negroes.

At Washington, Charles Sumner sat himself down to the task of writing a Fourteenth Amendment to prevent the disfranchisement of the African citizen by the several states. He found it impossible to enlarge the suffrage without making mention of the word "male," in order to prevent its application to black womanhood. To have given the negro woman the ballot would have brought down upon the Republican party the wrath of a Nation not ready for universal suffrage. Suffrage for the black male was all the strain the radical party could stand.

Sumner's proposed amendment inserted the objectionable discrimination of sex for the first time into the organic law of the land. The woman's rights leaders were quick to perceive the significance of the phraseology which would make it more difficult than ever for them to obtain the vote. Sumner and the Abolitionists had abandoned the suffragettes in the name of that negro philanthropy which owed so much to the courage of white womanhood.

The menace of the Fourteenth Amendment invigorated the cause that had lain dormant during four years of war. A brilliant, dreamy-looking young journalist, Theodore Tilton, came forward with the proposal of the formation of a National Equal Rights Association to demand suffrage alike for negroes and women in one amendment.

A call was issued to the scattered membership of the woman's party to come together in New York City at the Church of the Puritans in Union Square. Here was held the first woman's assembly since before the war, and here was begun the movement proper for woman suffrage. Nearly twenty years had elapsed since Seneca Falls when Mrs. Stanton boldly had demanded the right of suffrage and Lucretia had thought it premature. Since that time the activities of women had been directed mainly to the acquirement of legal, social, and economic rights. It was the prospect of the negro's being boosted over their heads that attracted their attention at this time to the subject of the ballot.

It was decided by the members of the rejuvenated woman's movement that their organization should adopt the name American Equal Rights Association, and that its stated purpose should be to obtain the ballot for white women, and negroes male and female. A memorial to Congress was adopted quoting a part of Sumner's great speech, "Equal Rights for All," and demanding that the proposed Fourteenth Amendment to the Constitution should grant equal suffrage to men and women.

Lucretia was particularly desirous that there should be a preamble to the association's constitution, which would preserve for posterity the information that the new organization was the outgrowth of the woman's rights movement. Mrs. Stanton was suggested for president, but she hastily expressed a desire to see Lucretia first in that office, that it "might ever be held sacred in the memory that it had been filled by one so loved and honored by all." She concluded with the promise that she would be happy as vice-president to relieve her aged friend of the arduous duties of office if Lucretia would but give the blessing of her name.

Lucretia was escorted to the chair occupied by her throughout the society's existence. During the course of a few remarks she rejoiced in the inauguration of a movement broad enough to cover class, color, and sex. She admitted happiness to lend her name and influence to the movement if only it might encourage the young and strong to carry on the work too strenuous for her seventy-three years.

In some closing remarks she called the attention of the members of the association to the fact that all great achievements in the progress of the human race must be slow, and are ever wrought out by the few, in isolation and ridicule. "Let us remember," she concluded, "in our trials and discouragements, that if our lives are true, we walk with angels—the great and good who have gone before us."

Lucretia's active days were past. The years had been kindly, but each one piled on so many before had left its trace. Her mind was vigorous and her indomitable interest in human welfare buoyed her aloft despite feebleness of body. Yet she never fully had recovered from the death of her daughter Elizabeth in the fall of 1865. This had produced a noticeable listlessness. She rallied under the excitement of a social call, a little opposition in conversation made her seem as well as ever, but in the absence of such incentives to effort, she was dispirited, and often tortured with dyspeptic pains.

There were times when she dreaded the labors of public life. This is pathetically illustrated in a letter written by her while on a visit to New York State, at the home of a niece. Elizabeth Stanton, Susan B. Anthony, Lucy Stone, all so much younger than Lucretia, took lunch together. "Elizabeth was like herself, full of spirits, and so pleasant. . . . . This Equal Rights movement is no play—but I *cannot* enter into it! Just hearing their talk and the reading makes me ache all over, and glad to come away and lie down on the sofa . . . . to rest. . . . . I hadn't much rest! Tomorrow we lunch at Sarah Hicks', and then come back to company to tea; something all the time. On First-day I dined at Hannah Haycock's after Fifteenth st. meeting; found S. B. Anthony waiting for me to go somewhere in a carriage with her to meet Horace Greeley and an Hon. Mr. Griffing. I just *couldn't* do it. Moreover, Susan and some others were to meet in Joralemon st. to discuss enlarging the 'Friend' to admit Equal Rights, and they wanted me to go hear Beecher and have him talk with us afterwards, preparatory to his speech in Albany—but I *couldn't* do that any more than the other! There is no rest!"

Driving, indefatigable Susan begged her to write a message, if only a line, for the annual Equal Rights Convention at Albany, but this equally taxed the woman never facile with the pen. Susan at forty-six was full of energy. Her proddings came hard on the failing strength of the woman who had been through so many exhausting battles, and now sought only a little quiet.

A month to the day after the opening of the convention that had resolved itself into the Equal Rights Association, Lucretia was visited by Susan and two gentlemen with wives, and there was "a great deal of talk; and there was a great deal of fault-finding," said Lucretia afterwards. One apparently did not satisfy Susan on the woman question, or she him on the negro problem, "and so we had it. I weary of everlasting complaints, and am glad sometimes that I shall not have much more to do in any of these movements. One thing is certain; that I do not mean to be drawn into any party feeling."

Yet she honored Susan's and Elizabeth's "devotion to their great work," and meant to "try to coöperate as circumstances admit." She regretted that the Equal Rights Association estranged many formerly staunch supporters of the woman's movement. It had the approval of the Boston intellectuals to a considerable number, but Wendell Phillips was distinctly cool, and the conduct of Garrison, Gerrit, Smith, Higginson, and the negro Douglass, was chilly. These men feared that the proposition of votes for women would jeopardize the chances of the negro who, it was plausibly explained, was more in need of the ballot in the South than were women of the North.

It was the negro's hour. The schism inevitable in every reform was under way. Blunt Susan expressed her opinion that this was "harvest time for the black man, and seed-sowing time for woman." She was one of the few leaders not deceived by the inducement offered her sex that if its members would abandon opposition to the proposed Fourteenth Amendment, woman suffrage would be provided for by law as soon as the negro had been entrenched; a promise kept after much persuasion—fifty-four years later.

The slightest opposition to the Fourteenth Amendment called forth hisses and denunciation from audiences that formerly had booed the mention of negro freedom. Equal rights leaders were everywhere waylaid and implored to avoid all discussion on the impending amendment. Only the Reverend Samuel J. May, Parker Pillsbury, S. S. Foster, and Robert Purvis, of the old Abolition school, remained loyal to the women. Purvis confessed shame to vote before his wife and daughter, but shame or no shame, this was what the radical Republicans were bent on making possible. Northern women and beaten patricians of the South were seated in a game where black cards took all the tricks.

When it was discovered that women Abolitionists were to have no voice in Republican party councils, that the sex had been sacrificed on the altar of expediency, Elizabeth and Susan turned to the hated Democrats who, with a logic that was only political, now became the vocal adherents of woman suffrage (the while denying the ballot to the negro).

Grandiloquent Republican phrases uttered in support of the Thirteenth Amendment were tauntingly tossed into Republican teeth by gleeful Democratic Congressmen who asked if Chinese coolies and Indians were not brothers, and why exclude fifteen million women in the noble scramble for suffrage?

The Republican press rather weakly wagered that women who were in favor of the ballot for themselves would even go so far as to discard the highly feminine virtues of "hoops, waterfalls, and bandeaus" if granted the privilege of voting. Equal rights women were withered old maids who couldn't get a husband even with all the arts of construction in "waterfalls" and "the employment of cotton-padding."

The question was not put whether the Nation was ready for woman's suffrage. The question asked was whether equal right's women would support negro suffrage after their own claims had been denied. Lucretia thought women had a right to be a little jealous at the addition of so large a number of men to the voting class, for colored men would naturally throw all their strength upon the side of those opposed to woman's enfranchisement.

Even Edward M. Davis was hostile to his mother-in-law's position on the Fourteenth Amendment, and spoke to that effect in her presence at a public convention where she occupied the chair. He was replied to by the presiding officer, with her customary tolerance. Lucretia realized that it was her son-in-law's honest opinion that if women sought suffrage in the Fourteenth Amendment, the defeat of the negro's claim was assured. Davis was undoubtedly right.

The Fourteenth Amendment, and a Fifteenth Amendment, like the Thirteenth, became law, and women for a half century were to be helplessly mired in an increased male opposition. In January, 1868, Elizabeth Stanton and Susan B. Anthony began the publication in New York of a weekly paper called "The Revolution," to promulgate their ideas in the long struggle which now confronted their sex. In "The Revolution's" office they hung a portrait of Lucretia Mott who, by the language of the Fifteenth Amendment, was the civil and political inferior of the negro she had helped to free.

CHAPTER XXVI.

The Death of James Mott

The summer and autumn of 1867 were seasons of quiet happiness to James and Lucretia. Both were in better health and spirits than for several years past. Their surviving children, all but one, were living within easy distance; grandchildren were growing up, and friends were everywhere. A colorful, peaceful sunset, after midday storms, suffused a tender glow on the porches of Roadside. It was an hour of pleasant recollections. Lucretia had either outlived her enemies, or they had grown to partially believe what she so long had taught.

Life was not all bucolic peace. There were days of activity and excitement, for Lucretia could not cut herself apart from the world, nor would the world permit her. The couple had pleasant rides together in the new leisure, sometimes to the city, or neighboring town of Germantown, and occasionally through the winding country into hilly Montgomery or fertile Chester counties. Lucretia enjoyed riding with her husband for the sake of his company, although she admitted sometimes to sleep. Caring nothing for crops or landscapes, she took her knitting with her and worked while she rode. The labor required no eyesight and was not a bar to conversation.

She and James were much in demand at weddings, especially of young couples who were children of old friends. They liked to hear Lucretia's remarks upon such occasions for they knew her admonitions were based on theory and practice happily blended.

Fame and popularity and the burdens of nearly three-quarters of a century did not vitiate Lucretia's interest in mankind. She still held opinions on numerous matters that were not popular, even though she, personally, had become acceptable to polite society. The fawning smiles of fortune never lulled her into a rocking-chair old age which accepted things as they were. No one enjoyed approbation more than she, yet she never let this trait of character divert her from the path of duty, no matter how unpleasant the consequences.

Attending a wedding officiated by the mayor of Philadelphia, that officer heard her murmur in an undertone "husband and wife" after

he had pronounced the couple to be "man and wife." Asking the elderly witness why she made this distinction she replied that the marriage
ceremony left man still a man and woman still a woman, that the
magistrate had only to pronounce the new relation in which the couple
stood, "husband and wife." The old formula left the woman a mere
appendage. The mayor was impressed with the reasonableness of the
argument, and thereafter never again used the term "man and wife."

The mornings at Roadside were the part of the day spent most in
contentment. Lucretia's practice was to arise before anyone else in
the house was stirring, and in the dewy air to pick her basket of peas
or similar task, usually completed by seven o'clock. Nothing so
refreshed her as the odor of the moist earth in the early morning
before the hot sun had parched it. A slight shower was no hindrance
to this practice; her tiny form would take shelter under the pea vines
until the heavens were dry again. She liked also to pick raspberries
and blackberries with James in the summer afternoons; she hardly as
tall as the vines, he head and shoulders above them, together at their
task.

During the summer and early fall of 1867 there was unusual
social activity at Oak Farm and Roadside, and a bustle of young people. James commenced a round of visits of the meetings about Philadelphia, where he spoke at each. He was no orator and seldom had
felt called upon to engage in this kind of work, satisfying himself
customarily with the business side of reformatory and church conventions. But he was a man ripe in experience, and great in the virtues
of tolerance and kindliness. For the first time he was "concerned"
to make such a tour in order to speak to the young people on the
subject of education and to interest them in the success of Swarthmore
College.

In the autumn of the year he and Lucretia spent a week near Boston; their last trip together. Lucretia preached Sunday morning in
the hall of the Parker Fraternity. At the close many persons crowded
up to speak to her, among them Lord and Lady Amberly, parents of
Bertrand Russel, the philospher. A daughter born soon after the
English couple's return to their homeland was named Rachel
Lucretia.

Lady Amberly announced the event to her American friend:
"Your picture hangs up in my room, and she shall be taught to

venerate and love her unknown and far-off namesake, whom I hope some day she may resemble to some extent, in all those noble, true, and feminine qualities which will always make yours a known and honored name to all lovers of truth, justice, and humanity."

The close of the happy summer and autumn was accepted with reluctance. A few months were to change the happy ripeness of life. Perhaps with a premonition of what might any day happen the elderly parents bade a sad farewell to their son and family as the latter embarked for an extended European tour. The lively house at Oak Farm was sold. Winter settled down bleakly on Roadside.

About the middle of February the couple decided to visit Brooklyn, where dwelt a married daughter, and to attend the wedding of two young people, children of old friends, who particularly desired their presence. James contracted a cold on the way which he diagnosed as trifling, but which soon developed into pneumonia. During the first few days of illness, he several times uttered the wish to be at home. This being impossible, he resigned himself to the situation, then unexpected, saying: "But I suppose I shall die here, and then I shall be at home; it is just as well." Throughout his illness he was the object of the unremitting attention of his younger brother Richard, a former member of Congress, who chanced to be visiting from Toledo, Ohio.

Early on the morning of the 26th of February the life of James Mott quietly ended. He breathed his last in peaceful sleep while his wife, worn with the night's watch, rested her head on his pillow and slept, too, as life slipped from the figure at her side; with him in death as she had been at his side in every thought and action in the fifty-seven years of their wedded life.

In the silent dawn of winter morning their daughter looked with awe upon the two still faces, one calm in the repose of death, the other serenely unconscious of the sorrow that would greet her awakening.

What had she to awaken to? All in life that was worth while had gone—gone without good-bye. Her dear one had slipped away without her knowledge, never to be seen again. Frail as was Lucretia, the family feared she would not survive the shock. But her mind was susceptible to great adjustments. Though much broken by the heavy affliction that had come so suddenly, she bore the stroke better

than expected. Her etherealized frame which seemed ready to succumb at the slightest touch, recoiled to the blow. The strong man,
though nearly eighty years of age, had been of such robust health
that no one had thought but he would outlive the frail wife.

Lucretia took up her daily life as nearly as possible in its accustomed routine and tried to fulfill the duties that remained with cheer-
fulness and resignation. She bore along, remembering with satisfaction the outburst of sympathy her husband's death had aroused. How
out of the fulness of their hearts friends had spoken words of love
of the good man who had been so kindly and so patient to friend
and foe.

The world was better because he had lived in it; the world had
rarely been blessed with such a light as had been his wedded life.
What he had been as a husband, no one knew so well as herself; what
he had been as a father, only his children could depict; what he had
been as a friend, a vast multitude could testify with glowing hearts;
what he had been as a public benefactor, an untiring philanthropist, and
a true and courageous reformer, the record of his long and most
beneficent life showed in luminous characters. Said William Lloyd
Garrison, "He seemed to me to lack nothing as a good and noble
man."

Nothing better summarized the beauty of the character of the
man who at the time of his death was president of the Pennsylvania
Anti-Slavery Society and the Pennsylvania Peace Society than his love
for children. He had often pressed upon parents the duty of teaching by gentleness. He would say, "Never threaten, and never promise
reward, and be very careful to consider before you say 'no'; say 'yes'
as often as you can." And when he heard of punishment inflicted on
children he would counsel patience, saying, "I wouldn't punish them
for trifles; they grow older every day, and will soon know for
themselves."

Although Lucretia resumed the tenor of her way a sense of desolation was with her to the end. She never again slept in the chamber
which she and her husband had occupied together, but took for herself
a tiny room with a window to the east, commanding the sunrise. With
this room the last memories of the woman are associated.

She now rarely attended Sunday meetings, poignant with memories
of a lost companion. She cared less for public gatherings of any
kind. Her delight was to attend the midweekly meeting in Philadel-

phia, which was attended by children from the Friends' Central School. She liked their fresh young faces and said they helped her to forget her own increasing feebleness, and mitigated her loneliness.

It was difficult to realize that James was actually gone, the strong man upon whose arm she had leaned through many years of persecution, the silent man always at her side with sympathy and understanding when the world mocked or sneered.

Scarcely a day passes that I do not think, [she wrote] of course for the instant only, that I will consult him about this or that. . . . . It discourages me to find that my memory is failing. When I found this morning that I had written the same thing twice, I put aside my pen, went into the garden and gathered peas for dinner, came in and shelled them, and have since read the "Radical," and looked into "Friends' Intelligencer," and some other periodicals, and wished we only took half the number.

She wrote a daughter: "Are you thinking this day, that two months have passed since the memorable night and day? Every day and night since has been counted by me, and the untiring subject of thought finds expression wherever there are ears to hear and sympathetic hearts to beat in unison. . . . . Mine are not tears of bitterness, but of tenderness. Excessive grief is lamentable, if not reprehensible. I do not mourn, but rather remember by blessings, and the blessing of his long life with me."

Life at Roadside became very quiet to the woman who always had loved action. "Maria and I are day after day alone. Edward comes out to a late dinner. Ellis and Margaret drove over the other evening by bright moonlight, and passed an hour or so on the piazza. But oh! the great blank! Your dear father was ever there these warm summer evenings, and we seem to miss him more there than in the house, if that is possible."

She felt, too, the absence of Robert Collyer, who was in the Middle West. "We were saying the other evening as we sat on the piazza in the moonlight, Edward, Maria, and I, how few friends we had left to come and sit with us, as Robert Collyer used to do, and how we missed in a thousand ways the beloved occupant of the large chair out there," where James had been wont to sit.

"Tom and Fanny are here for a few days, and their merry laugh takes us back to the happy days of Roadside, before the glory departed. Alas!"

CHAPTER XXVII

FREE RELIGION

Early a transcendentalist, as Lucretia grew older she became increasingly rationalistic. She made many startling statements about religion which in former years might have led to disownment from the Quaker church. The Civil War had shown her to have been so early in the right of Abolitionism that she was considered a prophet among her people, and what she said was accepted by lesser lights with possessive pride, especially by members of her church who did not grasp the full significance of her radical utterances.

What if she did say that religion in time would become so practical, so living, that she wondered what use the increasing number of churches would be put to, as civilization outgrew them? What if she did preach natural religion, philosophy, and skepticism of what lay beyond the grave? What if she did say that a great deal of time and effort had been spent in the sphere of poetic fancy, picturing the glory and joy of a kingdom hereafter, when what was chiefly required of man was to come into the divine government *now* on earth? What if she did charge that people were changing their ideas of religion even though they clung to the form of ancient creeds? What if she did deny that the daily minutiæ of man were controlled by an Almighty God influenced by a council of saints and the prayers of priests? What if she did preach a religion which was defiant of antiquity and old interpretations?

After all, she was a very famous person, and famous persons are entitled to make bold utterances.

Quakers who had not had a fresh thought since adolescence blinked benignly as Lucretia charged, "What feeble steps have been taken from Popery to Protestantism! Our ecclesiastics, be they Bishops, or Quaker Elders, have still far too much sway. Convents we have yet, with high walls, whose inmates having taken the veil, dare not give range to their free-born spirit, now miserably cramped and shrouded."

No one complained when she made the startling statement that Jesus had not taught any new principle; that Christians made a mistake when they dated the commencement of true religion eighteen hundred years back, and that no nation had a spiritual language exclusively its own; that there was a religious essence in man; that the records of all ages showed this instinct in man, varying in accordance with the circumstances of birth and education, and the exercise of free agency. She admitted that where there was ignorance there was barbarism and superstition. But, she affirmed, all through the ages there had been striking instances of righteousness, goodness, and truth among pagan peoples, and these to a far greater extent than Biblical history furnished.

Having witnessed Indians at their strawberry festivals and dances and religious operations, she had thought there was, perhaps, as much reasonableness and rational worship therein as in passing around the little bread and wine, or in some of the peculiarities of her own people the Quakers, for all sects, all denominations, she affirmed, had their tendency to worship in the letter rather than the spirit.

She boldly prophesied the coming of the day of universal religion. The Great Spirit of the Indian, the Quaker "inward light" of George Fox, the "blessed Mary, mother of Jesus," of the Catholics, or Brahma the Hindoo God, would eventually be deemed the same thing, and when this was accomplished there would "come to be such a faith, and such liberty" as should "redeem the world."

A startling attitude for a person on the brink of the grave was her cheerful doubt of even well planned prognostications of what lay the other side of death. Being intellectually honest, she came close at times to agnosticism. Scattered over a period of forty years there are but few references to immortality in her writings. As early as 1840 she had told Elizabeth Cady Stanton that "no one knows any more of what lies beyond our sphere of action than thou and I; and we know nothing." This summed her attitude towards what she often described as the "unprofitable speculations" of churchmen on the subject of Heaven.

She was content to leave the impenetrable mystery of death in the hands of Infinite Beneficence. She is known to have written but one letter regarding the future, and this was in reply to a friend who, in the agony of heavy bereavement, had written her for consolation. Lucretia's reply, written a few years after her own dear husband's death, during a period of loneliness and mourning at an age past seventy-five, illustrates how the writer clung to principles.

She wrote how gladly she would send a consolatory letter, "but alas! While the faith of many sympathizers with the bereaved can present beautiful pictures of the blessedness of the departed, and their assurance of a happy reunion, I can only say with the Apostle, 'It doth not yet appear what we shall be,' and try to be satisfied with the consciousness that *now* are we the children of God; with the fullness of hope, and such an earnest of the kingdom of Heaven as may be in completion hereafter—and always with the *idea* that our nearest and dearest immortals are waiting for us."

After the death of a grandchild, a friend criticized how little faith had Lucretia because she failed to dwell on the nearness of Heaven "as a known fact," to which Lucretia had replied that it was because "we have so much faith, and a firm trust that all will be well, that we indulge no vain curiosity as to 'what we shall be.'"

When a stricken sister described the death of one of her children as a "special Providence," and pictured her little son "in an angelic embrace in the ethereal world" with his grandmother, Lucretia replied that "it is a beautiful thought—would that its reality were capable of demonstration," but, she asked, "why speak of 'special Providences?' We can but consider them 'dark and inexplicable.' But when we come to look at all these seeming inflictions, as the operations of the natural laws, while the pang of parting with our loved ones is none the less, we are not left so in the dark, nor do we take such gloomy views of 'the ways of Providence.' In thy letter thou says, 'Charlie's death was so decreed. It is beyond mortal power to say *why* decreed.' I would ask if it is not equally impossible to *prove* it 'so decreed?' While, on the other hand, tracing all effects in nature to their legitimate causes, we may with more knowledge say why death ensues when malignant disease visits; and why malignant disease visits our abodes, in these populous cities, where the poor are crowded into unventilated rooms, and in the universal linking of our interests and our sufferings, 'strikes down our fairest and our best beloved.' . . . .

"We mourn the dead, because nature has so constituted us; not on their account always, nor is the sorrow purely selfish. When people die before they have lived half their days, it seems contrary to the design of their creation; the world loses their usefulness, and they lose so much of the enjoyment of life, that all these considerations inspire sadness at their departure. . . . . "

287

Thoughts such as these were rare in a day when people preferred to believe that children who died young were gathered in an early harvest to sit with the angels in a sort of socially registered heavenly Blue Book. The anodyne was expressed in the slogan "The good die young."

It was easier and less expensive to say that death was due to God's providence than to carry on a campaign for improved sanitation. The shift of blame to God raised no objections from gentlemen of wealth who rented squalid homes to poverty-stricken tenants, and were not infrequently elders in the church. Such men controlled religion and made city ordinances, and had a mighty advantage over the non-elect.

Lucretia's interest in rational religion led her, despite a feeble state of health and the burden of seventy-four years, to make the arduous journey to Boston when invited to attend a meeting for the purpose of organizing the Free Religious Association.

She was introduced to the audience as a loyal friend of liberal religion. The Free Religious Association came nearest to Lucretia's ideal of a religious organization than any she had ever known. No reform since the close of the anti-slavery struggle absorbed her attentions so warmly, except the cause of peace. With considerable regularity she attended the anniversary meetings of the new society.

The famous Thomas Wentworth Higginson described her appearance upon one such occasion: "Dear old Lucretia Mott spoke. She said that long ago in noting the failing powers of a speaker, she told her daughters she herself would stop speaking at sixty. Her daughters think 'mother takes a long time in being sixty,' as she is now past eighty and still spoke half an hour clearly and forcibly."

In 1873 Lucretia made what she thought would be her last speech to the association which had endeared itself to her from the beginning. At this time she expressed her satisfaction of a change in the association's constitution, made at her suggestion, that a purpose of the society was to encourage the scientific study of the religious element in man rather than the scientific study of "theology." Dilating on the point, she told her audience of a visit from Dr. Channing years ago at her house and how, when he attempted to advocate his views about what everlasting progress there should be in the hereafter, she had told him it was as interesting to her as any speculation on the subject to which she had ever listened, but he must allow her to say that it was speculation still.

LUCRETIA MOTT, SOCIAL PIONEER

At the age of eighty-three Lucretia made her last address on the Free Religious platform. Coming towards the end of the program, she opened her remarks with the apology that it seemed to her very kind in an audience to be willing to stay and "listen to the humble words of an old Quaker woman." Accepting some flowers that were brought up to her, she related many interesting personal reminiscences of days when she had been a pioneer in free religion and had found few comrades with whom to commune.

Her voice was heard not again on the platform of the Free Religious Association, but she was not forgotten. At the thirty-third annual convention held at Boston, June 11, 1900, an address was given in her memory as one of the country's great leaders of liberal religion. Said a speaker upon that occasion:

Those of us who were privileged to attend the earlier meetings of this Association, in Horticultural Hall and the old Tremont Temple, remember that saintly yet fragile figure—but not too saintly to be human or to fight vigorously for the things that she believed to be true, especially if they were unpopular—Lucretia Mott. She certainly is to be numbered among the saints of Free Religion.

CHAPTER XXVIII
PACIFISM

In the last decade of Lucretia's life the peace movement overtopped all other interests. Even votes for women did not take hold of her as did the campaign to abolish war. After her husband's death she succeeded him as president of the Pennsylvania Peace Society.

Despite the Franco-Prussian War in Europe and civil war at home recently ended, Lucretia was encouraged to believe that the battlefield would eventually be abolished by an enlightened people, just as slavery had been abolished when first the task had seemed impossible. Her influence for peace was greater because of her untarnished record of obedience to principle during the Civil War. It was remembered that she had been an early member of the non-resistant society founded by Garrison which had embraced pacifism so thoroughly that it had emanated an offensive stench to the nostrils of even the members of the American Peace Society.

The first pacifist of the century to attempt on a large scale the organization of public opinion in the interests of practical peace had been, not Garrison, but Elihu Burritt, "the learned blacksmith." Burritt was an idealist who did much hard labor. In association with William Ladd of the American Peace Society he had assembled an international congress of delegates in place of visionary utopias previously conceived by idealists, thereby taking a practical step towards the idea of international unity and open discussion.

When the Oregon question had threatened war between England and the United States, he had mobilized the working classes of both countries to express anti-war sentiment, a novel idea in days when working men shared no part in foreign affairs except as cannon fodder. On a large scale he had utilized the press by incisive bits of peace propaganda called "olive leaves," and had organized Olive Branch Circles in British and American cities to exchange sentiments on the mutual profits of trade to be derived from peace.

Merchants and mayors of English cities wrote to merchants and mayors of American cities, and vice versa. Plymouth, England, memorialized Plymouth, Massachusetts, and new Boston greeted old Boston. As many as 3,525 Philadelphia women had responded to

Lucretia's plea and signed a friendly address to the women of Exeter, England, in one of the largest of these letters.

Lucretia had written friends in Ireland that she hoped Elihu Burritt and other lovers of peace "in this land and yours" would avert the impending danger of war between the countries. "Our politicians and demagogues may make a great bluster, and your nation may expend much in preparation for battle; but let the moral power of the friends of peace be exerted and we may hope the sword will be stayed."

What share peace propaganda had in the settlement of the Oregon question cannot be identified with certainty. Perhaps the alliance of Southern cotton fields with British capital had more to do with it than olive branches.

Successful in some degree in preventing a third war between America and the mother country, Burritt and his associates had been signally unsuccessful in avoiding the clash with Mexico. A forest of olive trees could not have obstructed the course of Manifest Destiny in 1846.

The determination of the wars of the Revolution and 1812 had ushered in an era of intense nationalism in America. Self-glorification and conceit require no organized societies. On every hand and in every paper it was heard or read that "ours is the elect nation for the age to come . . . . we are the chosen people . . . . the only free men on earth." The sentiment had grown that the Stars and Stripes should wave in unbroken ripples from Bar Harbor, Maine, to the Golden Gate, even from Hudson's Bay to the Isthmus of Panama. Manifest Destiny champed its bit. The eagle spread his wings and shrieked defiance.

The controversy over Texas and California—evidence that "greedy" England might be thinking of seizing land "patriotic" Americans wanted—bred suspicion and jingoism. On March 4, 1845, James K. Polk took the oath of office as eleventh President of the United States. Everything was in readiness for the greatest land grab in American history. Polk was not one to graft olive branches onto the tree of statesmanship. The easiest way to keep California from going British was to annex it to the United States. Accordingly, Polk acted the bully over the issue of the eastern boundary of Texas, and ordered troops to take up a position in the valley of the Rio Grande in the disputed strip of territory between Texas and Mexico.

General Worth had led the army of occupation; in contemporary language "gallantry leading the way in the first venturous crossing of the Colorado," and had pitched camp on the left bank of the Rio Grande, opposite Matamoras. A tense situation created, it was not long ere guns were discharged, blood had been shed, and the manpower of America was called to "defend" its institutions—mainly slavery and the real estate business.

The war spirit zoomed. On every hand Lucretia heard the cry, "Our country has been invaded and Amercian blood spilled on American (proposed) soil." She heard, too, the musical productions of the pre-tinpan alley played by every orchestra in the country. The Nation resounded to the stirring music of "General Worth's Grand March" and "General Worth's Quick Step," and songs warranted to excite the pulse if they did not nourish the brain.

From Europe Burritt had sought Lucretia's aid in obtaining for him a list of all the Sabbath schools in Philadelphia with the names of the superintendents in order to establish a correspondence on the subjects of peace, love, and liberty. Lucretia confessed she had not faith enough in the efficacy of the measure, nor indeed in Sunday school operations in general, to enter into it very heartily.

She did, however, take the letter to the agent of the Sunday School Union, but he declined to furnish the list, giving the excuse that Sunday schools only instilled general principles, leaving details to other schools and parents. Lucretia came away ruminating on the maxim that when a Nation is at war it is best for churches not to be too specific about the brotherhood of man and the peace that passeth all understanding.

The Immediate Emancipationists, one hundred per cent. strong, repudiated the slaveholders' war, as they identified it; and one hundred per cent. Americans were confirmed in the belief of many years growth that humanitarianism had gnawed out the heart of patriotism. Like a worm in an apple it had consumed the sterling virtues of mankind which were the worship of the prevalent religion and the defense of the prevalent flag.

No expression can be found in Lucretia's letters to show that she was thrilled by the exploits of that graceful and dashing cavalier, her kinsman Worth, whose tall and erect form had been the first to enter Mexico City, where he had cut the flag that waved from the national palace and unfurled the Stars and Stripes in the land of the Montezumas.

Fortunately for Lucretia the war with Mexico had been not more than a series of setting-up exercises for the American armies. There had been no need of a Criminal Syndicalism Act, and she had not been silenced by law. In fact, opposition to the war had been openly and vociferously carried on in many parts of the North where there had been talk of secession.

While the roll of drums and the treble of the fife were being heard in the land, a Hicksite minister by the name of Jackson inopportunely published a small treatise entitled "Reflections on Peace and War." The author's purpose had been to demonstrate that war was at variance with the Christian religion, and to question the divine inspiration of the Jewish wars of the Old Testament. The book aroused a storm of criticism (not among irreligious politicians or money-mad capitalists so often accused of fomenting wars, but among the church people of the Nation who preached the principles of Christ).

Most Quakers were opposed to the book on "principle," many were afraid to suffer it in their homes; very few read it. When at a Quaker meeting in Ohio Lucretia had recommended it to women in place of the frivolous periodicals of the day, a spirited reply had been made by a local minister who expressed astonishment that a Quaker minister should recommend a book "that despised the Bible."

Long before the publication of Jackson's book, and antedating the formation of the New England Non-Resistance Society, Lucretia had expressed the opinion that war had no divine sanction. Repeating this thought to Garrison in days when he was still a Calvinist, he had been at first startled, not to say shocked, as he described it "on hearing the determination from her lips, that she did not believe God ever authorized or sanctioned war, in any age or nation. . . . . Not that I," commented Garrison, "had any doubt as to the prohibition of all war in the New Testament, but I had never thought of questioning the integrity of the Jewish record. 'How do you dispose of the statements made in the Old Testment,' I asked, 'that the Lord commanded Moses, Joshua, and others, to wage even wars of extermination?'"

Quietly the Qaukeress had replied, "I can more easily believe that man is fallible, than that God is changeable."

Had Garrison not been converted to the idea of the total sinfulness of war, America would have lost a cog in the movement for world peace. Education was a remedy proposed by Lucretia. The need for this she preached in many sermons. She was convinced that when men evolved to a disposition to redress national grievances by means other than physical, they would find a way to accomplish that end. It was necessary first to bring them to the proper way of thinking.

Of course, there were many persons who accused her, in this as in Abolitionism, of having no practical or specific plan of relief; but a survey of man's progress demonstrates the truth that first there must come the seer with vision, and next the educator to wing desire, and thirdly the man of action to give shape to dreams. Too often the statesman, who takes up the burden at the point where popular opinion has been crystalized by the pioneer, is accorded a share of fame in excess of his deserts. The world requires the dreamer and the teacher and the motivator, and although there is truth in the accusation that the dreamer is scarcely ever the man of action, seldom is the latter the prophet of man's noblest aspirations.

Long before Lucretia's death practically every modern plan for securing peace had been anticipated. A plan almost identical in outline to the draft which created the twentieth century League of Nations and the world Court had been an essay winner as early as 1840. Late in life Lucretia addressed a meeting at New York convened to lay plans for the calling of a world's convention of women in behalf of international peace, and to advocate the settlement of differences between nations by an international court.

While she was president of the local State peace society she rarely allowed anything to interfere with her attendance at executive meetings. A few months before death she attended such a meeting for the last time, but was not strong enough to remain throughout the session.

She would not have been surprised, if she had lived into the twentieth century, to have observed that the clergy which in her day supported war as an ordinance of God, rallied on both sides in the World War, bringing with them in the name of patriotism the split blessings of Almighty God. More to her satisfaction would have been knowledge of the modern church program of pacifism. She might say of modern clerics that, right or wrong, they are more nearly followers of Christ than they have been these nineteen hundred years.

CHAPTER XXIX

FALLING PETALS

"Having known Lucretia Mott, not only in the flush of life, when all her faculties were at their zenith, but in the repose of advanced age, her withdrawal from our midst seems as natural and as beautiful as the changing foliage of some grand oak from the spring-time to the autumn."—ELIZABETH CADY STANTON.

Old age is apt to follow great personages, like the moon the sun, to distort the shadowy shapes of those who have lingered too long. But the years were kind to Lucretia, and she grew venerable without the caricature of mental affliction. She suffered no serious decay, yet year by year, month by month, and finally day by day, the body weakened, the spirit no longer could apply the lash, and she laid herself down to die, serenely and without fear.

She had faith in the universal fitness of Creation; death must inevitably dissolve the physical body. On her death bed she held fast to her integrity, saying: "I do not dread death. Indeed, I dread nothing; I am ready to go or to stay, but I feel that it is time for me to go"; and again, "I am willing to acknowledge all ignorance of the future, and there leave it. It does not trouble me. We know only that our poor remains

'Softly lie, and sweetly sleep
Low in the ground.'"

At half past seven o'clock on the "eleventh day of eleventh month," 1880, the torch flickered out. She was laid to rest Sunday afternoon in the Friends' burying ground at Fair Hill on the Germantown Road in the presence of a large concourse of about two thousand persons, many of whom were representatives of the race she had done so much to free. Before death she had commanded her family, " . . . . remember that my life has been a simple one; let simplicity mark the last done for me."

In the house at Roadside there had been the Quaker season of solemn silence, after which short remarks had been made by those who felt moved to speak. A friend quoted the passage, "Know ye not that there is a prince and a great man fallen this day in Israel." The coffin was carried to the highway by sons and grandsons, and the long procession moved down York Road towards Philadelphia bearing Lucretia on her last journey on the highway to the city over which she had so many times traveled on errands of mercy.

Fair Hill cemetery was a little mound-shaped enclosure, sloping up all sides to the center, and filled with trees and shrubbery, with graves marked only by marble blocks not more than six inches high. In the loftiest part of the mound an excavation had been opened by the side of the body of James, beneath the spreading branches of an aspen tree, and hard by a weeping willow. A quiet, peaceful, secluded spot in the bustle of life.

A profound silence hushed the mourners while the last preparations were made, broken only by a few words by Dr. Henry T. Child. The little coffin, scarcely larger than a child's, was reverently lowered. A voice could stand the suspense no longer, and cried, "Will no one say anything?" And another responded from a full heart, "Who can speak? The preacher is dead!"

Death stills tongues which have spoken, but can never still the truth of words once uttered. The preacher died, but sentiments that were always raised whenever an unpopular truth needed defense, wherever a popular evil needed to be testified against, and wherever a wronged man or woman needed a champion, will live as long as men pay homage to truth and purity.

For this reason we choose not to close the life of Lucretia Mott at the fresh mound. Let us recount in further detail the nearly twelve years of Lucretia's life after the parting of James. There were drives to the beautiful old meetinghouse at Jenkintown, silent and secluded in its location amidst the "Oaks of Abington," one of the most peaceful spots imaginable. Lucretia loved the fine old building, prim and full of dignity, and its noble setting off the York Road. There were trips into the city, visits to the House of Industry, and the Race Street School, meetings at the Old Colored Home, and interest in Freedmen's societies, the peace society, and suffrage conventions, as well as attendance at the midweekly meetings and yearly meetings of Friends at Philadelphia, and occasional participation in the convocations of the Free Religious Association at Boston, a part of which has already been recounted.

FRIENDS' MEETING HOUSE AT JENKINTOWN, PENNSYLVANIA, WHERE LUCRETIA
MOTT WORSHIPPED AFTER HER HUSBAND'S DEATH

Photo by courtesy of Thomas Knight, Philadelphia

There was much to do and many people willing to help. There was solace in the general kindness that everywhere greeted the aging crusader. Instead of averted faces and open condemnation, she was met with manifestations of tenderness and veneration. The quaint little figure of an older day became a venerated object in the bustle of city streets. It was not an unusual occurrence for her to be addressed by strangers with the request that they be allowed to take her hand a moment. Once a woman in deep mourning brushed her by and murmured as she passed, "God bless you, Lucretia Mott."

Fostered in an atmosphere of love and appreciation, her face became transfixed like a saint's. Each year stole something from her physical vigor, and added to her grace of manner. She had lived to see the triumph of a great cause, and her heart was filled with thanksgiving. But as year after year removed old associates and loved companions, a sense of loneliness stole upon her despite her long habit of being constantly engaged in activity to drive away the blues. The younger generation growing up around her could not quite take the place of departed friends, though its members tended her declining steps with care and devotion.

The peace of these years was broken only by internal dissensions in the woman's ranks coming to a head in the white heat of Reconstruction. There were, too, inevitable differences of religion, and divergent views about divorce.

In time Susan and Elizabeth formed the National Woman's Suffrage Society, and Lucy Stone and Mrs. Howe effected an opposing organization named the American Woman Suffrage Association. The president of the American society was potent Henry Ward Beecher, a gentleman (before the fall) more eminently respected than Susan or Elizabeth. Lucretia was not so much interested in the turn towards suffrage as she had been in the earlier struggle for economic and legal equality. Though she retained interest in the woman's movement, she resolved not to be drawn into party spirit. But she could not restrain casting her primary allegiance with the founders of the movement, who were allied with the national party, while she retained friendships also with many old anti-slavery companions in the American Society. These included Robert Collyer, Garrison, Julia Ward Howe, Beecher, Lucy Stone, Colonel Higginson, Grace Greenwood, Lydia Maria Child, Phœbe A. Hanaford, S. S. Foster and wife, Samuel J. May, Mary Grew, George W. Julian, and Gerrit Smith.

The opposing wings did little harm to each other, but the spectacle of friends arrayed against each other in a mutual cause, led to efforts of compromise and reconciliation. Elizabeth proclaimed herself willing to resign as president of the national society if the two factions could be brought together under the generalship of either Beecher or Lucretia. A conference was called to meet at the Fifth Avenue Hotel in New York. Lucretia, who now rarely left home, went all the way from Philadelphia to use her influence in effecting a reunion. The result was a protracted but fruitless conference of four hours. Lucretia's friendly offers which had never before been disregarded failed to effect a purpose.

At this importunate hour, while the national society was busy shaking its skirts of charges of free-loveism (engendered because of Mrs. Stanton's views on divorce), there injected herself into the woman's ranks startling Victoria Woodhull, whose similarity to the good queen ended where the name began. Victoria and her sister, Tennessee Claflin, issued "Woodhull and Claflin's Weekly," in favor of spiritualism, woman suffrage, birth control, and eventually Victoria Woodhull for President of the United States. The sisters defended, and supposedly practiced, "free love." They had had a spectacular career in Wall Street as stock brokers, incongruous with their school education and police records. Their success was explained by rumors that they were protégées of old Cornelius Vanderbilt, and likewise had the aid of spirits, perhaps specters of deceased Wall Street operators who combined the advantages of mundane experience with that of supernatural observation.

Victoria's decision to enter the woman's field was received with shivers of apprehension by the leaders of the movement, who had little sympathy with the most of her principles. In the rôle of free lance, Victoria appeared before a Congressional committee and read a paper urging that women were already entitled to vote under existing constitutional provisions, and that a Sixteenth Amendment was not necessary to confer the ballot. Her paper was so much superior to anything on the subject yet produced by more experienced women that it was generally conceded to be the work of one of the brilliant legal minds of the day.

Elizabeth and Susan were delighted with the paper. Quick to take up the cudgels in defense of any woman under fire, they admitted Victoria into their ranks, believing her a martyr to Victorian cant (the Queen's brand!). They accepted the advice of a tried politician that they could not let go a promising worker because of divergent opinions on alien subjects, if they wished to gain power.

Victoria was presented at a convention to the suffragette public carefully sandwiched on the platform between Elizabeth Stanton and Lucretia Mott for the purpose of conveying the impression of respectability. Rising to the occasion, the notorious convert gave a "Great Secession Speech" in true dramatic style and with plenty of fire and adjectives. She let it be known, if the next Congress refused to give women all the fruits of citizenship, women would call another convention and frame a new Constitution of the United States and, if necessary, a new government. "We mean treason, we mean secession, on a thousand times grander scale than was that of the South," exulted Victoria.

Such a valiant speech had not been heard since days before the war when Wendell Phillips and William Lloyd Garrison had hurled their white-hot bolts into the Nation's face. Victoria sat down in a glow of excitement. Her palpitant frozen beauty moved even Lucretia, who had had her doubts. Paulina Wright Davis was hypnotized, and Horace Greeley joined Vanderbilt in masculine admiration.

Victoria on the platform increased the cry "free love." Even Lucretia's name did not escape the charge by some quirk of excited reasoning. The opponents of the woman's movement were convinced anew that their fears had been always correct. The members of the American Society thanked their lucky stars they were no longer associated with such radicals as Elizabeth Cady Stanton and Susan B. Anthony. Lucy Stone's retention of her maiden name simmered into comparative respectability.

In order to test Victoria's theory of the right of women to vote, Susan cast a ballot at an election, and was promptly arrested and convicted on the charge of voting without lawful right.

When Victoria offered a motion looking forward to the formation of a new political party to elect herself to office, disillusioned Susan awoke to the fact that Victoria was making a tool of the woman's national society. Whereupon Susan adjourned the meeting and ordered the janitor to cut off the lights, and Victoria sputtered out in darkness like a fallen star after a meteorical flight across the suffragette heavens.

Meanwhile death continued to weave in and out among Lucretia's family and friends, delaying always to cut down Lucretia as though unable to bring itself to the task. Beloved sister Elizabeth, cherished companion of seventy years, died within two years of James. Lucretia missed her sorely, and passed her house with an aching sense of desolation and the feeling of "a lone, lorn one left behind." She grieved to a daughter, "It is time for me, too, to rest 'low in the ground,' beside your father's earthly all, and so near two dear daughters."

Five more of the family passed away in the course of the next half dozen years, including youngest sister Martha. Separation from Martha, a fellow laborer, supporter, and sometimes her leader in the woman's movement in respect to new ideas, confidante in domestic as well as public careers, was almost too much to bear.

In the autumn of 1869 Lucretia performed the sad duty of visiting Nantucket to attend the funeral of Nathaniel Barney. Again in the summer of 1876 she visited the home of her childhood and reviewed the old landmarks she had known and loved so well, taking grandchildren and great-grandchildren with her that they might see the land of her fathers and mothers, and drink at wells of inspiration where she had imbibed. She fondly promised herself she would go again, but never regained sufficient strength to undertake the arduous voyage. Weeks slipped into months and months into years before she admitted that she would never more see the land of rolling moors and windswept hills and weather-beaten wharves, the far-flung island over which the spirit of Tristram Coffin and Mary Starbuck ever lives.

Seventy-seven years of age, she attended the funeral of Thomas Garrett, the staunch Moses of fugitive slaves. In attendance were negroes and whites. An intelligent black man, a Methodist minister, and Lucretia were among the speakers. A mourner described her words as a benediction.

One by one she bade farewell at the grave to the companions of her long fighting life. Others became so feeble as to appear decreasingly in public. Giants who had faced the turbulence of the world became the charges of children and grandchildren. Lucretia wrote of herself in 1872, "I fail every week . . . . I weighed yesterday— only seventy-six and a half pounds now!"

Wherever she went she was accompanied by a member of the family or an intimate friend, for as she complained, "I have arrived at the state not to be trusted alone"; then the independent spirit of the spitfire of Nine Partners asserted itself, and she concluded, "therefore I shall soon give up going anywhere." This decision she no better kept than the earlier one to give up speaking at sixty. The wilful spirit continued to preside at occasional meetings.

Her time at home was utilized in the old-fashioned practice of preparing household rags to be woven into carpets, and in turning sheets, hemming towels, or darning stockings. Her reading favored Dean Stanley. His valedictory address at St. Andrews was a preeminent favorite. A newspaper clipping of it became so worn with use that a friend sent her a new one neatly pasted in a small blank book. This she carried in her pocket, more to lend than to read, for she knew much of it by memory.

No characteristic of her long life more marks her freedom from sectarian bigotry than her delight in reading what she called Truth wherever contained. In youth she had revered the writings of Channing, but now she had room in her heart and mind for Stanley. His "Hope of Theology" she kept beside her until her dying day, offering it for a glance to visitors that came to her bedside. Copies of an address by him made on his American tour she bought in large quantities to give away.

Even when she had lived more than eighty years she retained interest in current problems with all her former relish. It is said she was better informed upon the presidential campaign of 1880 than many persons with easier channels of information. In the twilight hours of life she not only recited the poetry of buried generations, but read with thrilling effect the poems of modern day. In the cool of evening she liked to repeat in tones of liquid sweetness whole pages of Cowper's "Task" or Young's "Night Thoughts" or Milton when his lofty strains did not jar upon her wider sense of justice.

Susan B. Anthony remembered how the woman spent an entire evening reading aloud to her household Arnold's "The Light of Asia." In after years Susan recalled the deep and tender voice and its moving sweetness when to young souls about her the woman of more than eighty-seven years read the parting words of Lord Siddartha to his wife and love, as he left her to go forth to save the world:

> My chariot shall not roll with bloody wheels
> From victory to victory, till earth
> Wears the red record of my name. I choose
> To tread its paths with patient, stainless feet.

At the silver anniversary meeting of the woman's movement held at Apollo Hall in New York City, it was especially announced that Elizabeth and Lucretia would be present during the ceremonies. A laurel wreath was presented "to the founder of the Woman's Rights movement, the venerable Lucretia Mott," and it was resolved by the convention "that Lucretia Mott and Elizabeth Cady Stanton will evermore be held in grateful remembrance as the pioneers in this grandest reform of the age."

Another event of interest was the centennial anniversary of the old Pennsylvania Abolition Society held in one of the largest halls in Philadelphia. The place was thronged and the platform crowded with those who had been active in reform. United States Senator Henry Wilson presided and after one or two speakers had been introduced, uttered these words: "I propose now to present to you one of the most venerable and noble of the American women, whose voice for forty years has been heard, and has tenderly touched many noble hearts. Age has dimmed her eye and weakened her voice, but her heart, like the heart of a wise man and wise woman, is yet young. I present to you Lucretia Mott."

As Lucretia came to the front of the platform the vast audience arose with tumultuous applause, waving hats and handkerchiefs, and cheering loudly. The recipient of the honor stood motionless for a time, frail in body, a light beaming in her face, when, in the hush that fell, she raised a voice slightly tremulous, but clear and impressive, and slowly repeated the lines:

> I've heard of hearts unkind, kind words
> With coldness still returning.
> Alas! the *gratitude* of man
> Hath oftener left *me* mourning.

Thus she forgave and forgot the unkind words that had been said of her so many years.

The personal ovation was continued the next year at the Centennial Anniversary of the Declaration of Independence. The year 1876 was one of patriotic exultation and enthusiasm throughout the Nation.

As popular thought turned with the interest of the hour to the under-lying principles of American goverment, women renewed demands for political equality and requested a place on the official program. This was denied. Mothers might popularly be accredited with mold-ing affairs of state equal to that of men by their benign influence in the home raising little generals and statesmen and washing their socks and dishes, but this boasted office of influence entitled them to no place on the long and varied program in memory of the founders of the Nation.

The centennial celebration was a gala male affair. Colored men —only a few years since harried in the Federal courts while women protected them—marched by with flaunting banners, citizens and voters of the United States of America. It was a brave occasion, and the newly enfranchised citizens appreciated what had been done for them—by their sex. Women on the sidewalks watched them carry banner after banner emblazoned with the names of Garrison or Phillips or Douglass. They searched in vain for a tribute to Lucre-tia Mott, or the author of "Uncle Tom's Cabin," or any other woman of the anti-slavery conflict. The year 1876 was a year of jubilee to a ransomed male nationality, white and black.

At twelve o'clock noon, July 4, the National Woman Suffrage Association met in the First Unitarian Church, where Dr. Furness had preached a half century, its pulpit now filled by a worthy kinsman of the Reverend Samuel J. May. Lucretia took her place on the plat-form as the convention's presiding officer. Commencing to speak, there were calls from the audience that she ascend the pulpit in order that she might be better seen. As the eighty-three year old president climbed the long winding staircase into the old-fashioned octagon pul-pit, she paused on the way and remarked humorously to the audience: "I am somewhat like Zaccheus of old who climbed the sycamore tree his Lord to see; I climb this pulpit, not because I am of lofty mind, but because I am short of stature that you may see me."

As the countenance of the woman appeared above the pulpit, the crowd marked the tender, placid face, so engraved but unmarred with lines of age, and the body that seemed slowly slipping away from earth, that one might almost expect to see it gradually dissolve into space and join the angels above. They knew it might be the woman's last appearance among them. By happy inspiration the Hutchinson family of singers broke into "Nearer, My God to Thee." The effect was marvelous. The audience at once rose to its feet and joined in the words of the hymn. Never was the beautiful song sung with more fervent expression, while the object of the subtle flattery quietly awaited until it was finished, without the least suspicion of the personal application of what she considered was a part of the regular service.

An eye witness remarked: "The dear old soul is so much stronger than her body, that it would seem that she must have greatly overtasked herself; though an inspired soul has wonderful recuperative forces at command for the temple it inhabits."

Lucretia's participation in the centennial celebration was not her last public appearance, but the spirit that had never failed to whip the declining body to just one more task, found it more and more difficult to attain its ends. Edward H. Davis was often sent as a proxy in causes dear to his mother-in-law, and became good-naturedly resigned to being introduced as "Lucretia Mott's son-in-law" on public occasions. To him was indebted for a number of years whatever life was found in the woman's movement in Pennsylvania, and he spared neither time, money, nor personal effort, to hold up the torch trembling in the hands of the aged pioneer.

John F. Hume saw Lucretia during one of her last appearances as a presiding officer and recorded: "She was then an aged woman, but her eye seemed to be as bright and her movements as alert as they had ever been. Framed by her becoming Quaker bonnet, which she retained in her official position, the face of the handsome old lady would have been a splendid subject for an artist."

July 19th—the day of the original Seneca Falls convention—was celebrated in 1878 at an assembly held at Rochester in the church of the same Unitarian society that had opened its doors to the women in 1848. It was a happy thought that transferred the thirtieth anniversary meeting of the woman's rights society from its customary meeting place at New York City to the little up-State town where feminine freedom had been born.

Noble Quaker Amy Post, seventy-seven years old, assisted in the arrangements, and so did Mrs. Frances D. Gage and Frederick Douglass. But it was only too clear that the ancients present would soon cease to answer the roll call. Names that once had been familiar on the platform were becoming historically remembered. At the reunion new faces predominated.

The Rochester convention was the last annual woman's meeting which Lucretia was able to attend. In the old Unitarian Church she had launched the movement; in the new church of the same society she bade it public farewell. Her family had especially requested that she be not urged to attend, but on reading the call she had quietly announced her intention to be present, and with ever faithful Sarah Pugh as her companion, had made the journey in the intense heat of July.

What changes she had lived to see in the popular estimate of herself! Once considered a dangerous innovator in the social and religious world, the slow-moving masses that feared her a half century ago as an infidel, a fanatic, and an unsexed woman, had followed her footsteps until a broader outlook had expanded their vision. They now revered her as a prophet and a saint. Yet Lucretia Mott had changed the bold background of her views only in the perfection of details.

The "vagaries" of the anti-slavery struggle had been coined into law. The "wild fantasies" of the Abolitionists were now the Thirteenth, Fourteenth, and Fifteenth Amendments to the Constitution of the United States. Infidel Hicksite principles which had shocked Christendom were now corner stones of the liberal religious movement in America. Woman's demands for social, civil, and political equality—grinned at by editors from the Atlantic to the Pacific—had been recognized in a measure by the courts and legislatures of Great Britain and the United States. The colleges, trades, and professions gradually had been opened to woman's admission. Followers of Blackstone and St. Paul were ready to defend the new doctrines in the name of conservatism, patriotism, and true religion, as formerly they had led the attack with the same weapons.

Seated on the platform at Rochester, Lucretia listened to letters received from Garrison and Phillips, for already disagreements engendered by Reconstruction were dying out. The participants realized that the years which had been so ripe and full were now few and numbered. There was no heart left for petty bickerings. They had fought side by side too often in their virile days to be strangers in the hour of death. They walked beside still waters in the valley of death and their hearts were tender for each other and the names of comrades who one by one had dropped from sight each anniversary meeting.

Lucretia spoke several times in her old, gentle, half-humorous but convincing manner and was heard with rapt attention. She never seemed more hopeful of the triumph of woman's principles than on this occasion. Her enthusiasm for the cause for which she had so long labored seemed reinvigorated. Her eyes sparkled with laughter as, in her happiest vein, she recounted amusing reminiscences of encounters with opponents in early days. She said little of herself, how, always apt in Biblical quotations, she had proved herself a worthy antagonist on the platform and had slain many an Abimelech with short texts of Scripture that had been like millstones upon their heads.

In the overcrowded, heated church, the gentle, frail figure in dove-like Quaker costume spoke on, the petals of the full-blown rose trembled on eternity as they awaited the faintest touch of sunlight from Heaven to strike them gently down. Happy memories crowded fast in mind, all the conventions she had presided over, legislatures besieged, the petitions and tracts circulated, the never-ending debates kept up in public and in private, all the causes for which she had given her strength and her mind and her soul—temperance, world peace, non-resistance, liberal religion, the freedom of a race, the freedom of a sex; always freedom. Prominent in her mind since childhood had been the thought of woman's equality with man, and though often crowded by other reforms, never forgotten, and never despised.

What a far cry from that day when the men of Philadelphia had crashed rocks against the windows of Pennsylvania Hall!

Another decade and perhaps not one of the old leaders would be left, but they had smoothed the paths of rocks for those who were to come. Lives of multitudes of men and women would be gladdened by the sacrifices they had made and the truths they had spoken, though posterity might forget the names of the pioneers, and even belittle their deeds, or fail to realize that the great temples of human happiness owe their existence to radicals who grub the lands on which they stand.

In the course of the convention Lucretia whispered to Elizabeth, "How thankful I am for these bright young women now ready to fill our soon-to-be-vacant places. I want to shake hands with them all before I go, and give them a few words of encouragement. I do hope they will not be spoiled with too much praise."

While she talked on about those olden days the body weakened. Dr. Moore, at whose home she was a guest, fearing the consequences of her efforts, stood up in the audience and attempted to attract her attention. Anxiously he called for her in the midst of her closing remarks. As she reluctantly descended the platform she continued speaking, moving slowly down the aisle, shaking hands with spectators eager for the accolade of her touch, even as the vicars of Christ touch hands with St. Peter.

The audience sensed that "the soul of the woman's movement" was marching off the stage of radical reform. Simultaneously it arose to its feet, and on behalf of all Frederick Douglass, the black man, called after the retreating figure:

"Good-bye, dear Lucretia."